ILLINOIS WESLEYAN UNIVERSITY

Continuity & Change

1850-2000

Minor Myers, jr. • Carl Teichman

Illinois Wesleyan University Press
in cooperation with
WDG Publishing

ILLINOIS WESLEYAN UNIVERSITY

CONTINUITY
&
CHANGE
1850–2000

Minor Myers, jr. • Carl Teichman

Frontispiece: Hedding Bell from Hedding College in Abingdon, Illinois that merged with Illinois Wesleyan University in 1930. This monument was erected with contributions from students and dedicated in 1934.

Illinois Wesleyan University Press
in cooperation with
WDG Publishing

Illinois Wesleyan University:
Continuity & Change
1850-2000

Published in partnership with
Illinois Wesleyan University Press
and
WDG Publishing

Creative Director: Duane Wood
Design: LeeAnn Williams, Kristine R. Smith

All images are from the Illinois Wesleyan University archives unless otherwise noted.

Copyright 2001 Illinois Wesleyan University Press

First published in the United States by:

WDG Communications Inc.
3500 F Avenue, N.W.
Post Office Box 9573
Cedar Rapids, Iowa 52409-9573
Telephone: (319) 396-1401
Facsimile: (319) 396-1647

Library of Congress Cataloging-in-Publication Data

Myers, jr., Minor, 1942-
   Illinois Wesleyan University : continuity & change, 1850-2000 / Minor
Myers, jr., Carl Teichman, Bob Aaron.
          p. cm.
Contemporary photography by Marc Featherly.
Includes index.
   ISBN 0-9651620-4-4 (alk. paper)
1. Illinois Wesleyan University--History. I. Teichman, Carl, 1956-
II. Aaron, Bob. III. Title
   LD2433 .M94 2001
   378.773'59--dc21
                                        2001005138

10 9 8 7 6 5 4 3 2 1

Table of Contents

Illinois Wesleyan University: Continuity & Change, 1850-2000 is dedicated to all the

students, alumni, faculty, and staff—past, present, and future—who love this University

and share these sentiments:

Come all ye students now, let every loyal man

Join in a song, in accents strong, for dear old Wesleyan.

And as the chorus swells the air, we'll hand in hand unite

And with a cheer, both loud and strong, we'll wave our banner bright,

Dear old Wesleyan, our own dear old Wesleyan,

No other shrine can brighter shine,

Than our dear Wesleyan.

Dear Old Wesleyan

150 Years of History...Past is Prologue

Charles William Eliot, a reform-minded educator, was president of Harvard for 40 years, 1869-1909. He was honored one night at a dinner party by faculty who toasted his achievements. The competition was keen when it came to piling plaudits on the campus chief executive. "Since you became president," one unctuous professor told Eliot, "Harvard has become a storehouse of knowledge."

Eliot, tongue-in-cheek, replied: "What you say is true, but I can claim little credit for it. It is simply that the freshmen bring so much and the seniors take so little away."

While many "spins" might be placed on this fable, we choose to focus on the notion that no one person is responsible for any organization's achievements, including a great university. That's the message of this book— a message in the spirit of an aphorism credited to Sir Isaac Newton. When the great English scientist was asked why he was able to see so far, he reportedly credited his achievements to the fact that he stood on the shoulders of giants—his predecessors.

That's what *Illinois Wesleyan University: Continuity & Change, 1850-2000* is all about. It's about those who preceded us—about how and why they built this great "storehouse of knowledge." It also is about some of the great personalities who have populated this campus over the last century and a half—their dreams and their accomplishments. Consequently, this is a book about people and ideas.

As the authors pawed and pondered over numerous history-laden documents—for example, President William H.H. Adams' handwritten Civil War memoir, including how he recruited African-American troops for the Union Army—we were struck by how the University was often close to events that shaped our nation and the world. Oftentimes this vicarious experience was through the achievements of alumni whose careers and intellect were shaped by early adulthood experiences at Illinois Wesleyan. For example, a touch of Illinois Wesleyan was at the pinnacle of national power when an alumnus of the 1850s, Adlai Stevenson, served as Vice President of the United States in the 1890s, or when Scott Lucas, class of 1914, was U.S. Senate Majority Leader during the politically turbulent early Cold War years. The University got a peek at the frontiers of science through Carl Marvel, class of 1915 and a National Medal of Science winner, whose innovations in chemistry helped pioneer synthetic rubber during World War II. A handful of Illinois Wesleyan alumni also were there when science was put to work to harness atomic energy, and one alumnus was an eyewitness, when that terrible atomic weapon was unleashed in the skies over Japan to end a war. Alumni have taken the University to the world's great opera houses, the sound stages of Hollywood, cutting-edge research laboratories, the top of professional athletics, and the corridors of some of

America's greatest corporations.

But, great events over the decades also have directly touched Illinois Wesleyan. The years of the Great Depression saw across-the-board belt-tightening, including tuition payments in the form of farm produce—not dollars, which was a humbling experience. And, of course, the world's battlefields sad-dened the Bloomington campus as students-turned-soldiers were consumed by gunfire and disease, never to return. Great crises of a more local nature also shaped the University's evolu-tion—landmark events like the 1943 Hedding Hall fire, which crippled but didn't crush the campus, as well as the inevitable financial ups-and-downs that, at times, brought the University to the brink of bankruptcy. Yet, the University rebounded from these and other setbacks with a fierce determination reminiscent of the moniker attached to the remnants of the great building destroyed in the 1943 blaze—Duration Hall.

Through it all, Illinois Wesleyan was on the cutting edge. A one-armed Civil War veteran, John Wesley Powell, brought a new approach to teaching science to students in the 1860s with path-breaking explorations of America's frontier. And, in the 1890s, a new and powerful telescope—a scientific instrument reputed to be the eighth largest in the world at the time—gave students and faculty a wonder-ful teaching tool to study the heavens. Seven decades later, the Illinois Wesleyan community got an idea of what it was like to touch the heavens, when *Apollo VIII* commander Frank Borman visited the campus shortly after circling the moon. And, a century after Illinois Wesleyan inaugurated its wonderful telescope, the University's scientific genius was seen again, when the $25-million Center for Natural Sciences caught the attention of Project Kaleidoscope, a science-education program sponsored with support from the National Science Foundation and other groups.

This book also is a tribute to bits of Illinois Wesleyan legend and lore that are no longer part of our "academical village," to use a term coined by Thomas Jefferson. *Continuity & Change* gives us the opportunity to reflect on important—but ephemeral—aspects of the University such as the law school, home-economics program, oratory department, corre-spondence school, graduate courses, and the Wilson School of Art. While these entities did not survive to the 21st century, they con-tributed mightily to Illinois Wesleyan's maturity and development.

The great architect and city planner Daniel Burham had a credo: "Make no little plans, they have no magic to stir men's minds." As readers travel through the history of Illinois Wesleyan, they will be struck by the size and scope of the plans—the dreams—envisioned by our forebears. Some, like the ill-fated Pillsbury Plan of the 1920s, remained unfulfilled. Others, however, like the admission of women and

African-Americans to the University in the 1860s and 1870s, as well as construction of Evelyn Chapel, the Shirk Center, and various libraries and science buildings over the years were repeatedly fulfilled.

The tale of Illinois Wesleyan also is the saga of people who believed in the fundamental value of education and were willing to invest their treasure in the minds of youngsters. *Continuity & Change* will introduce you to countless benefactors from Isaac Funk to B. Charles Ames, class of 1950, and Joyce Eichhorn Ames, class of 1949, who graciously have put their money to work for the benefit of others. From generation to generation, these benefactors shared a vision of Illinois Wesleyan akin to what the Ames family said when they announced a new $12-million fund-raising challenge to fellow alumni: "We believe Illinois Wesleyan University has a unique opportunity to rank among the top 40 national liberal arts institutions in the United States within the next few years. For this reason, we are willing to make a substantial commitment of funds if our fellow alumni will join with us to achieve this goal."

As a consequence of this type of support, Illinois Wesleyan has been most fortunate over the past decade: raising $115 million, constructing about $90 million in buildings, and increasing enrollment from 1,800 to 2,000 students, as well as increasing the quality of those students. *Continuity & Change* is the story of how Illinois Wesleyan positioned itself over the years to achieve its contemporary success. This success also includes being ranked among the nation's most selective liberal-arts campuses by *U.S. News & World Report;* being ranked 12th nationally by *Kiplinger's Personal Finance Magazine* among private colleges and universities in delivering high-quality education at an affordable cost, and being ranked the 8th "most wired" college in the nation by *Yahoo! Internet Life.*

So, as you read about the Illinois Wesleyan University adventure take pride in *your* University's success—success nurtured and cultivated through hard work and genius by men and women over a century and a half. The authors hope that you will chuckle at campus capers like a Pajama Parade or the Uprising of the Mules and that you will take pride in the University's Goldwater Scholars, 1997 national basketball championship, and faculty research and writings.

And, as you read with pride about *your* University's accomplishments, you might hum the lyrics of *Fight Wesleyan:*

Fight Wesleyan, keep a-fighting every man,
Our team will stay, right in the fray
And Wesleyan will win today,
So plunge through that line
Make a touchdown every time,
The crowd a' yelling, the cheers a' swelling.
Fight, Fight, Fight, Fight, Fight,
Fight for Wesleyan.

Minor Myers, jr. • Carl Teichman

The authors want to thank countless individuals and organizations for their assistance in the researching, writing, editing, and publishing of *Illinois Wesleyan University: Continuity & Change, 1850-2000*, a project that unfolded on a crash course over 18 months.

Several organizations—on and off campus—played key roles in providing primary and secondary-source documents, as well as rare and valued photographs that illustrate the remarkable history of our University. Among these organizations are the U.S. Senate, U.S. Geological Survey, U.S. Marine Corps, Illinois State Historical Society, American Chemical Society, McLean County History Museum, and the University of Arizona, as well as Illinois Wesleyan University's Sheean Library, particularly the University Archives, the *Argus*, the *Wesleyana*, and the Office of University Communications.

Several histories of Illinois Wesleyan University and memoirs were invaluable resources in preparing this manuscript. Among those references, we respectfully acknowledge: *The Illinois Wesleyan Story, 1850-1950* by Elmo Scott Watson; *The Professor Goes West* by Elmo Scott Watson; *Illinois Wesleyan University: Growth, Turning Points, and New Directions Since the Second World War* by George Vinyard, class of 1971; *A Personal Memoir of the Bertholf Years at Illinois Wesleyan University, 1958-68* by Lloyd M. Bertholf; *Pictures at An Exhibition:*

Illinois Wesleyan University, 1968-86 by Robert S. Eckley; and *Through the Eyes of the Argus: 100 Years of Journalism at Illinois Wesleyan University*, by Jennifer L. Barrell '94 and Christopher J. Fusco '94.

The authors gratefully acknowledge the painstaking and diligent research of three Illinois Wesleyan students without whose professionalism and dogged determination this volume would not have reached the printing press. Sara Scobell, class of 2000, who was named a 1999 Lincoln Academy Scholar by the State of Illinois, was selected to be a principal researcher for this volume. Her meticulous efforts, combing through large stacks of dusty documents, enriched this volume, adding color and broadening its scope. Her scrupulous attention to detail and Sherlock Holmes-like persistence in searching for evidence did much to ensure the accuracy of information presented here. Following Ms. Scobell's graduation, Kathryn L. Weber, class of 2002, an English major, and editor-in-chief of the *Argus*, very ably and enthusiastically took over research responsibilities. Katherine Edwards, class of 2002 and an English-literature major, played the pivotal role of photo researcher. She sifted through thousands of aging negatives, photos, and slides—some tucked away in basements and musty file cabinets that were untouched for decades—probing for just the right photo to illustrate a point. Her valuable work was made more difficult because so many precious photographs were lost in the 1943 Hedding Hall blaze. Each of these students showcased on-the-job research, writing, and analytical skills that are so fundamental to a quality liberal-arts education.

The photography component of *Continuity & Change* would not be possible without the efforts of Marc Featherly, university photographer and a member of the Office of University Communications staff. Many of his photos—as well as those of others—taken over the years illustrate this volume. However, he also spent numerous hours—often after midnight—in the precise and tedious process of copying photos out of timeworn University publications, photos for which negatives were unavailable. Additionally, he spent countless hours doing photo research and in the darkroom developing batches of film so that the authors could review photographs for possible inclusion in this volume.

The Office of University Communications also was instrumental in bringing *Continuity & Change* from concept to reality. And, the staff, as always, took on this sizable and persistent project with good cheer and their trademark professionalism even as they grappled with a myriad of other projects—ranging from news-media inquiries to news releases, feature stories, writing various publications, preparing slide shows and videos, and quarterly production of

the *Illinois Wesleyan University Magazine*. The communications staff played several roles in preparing this volume, including legwork in pinpointing sources of information and photographs, fact-checking, proof-reading, and reviewing copy. Consequently, many thanks are in order to: Stew Salowitz, class of 1976 and director of news services; Sherry Wallace, assistant director of University communications; Tim Obermiller, editor, *Illinois Wesleyan University Magazine;* and Tina Williams, office coordinator. In addition, special thanks is owed Bob Aaron, former director of University Communications, for his tireless efforts with all aspects of this manuscript.

And, of course, thanks also are in order for our partners in this project, WDG Communications of Cedar Rapids, Iowa, particularly Duane Wood, publisher, LeeAnn Williams and Kristine Smith, graphic designers and JoAnn Wood, Shari Boyle, Linda Whitman and Vonda Olson, production. Their creativity and cooperation contributed much to the success of *Continuity & Change*.

But, most especially, the authors want to acknowledge the contributions of our predecessors—students, alumni, faculty, and staff. For without their vision, foresight, hard work, and diligence, this history of Illinois Wesleyan University—published on the campus' 150th anniversary—would have been impossible. This book is their story.

Minor Myers, jr. • Carl Teichman

I. From Illinois University to Illinois Wesleyan

T hat Bloomington would have a college seems a given, based on the eastern background of the early European settlers. Its form and specifics, though, depended very much on politics and details.

A lot of this history would have been conjectural at best were it not for John Barger, principal founder of Illinois Wesleyan who at the request of the University's Board of Trustees wrote five long columns on the institution's early history for the *Western Whig* in the spring of 1851. He was asked to do so by Methodist meetings of March 8, 1851.

In the decade from 1820 to 1829, 22 new colleges were founded in the United States. That number was increased by 38 during the next decade. Various factors, including economic conditions contributed to slowing down this movement, so that there were only 42 colleges established from 1840 to 1849. But in the next 10 years from 1850 to 1859 that number more than doubled to 92 campuses.

In the early 19th century colleges continued to be educational extensions of church denominations. In the years before the American Revolution Congregationalists, for example, established Harvard and Yale, Baptists created Brown, and Presbyterians launched Princeton and Washington and Lee.

Early Bloomington

Bloomington, Illinois, had begun life as Blooming Grove in 1822 as the first settlers of European stock arrived. James Allin, a shopkeeper originally from North Carolina, moved from Vandalia to Blooming Grove in 1829, recognizing the locale's commercial potential. Though there were barely 100 residents in the town, the entrepreneurial Allin led a movement to create a new county with Blooming Grove as the county seat. These efforts were successful when McLean County was created on December 25, 1831, with a renamed Bloomington as the county seat. McLean County grew to a population of about 4,000 by 1840, leaping to 10,399 when Assistant Marshal William McCullough counted heads in 1849.

Westward migration was a given in those American decades. Several factors coalesced to make Bloomington a developing center of population and economic activity. The extraordinarily fertile soils drew the farmers and the farmers drew the merchants, lawyers, and doctors. That pattern was common enough, but geography gave Bloomington a special boost as more than a railroad town. It was a railroad junction.

In the 1840s Chicago and St. Louis were prominent economic centers waiting to be linked by the spreading network of railroads. Tracks reached Bloomington from the south in 1852, and by 1855 it was normal to ride the 260 miles between Bloomington and St. Louis in 15 hours and 30 minutes. Perhaps less inevitable was the Illinois Central, which went north and south through the state like a backbone. Chartered by Congress in 1850, the Illinois Central tracks reached Bloomington in 1854. But the railroad's greater impact came later. By 1856 the Illinois Central was running a national campaign to attract settlers to Illinois on farms along its tracks. Land was $5 to $25 an acre and economic success for new settlers was all but guaranteed. Land sales were strong, and the

Chicago and Alton and the Illinois Central railroads crossed only at Bloomington. In addition the east-west railroad completed in 1870 offered still a third window to national commerce and economic growth. That the Chicago and Alton made Bloomington the location for its shops only intensified the pattern. And so by 1860 Bloomington's population reached 8,000.

Early Elementary Schools

Settlers of European stock moved west across America in the 19th century. Some towns have strong southern roots, others pure New England

editors, or ministers. Delia Mullin began with her log-cabin school for small children as early as 1825 in Bloomington. William Hodge ran a school in the village in the 1830s and Lemuel Foster, a Presbyterian minister, had a school in 1834. In the early 1840s Martha Tomkins operated a school for girls at the corner of Washington and Center Streets in Bloomington, while Dr. W. C. Hobbs had a school for boys.

There was a pair of academies in the late 1840s. The Baptist minister Charles E. Dodge opened the Bloomington Male Academy on September 4, 1848, where he taught reading,

Charles P. Merriman

James Allin

W. C. Hobbs

origins. Bloomington settlers came from Vermont through North Carolina, with many coming from inland states to the west. These settlers brought a general enthusiasm for education, with mixed backgrounds on how it was supported. New England used state funds to support common schools. Early Illinois followed southern and western models, depending more on local efforts which were not long in coming, though highly intermittent. Only in 1855 did Illinois establish a system of public schools, while state-supported universities started only in 1857.

Early education at every level in Illinois was dependent on entrepreneurship or public benevolence, often both. Teaching offered an extra source of income for doctors, lawyers,

penmanship, English grammar, arithmetic, and geography for $3 per quarter and more advanced courses for $4 and $5 per quarter. About the same time George W. Minier and Mary M. Spaulding opened the Bloomington Female School. The primary department covered reading, spelling, and arithmetic, while the advanced department delved into astronomy, ethics, history, and elocution.

Merriman Dreams, January-May, 1849

A key figure in Bloomington and its vision was Charles Merriman, editor of the town's newspaper *The Western Whig*. He was first to imagine a college in Bloomington, just as he was later to be a partner with Jesse Fell in transforming his old paper into a new one, which he named *The*

Pantagraph. With his classical background, Merriman knew that moniker meant "write all."

Records are unclear on Merriman's background, but it is clear that his life began with some uncertainty. He was born in Hatley, a town the residents thought was in Vermont. In fact, he was born in Canada, which probably explains his attending a Catholic college near Montreal and returning as a bilingual professor of mathematics at a seminary in Newbury, Vermont. Why he went to run a school in Athens, Georgia, is as inexplicable as the forces which brought him to Bloomington to take over a school in 1844. He started *The Western Whig* two years later. He was a community-minded citizen, who over time was president of the town board of trustees and mayor of Bloomington. But he is best remembered as newspaperman.

Merriman also is a sad character in this tale. Once he was the well-to-do editor and educational visionary. Yet, in later years, he was out of the newspaper business and reduced to running a bookstore, at least until he found an intermittent job as a language teacher at Evergreen City Commercial College and, ironically, Illinois Wesleyan.

Merriman's articles in 1849 left no doubt: Bloomington should have a college. Readers on May 19, 1849, found he was doing more than thinking or dreaming. He was ready to act.

Together with the Baptist minister Charles E. Dodge he proposed to establish "a seminary of learning in Bloomington." It would be called the McLean Collegiate Institute and it would teach ancient and modern languages, math, science, and philosophy, "together with all the usual branches of an English education." If he could raise $5,000, the institute would have a building and start classes by January, 1850. An advertisement ran at least twice, and a separate printed version had a plan for a building. No copy survives. A very distinct trait of the plan was explicit: the institute was to be free of "all political and sectarian bias." It would be a college for a community, not just for one denomination.

Merriman's advertisement invited subscribers to come forward. How many did is unknown and little more was heard of the McLean Collegiate Institute that summer, but Merriman was moving forward nonetheless.

Teachers' Institute, 1849

A teachers' institute was organized in the summer of 1849 by Merriman and George W. Minier, as well as three subscription-school teachers: A. H. Brown, Joseph Macon, and Henry Louis Shafter Haskell. The quintet met on Friday nights and at one of these conclaves Haskell was asked to discuss: "How can we best advance the cause of education in McLean County?"

Haskell argued that the county needed a university, "a fountain from which recruits would come for every branch of learning and science." Bloomington was a logical venue for a university because it was "eligibly situated on the projected line of the Illinois Central and other roads, with no colleges east of us or near us."

Likewise, in early summer 1849 *The Western Whig* announced: Mrs. R. Merriman, surely the editor's wife, will open a school in the north room of the Lucas house, on the first Monday in May, for a term of four months, and will teach the common branches of an English education. Terms were $3 per session, or 75 cents per month, for each scholar. The school was open to students regardless of age or sex.

If his wife was running a primary school in 1849, Merriman himself began making plans for the classical school he began advertising in February, 1850. In association with George W. Minier, the school would offer the elements of English education, mathematics, and philosophy, plus Greek, Latin, Spanish, French, Italian, and vocal music. These offerings sound like an academy or high school about to become a college.

Illinois Methodism

The early years of Illinois Wesleyan are incomprehensible without an introduction to Methodist vocabulary and organization. Methodists continued the tradition of Anglican bishops, but rather than have the bishop responsible for administering a diocese, the denomination organized a series of representative committees, assemblies, which together operated a Conference. Illinois in the late 1840s was divided into two Methodist conferences. Dividing by a line that ran roughly from Rossville in the east to Hamilton in the west, the Rock River Conference organized Methodists north of that demarcation, while the Illinois Conference incorporated the remaining southern portion of the state. Bloomington sat near the borderline.

The Illinois Conference had two colleges under its patronage in the late 1840s. McKendree College for men began in 1828, while MacMurray, which opened in 1846, was for women. The Rock River Conference had committed itself to starting a Methodist college in Evanston, now Northwestern University.

John Barger

There is little question that if the title founder of Illinois Wesleyan is bestowed on a single person that person is John S. Barger (1803-1876). Born in Kentucky, he knew colleges well by the time he arrived in Bloomington as a Methodist minister, serving as head of the Bloomington district from 1847-50. Indeed, no one could have known better that colleges are both born and face life-threatening situations.

For two years Barger had been the financial agent for McKendree College, beginning in 1837. Financial planning at that time concluded that McKendree would be on a firm fiscal footing if it raised an endowment of $50,000, a very large sum, but one which could be managed if the college sold 100 scholarships at $500 each. Such was the development plan adopted. Sales went well, but fiscal details are uncertain. Yet, it would appear that 100 commitments were made, perhaps being paid in installments by the "donors."

John S. Barger

The Panic of 1837, an economic downturn, intervened, sending McKendree into a tailspin. The scholarships gave a family the right to send a student tuition-free "in perpetuity." How long that was to last is unclear, but suddenly donors found they could not pay their scholarship commitments, and the college could find no students who otherwise could attend. McKendree refunded its donations, called in its scholarships, and hoped for $200 donations. As Barger put it in 1851, writing the history of Illinois Wesleyan, then barely a year old: "Thus vanished the endowment of M'Kendree College." Faced with debt of over $10,000, rather than an endowment of $50,000, the college suspended. More than anyone in Bloomington, Barger realized how dependent educational dreams are on fiscal resources.

McLean College Organization

Charles Merriman's dream for a college and his plans for classical education were certainly well known in the community, though his classical school was not announced until February, 1850. Yet, John Barger knew as well as anyone that the idea of a college had taken hold.

The annual meeting of the Methodist Illinois Conference met from September 19-26, 1849 in Quincy, Illinois. At these meetings Barger became a key figure in local college politics. He knew of the interests in the Bloomington community and he talked with his Methodist colleagues. The hint was passed back and forth, that if Bloomington organized a college, the Methodist organization might help it or take it under its control.

John Barger was the chief informant when the Committee on Education heard several informal proposals for setting up "schools of academic grade" in Bloomington and Jacksonville. The Conference named committees to hold talks with citizens in Bloomington and elsewhere about the "practicality and expediency of opening schools and erecting buildings as soon as circumstances shall justify." Certainly the most significant phrase in the documents of that meeting was the promise that if the conference embraced a school it would extend "its official patronage." The committee assigned the task of talking to the citizens of Bloomington about establishing a school to John Barger and Thomas McGee.

McLean Trustees Hear about the Methodist Thoughts, 1849

Barger's five contributions to *The Western Whig* in 1851 leave no doubt as to what happened next. "The friends of education in Bloomington, met, organized, and elected a Board of Trustees under the name and style of McLean College." Without a roster of names, Barger did record the composition: "In this board all the churches of the place, were represented; and several gentlemen, not connected with any church, but of high standing in society, were elected Trustees." Ultimately both Barger or McGee were added as the Methodists on the board, which was still operating with Merriman's hope of creating a non-sectarian college.

From that moment Barger played two roles. He was a trustee of McLean College, then only an idea with a non-sectarian board. And, he was also a representative of a denomination he hoped would patronize a new college in Bloomington.

Once formed complete with officers, the board did little. Whether Barger means something by his definite first phrase is unclear:

"But from some cause, this attempt at a College organization proved abortive. At the request of the Conference committee, a meeting of the Trustees was called on the evening preceding the fourth quarterly meeting conference of the Bloomington station, July 5, 1850. But failing to obtain a quorum (none present by the President and Secretary of the Board), the projected enterprise was considered defunct."

It is hard to know whether Barger was disappointed or delighted, given what happened the next day. He perhaps wanted a non-sectarian vision to be defunct, as he now saw the possibility of a Methodist reality. As though worried a still dormant rival might spring up over a year later, Barger in recording his facts in 1851 added: "No attempt has since been made to revive the undertaking."

Barger was not to be stopped. He foresaw a larger Bloomington, a new Methodist conference encompassing the central part of the state, and a major college in Bloomington. On July 6, 1850, less than 24 hours after he called the McLean College board defunct, Barger and McGee reported to the quarterly meeting of the Bloomington area. They had tried to confer with the trustees of McLean College, but they "from some cause [the same phrase again], have failed to perfect their organization." If no others would do it, the Bloomington station should go ahead, set up a college, open a school, and "provide as soon as shall be deemed advisable, suitable buildings." Quite simply, a college was both "practical and expedient."

As usual, things went to a committee, which reported on July 8 with vigorous recommendations. Concurring with Barger on every point, E. Thomas, L. Graves, and J. Allin recommended that the local Methodist group move ahead to create an institution of learning "under the patronage of the M. E. Church." The Bloomington-area group itself would appoint nine trustees "who shall take the necessary steps to perfect their legal organization under the statutes of this State."

Barger, Magee, and Allin immediately were named to the board, with Barger to coordinate finding the other six trustees and carrying the project to the September conference meetings. The quarterly conference opted for Illinois University as the name of their now independent rival.

In short order the board consisted of these nine: John Barger, H. J. E. McClun, L. Graves, Dr. E. Thomas, James Allin, James Miller, C. P. Merriman, W. C. Hobbs, and John Magoun.

Merriman had dreamed of a non-sectarian college and an alliance with the Methodist Conference probably was not what he had in mind, though he would be one of the first trustees of Illinois Wesleyan. But denominational association governed vision, as is evident in an analysis of the need for a new college in Bloomington.

Bloomington, Methodists learned, needed a college because others were too distant. Local students otherwise had to go to Evanston, Jacksonville, or Indiana. Completely invisible in this analysis were Knox, started by the Congregationalists in Galesburg in 1837, and Jubilee College at Robin's Nest, an Episcopal school under the direction of Bishop Philander P. Chase, the founder of Kenyon. The Literacy and Technological Institute of the Lutheran Church of the Far West, later known among other names as Hillsboro College (now Carthage) had started in 1846 and Shurtleff College though it dated to 1826 at Alton was Baptist.

Quarterly Meeting Conference of Bloomington Station

Barger reported that "very recently" Illinois University had been organized, and would be interested in discussing cooperation with the Methodist conference. He wrote in *The Western Whig* of May 21, 1851: "A Board of nine Trustees, citizens of Bloomington, have been appointed by the Quarterly meeting Conference of the Station, who are waiting

the approaching session of the Illinois Conference, to place the Institution under the control of the Church."

Rock River is Dubious, July 18, 1850

John Barger, Thomas McGee, and Wingate Jones Newman went to the Rock River Conference meetings in Plainfield, Illinois, on July 18, 1850. On July 19, they asked that Rock River Conference join with the Illinois Conference in taking the new Illinois University under its patronage, sharing in governance and supervision, particularly in choosing members of a Board of Visitors. They proposed particularly that the Rock River group elect visitors who would meet with the Illinois-conference group in September.

In that same session, papers establishing Northwestern University were under discussion, but Barger and the others also presented a proposal on "Illinois University." They addressed the Conference as the Board of Trustees of Illinois University and the Conference in turn referred the question to its Committee on Education. They were not the official visitors Barger had requested, but they did come to the September meetings in Bloomington.

Barger had much to learn as well as tell. He discovered that Rock River already had "friends of education in the city of Chicago" planning a new major university nearby, The North Western University. Rock River had an even grander collaboration in mind, for it would work with Methodist conferences in Wisconsin, Iowa, and Indiana. Barger probably was surprised when he found they even had in mind asking the Illinois Conference for help with the project.

Another issue was afoot, uncertain but logical. The suggestion was strong that the middle part of the state be made a third and separate conference, in which case Illinois University would be the obvious school for that Conference, just as North Western would be for Chicago, and McKendree and MacMurray were to the southern counties. On July 23, in the morning session, the Rock River group named a committee to confer with their colleagues in the Illinois Conference.

The Rock River Conference expressed interest in the project, but failed to offer "pecuniary aid" because it was pledged to support another Methodist institution, North Western University at Chicago, and trustees were named for that institution on July 23, 1850.

September 17, 1850

In mid-September John Barger was now a man of many hats. He was a prominent figure in conference politics, yet he was also the intellectual leader of the Illinois University board. He spoke constantly in both capacities.

Barger's report the next day says that on the evening of September 17 the Board of Trustees of Illinois University met to discuss an alliance with the Methodist denomination. They liked the plan and anticipated making a presentation to the Conference on September 19. Further, they voted to expand the roster of trustees from nine to 30, as Barger reported, "to extend the influence of the institution more generally through the Conference and over the State."

The Illinois Conference Meets, September 18, 1850

When the Illinois Conference opened its 27th annual session on September 18, 1850, the Bloomington university project met with more success and some unexpected travails. Barger and Magee presented a report, summarizing their meetings with Bloomington citizens "on the subject of a seminary of learning at that place." The Illinois University trustees were willing to work with the Methodists and willing to expand the board to 30 seats. The Conference agreed to his suggestion that a special five-person panel confer with the Rock River Conference and Illinois University trustees.

September 19, 1850

It was probably on September 19 that the special panel of five held a joint meeting with the Illinois University trustees and three Rock River Conference delegates. Barger reported what happened at a very amiable conference. The special committee reported back that the trustees of Illinois University "have tendered to the Conference the patronage and control of their Institution." In turn the committee recommended that "we accept the tender of the said Illinois University, and hereby adopt it as the University of Illinois." They submitted their report, together with an eloquent document from Barger and J. C. Finley on behalf of Illinois University. Barger probably wrote that one, too.

The document from the University board stressed the growth of Bloomington, the fertility of the soils, and the beauty of the country. It noted: "We cannot begin too soon. The increase of our own population—the increase of foreigners are pouring upon us. The tide of emigration is rolling its ceaseless current through us—and the great highway of nations uniting the extremes of Europe and Asia, will soon pass by our doors; and the wealth of the world will be poured into our treasury; and by the time we can acquire the experience necessary for the conduct of a College, the liberality of our people will have furnished the means, and the youth of our Country will be pressing to our Halls for that instruction which it is our duty to provide for them."

This was more than rhetoric. Since Barger, the assumed author, assured the Conference that: "Buildings fully adequate to conducting a large High School are now ready," and since the burgeoning wealth would provide ready, spontaneous support, the conference would have a college at virtually no cost. Indeed, as a trustee of Illinois University Barger assured his Conference colleagues that Conference patronage "will not for the present involve them in either expense or harassing responsibility."

It was a proposition hard to resist: control and public acclamation at no cost. There was some opposition to the idea in the Committee on Education, but the panel still reported it out favorably, and with no objections the conference voted to accept the offer. A year later Barger was moderately bitter. His reports had been received, he wrote, with "oblivious calm of indifference," and his eloquent statement on behalf of the trustees was never printed or distributed.

Barger was equally disappointed by the response of his northern colleagues. The three representatives of the Rock River Conference left Bloomington saying they thought the conference would encourage the project. All they did, however, was present a resolution of encouragement with the clear stipulation they could offer no "pecuniary aid."

The report by Barger and a colleague was a ringing endorsement of need for improved education in Bloomington, declaring: "We cannot begin too soon," especially as the area's population grew through immigration and its wealth increased. "It is our duty," the report proclaimed, to provide education under these circumstances.

The report was referred to the Committee on Education. Part of the committee's reluctance to move on the Illinois University proposal might have been tied to a previous Quincy Conference initiative to shift McKendree College to Bloomington.

"Because of this," Elmo Scott Watson wrote in his centennial history of Illinois Wesleyan, "they opposed, or at least reluctantly consented to, the establishment of the projected Illinois University under the patronage of the Illinois Conference. At least, Barger hints that there was such opposition, but states that it was not strong enough to make itself evident on the floor of the Conference."

Ultimately, the Conference adopted a resolution, "That the Illinois University be received under the patronage of this Conference in accordance with the request of the Trustees and committees of the Conference."

September 23, 1850

Within days, the McLean College Institute board was transformed. The original nine were now increased to 30, and the roster filled with Methodists. What some had hoped would be a non-denominational college was suddenly coopted. The new board gathered for the first time on September 23, 1850.

At that point the board signed a declaration of intent to form a corporation under the 1849 Illinois Act for the Incorporation of Institutions of Learning. The state statute mandates most of the text of that declaration: the number of trustees, subjects to be taught, the professorships to be established, and perhaps, most interesting of all, in this case—the name.

As the document was drafted and copied out for signature there was no doubt about the name—Illinois University. The Methodist Conference later printed the full minutes of all its September sessions. The printing probably was completed in October, and there can be no doubt, when the Methodist meetings finished in Bloomington, the local church leaders had opted to start Illinois University.

Manuscript records of the Conference even refer to the University of Illinois, and in fact when *The Western Whig* ran the first advertisement for the school on October 12, 1850, it announced that Reuben Andrus had been retained to head the preparatory department for the new "University of Illinois." Classes were to begin on October 28, and on November 27 a new advertisement appeared. It ran weekly through the spring reporting the curriculum at "Illinois University." That term continued at the head of the advertisements for the new school through April, 1852.

The beginnings of Illinois Wesleyan are distinctly odd and uncertainty about the name may encapsulate far more than early historians were willing to record.

Articles of
Incorporation
showing the addition
of "Wesleyan"
to the name.

Illinois Wesleyan began with a preparatory school and no president of the college faculty. At first there was a president pro tem, followed by a president in absentia, followed by a president who lasted a year. Only in 1856 would the denomination, which had claimed the name Illinois Wesleyan, offer funds to keep the school going.

The records are lacking, but it is not difficult to surmise what happened. John Wesley had founded the Methodist sect of the Anglican church, which in America declared itself to be a separate denomination in 1784, at which time Francis Asbury and Thomas Coke became its bishops.

Like other denominations, the Methodists had been active in establishing colleges, with varying patterns in the names. Methodist support in Connecticut had created Wesleyan University in 1831 in Middletown. Georgia Female College in Macon began in 1831 and changed its name to Wesleyan Female College in 1843. Ohio Wesleyan had begun in 1841, perhaps setting a model of combining state and denominational names.

In any event, in November, 1850, when the board began organizing, someone probably suggested Illinois Wesleyan as a formal name. There may have some reluctance, but the word Wesleyan was added to both copies of the original papers of incorporation with a carat showing where the word should be inserted.

In the meantime some were unsure of the use of the denominational ties, and thus the first newspaper advertisements continued for "Illinois University," with no mention made of a denominational attachment. The first announcements had said classes would meet in the Methodist church, a detail omitted later. Once maybe a misprint, but the same advertisement appeared again and again for a whole season.

"Wesleyan" had been inserted in the name when the document was filed in the courthouse on December 3, 1850, but the advertisements remained unchanged. The name Illinois Wesleyan was in place at least by April 23, 1851, when Barger wrote to the conference meetings in Peoria.

And so, "an Institute of learning of Collegiate grade" was established in Bloomington which "shall be known in law and equity or otherwise by the name and style of Illinois Wesleyan University."

Overleaf:
Main Street in early
Bloomington looking
toward the north.

II. Bright Beginnings to Disaster Averted

Students have long come first at Illinois Wesleyan. Indeed, there were students before there was either a president or an organized board of trustees. The first classes gathered at nine o'clock in the morning of Monday, October 28, 1850, at the Methodist Episcopal Church.

Built in 1836, this small church stood at the corner of Olive and Main Streets. There were seven students that day, aged 14 to 22 years. As planned, Reuben Andrus was there to begin instruction in language, geometry, algebra, philosophy, English grammar, orthography, and arithmetic. The advertisements had called him "an eminently successful practical teacher" and there is no reason to think those seven students did not get their money's worth at tuition rates running from $3 to $5 a quarter.

The all-male student body that first day included: Edwin Miller, Archibald E. Stewart, Edwin Fell, Fletcher Wilson, John Perry, George Stubblefield, and James Stevenson Ewing. James Ewing was the son of trustee John W. Ewing. He would later practice law in Bloomington with his cousin, Adlai Ewing Stevenson, another of Illinois Wesleyan's early students who would ultimately become vice president of the United States under Grover Cleveland. President Cleveland also named James Ewing, Minister to Belgium, where he served for four years. Archibald E. Stewart became a doctor, a farmer, a member of the Illinois legislature, a circuit-court official, an acting county superintendent of schools, and a newspaperman. Many years later Andrus would write about that first year: "The list of students was gradually enlarged until in January 1851 there were present in the classes forty five (45) persons, the maximum number for the year." Education went well in the first days of Illinois University as the institution continued to call itself in advertisements.

However, organization and funding were completely different topics.

Filing the Document with a New Name

Only when the Board of Trustees met on December 2, 1850, was William H. Allin instructed to have the September 23 declaration entered "on the records of McLean county and [to forward] one copy of the same to the Secretary of State in Springfield." The next day Allin filed the document with himself, for he was, in fact, clerk of the circuit court. Nine days later the board met again to elect officers and begin writing a new constitution, adopted on December 18, 1850. Early plans for a non-sectarian college were now transformed into one where a majority of trustees were to be members of the Methodist Episcopal Church.

When trustees met in Bloomington's courthouse in January, 1851, their agenda was about as comprehensive as it could possibly be: acquisition of a site for the University, building construction, choosing a president, assembling a faculty, publicity, and, above all, finance.

They had no way of knowing that discussions of a site would go on for four long years. Classes had begun in the Methodist church, with every expectation that the whole operation would move to the new church building to be completed in the summer of 1851. Yet all agreed a college needed a campus. In February, 1851, two trustees, William H. Allin and James Miller, later Illinois state treasurer, each offered 10-acre tracts for the new University's home. The

◀ North Hall

trustees voted to approve Allin's offer, a site located north of Chestnut Street and east of the Chicago & Alton Railroad. However, in May the trustees voted the conditions Allin offered unacceptable and debate dragged on.

Staffing went marginally better. Andrus had arrived for the opening of the school, but in July, 1851, he received a new title, and perhaps a demotion. Andrus was now professor of mathematics and natural philosophy, and he was to be joined by an old acquaintance from the McKendree staff, William Goodfellow, who was professor of natural science. Goodfellow, like Andrus, was a Methodist minister, but the older man now supplanted Andrus as head of the school. In addition, Erastus Wentworth was elected president.

The only known existing photo of the University's first home was taken in 1900, after it had been converted from a church into a livery stable.

The First President: Erastus Wentworth

Erastus Wentworth (1813-1886) was a natural choice for president. He was just finishing four successful years as president of McKendree, a role which made him well known to local Methodist leaders.

Wentworth was born a Congregationalist in Stonington, Connecticut, finished Wesleyan in 1837 and then combined teaching science with the Methodist ministry in New York and Vermont. Out of the blue, he was named president of McKendree in 1846, a position he accepted for the unexpected reason that the climate would be healthier for his wife. After four years he was ready to head back east to be professor of science at Dickinson, and he was not to be stopped by the new college in Bloomington, as the board heard from him

Reuben Andrus

William Goodfellow

in September. After four years in Pennsylvania, he spent the next eight years as a missionary in China, before returning to churches in New York and Massachusetts.

Reuben Andrus (1829-1887), who was named professor of mathematics and natural philosophy, had long McKendree associations. Born in New York, he came to Illinois quite young, started at Illinois College, but finished at McKendree in 1849. He already was ordained a minister.

William Goodfellow, a native of Wooster, Ohio, moved north to join his former student, Andrus. He had been in charge of the preparatory program at McKendree and he had experience at raising money for buildings, both useful talents in Bloomington. Whatever his title, Goodfellow appears in the records for months as though he is coordinating all aspects of the program. Only in July, 1852, did the board make the actual official, when it made him president pro tem at the same time the trustees tried to choose another president.

Admissions and Fundraising

Charles Merriman and John Barger continued their efforts for the college. They had hoped to appoint an agent to seek donations and students in early 1851, but when such an appointment did not materialize they printed a broadside circular instead, a document which captures a lot of changing circumstances.

First funds raised for the nascent university came from a source all-but-unknown today, but common in the 18th century, when artists would paint a great picture and visitors would pay a small fee to view it. Elisha Hunt was a Bloomington portrait painter. For most artists then, portraits were merely a way to make money. Great historical or religious scenes were real art, and like many of his artistic colleagues a great work would make a display to which the public would pay admission. Hunt produced his version of the Last Supper. It was placed on view in the new Methodist church, and *The Western Whig* of August 13, 1851, called it a "magnificent painting on which Mr. Hunt has spent a vast amount of labor," adding that 112 people paid a quarter each to see it. Proceeds of $28 arrived at the University in September, 1851.

In August, 1851, the University made the appointment it had been unable to make earlier in the year. Thomas Magee became the University's agent and started combing the countryside for financial support. *The Western Whig* reported in the spring of 1852 that Magee's efforts had resulted in $15,000 of local support. Further work on the East Coast found that the "liberality of friends in Boston, New York and Philadelphia" had made it possible to purchase a "philosophical and chemical apparatus" and add 500 volumes to the library. By year's end, Magee had raised nearly $17,000, but most of these funds were earmarked for buildings to house the University.

The Second Fall of Classes after a Successful First Year

On July 31, 1851, *The Western Whig* character-ized the preparatory school's inaugural year as successful, noting that the institution had 50 students, two faculty members had been select-ed, and that the trustees were seeking funds to construct buildings, purchase equipment, start a library, and endow professorships at $10,000 each. Despite this optimistic outlook, financial problems loomed.

In a reminiscence written decades later, Principal Andrus recalled: "There were classes the year through in arithmetic and English grammar—in the elements of Latin and Greek—also in algebra and geometry together with elocutionary and rhetorical exercises . . .

"After a vigorous campaign in the interest of . . . [Illinois] Wesleyan during the summer months at Quarterly meetings—camp meetings, etc.—the second year opened in September, 1851, in the basement room of the new M.E. [Methodist Episcopal] church, situated near the South East corner of the Court House Square . . ."

An advertising circular reveals Illinois Wesleyan was organized on four levels in the summer of 1851. The preparatory program had two divisions, the classical and the scientific. Classical tuition was $5 a term, while students who did not study Greek paid only $4. There were classical and scientific options for college-level work but the fee was $6 in either case. The circular listed not only trustees but students, by name. There were then 43 students listed for the preparatory program, 10 who were in the "classical" and probably college-level course.

During the late summer of 1851, Reuben Andrus and John Barger traveled through cen-tral Illinois advertising Illinois Wesleyan in an effort to attract students in conjunction with other publicity efforts. A "mass meeting" in Bloomington to explain the program must have been very persuasive, for things looked good when the 1851-52 school year opened. Surely the lower level of the new Methodist church

was more appealing than the old building, and enrollments were good. Of 101 students attend-ing the preparatory department, now headed by J.W. Sherfy, 20 were in the classical course and 81 attended the scientific program. However, at the college level, there were seven freshmen and a single sophomore in the classical course of study and 16 juniors and 10 seniors in the scientific course. Seventy-eight of the students were Bloomington residents, while J. Mayfield, called Terre Haute, Indiana, home.

Fall 1851 and Women's Education

In the fall of 1851 the question of women's education arose. Should girls be included in the new preparatory programs or the college? Solemnly, the board adopted a resolution in October, 1851, that ladies were "inexpedient" as students. In July, 1852, however, the board allowed the McLean Female Seminary to use the chapel and apparatus for lectures.

The Next "First" President: John Dempster

Waiting until June, 1852, to seek a president was leisurely to say the least. Goodfellow had been running things, and the board now elected his father-in-law president. John Dempster (1794-1863) was an odd choice, for even from the first it appeared Dempster would be an absentee leader.

Dempster was a distinguished man. His father was an alumnus of the University of Edinburgh, who had been sent to North America by John Wesley, the founder of Methodism. Born in upstate New York, Dempster managed to learn Greek, Latin, Hebrew, theology, and philosophy without attending college. He became an itinerant Methodist minister at age 21 and his work took him all over America and as far away as Buenos Aires, where he spent seven years. In 1847, however, he was in Concord, New Hampshire, starting a Biblical institute. It flourished and later moved to Boston, where

John Dempster

it became the oldest segment of Boston University. He resigned his post in Concord, when he was elected president of Illinois Wesleyan by the trustees on June 7, 1852.

However, Illinois Wesleyan University founder Reuben Andrus wrote in his *Reminiscences* that: "Dr. Dempster's appointment to the Presidency was understood to be only nominal . . . and to this arrangement he consented in deference mainly, it was believed, to the wishes of his son-in-law, Prof. Goodfellow." Consequently, the Board of Trustees appointed Goodfellow to act as president pro tem of the University in Dempster's absence.

Dempster's role at Illinois Wesleyan is still debated, if only to discover what it was. Some historians write that he resigned his Concord position once he was chosen president in Bloomington, while others maintain he was never in Bloomington, even once. There is no doubt that he did preside at the first commencement, but his strange presidency ended in June, 1854, when he concluded that he would start another Bible institute in the Chicago area. He headed north and began what is now Garrett Theological Seminary of Northwestern University.

Andrus Leaves

One of the stranger events in the first few years of Illinois Wesleyan was the departure of Reuben Andrus. At the first session of the July, 1852,

board meeting, trustees heard that Andrus did not want to continue as professor of mathematics and natural philosophy. However, the next day they elected him to just that position. He also was chosen corresponding secretary of the board. The very next day, as the same meeting continued, he was made fiscal agent as well, whereupon he resigned as professor. The board then turned to electing a new mathematics professor, only to find Andrus one of the nominees, though someone else was chosen.

Chances may be Andrus was miffed after being passed over for president, for he went on to a most interesting career. He was next principal of an academy at Springfield, president of Quincy College (later named Chaddock) from 1866-67, and served as president of Asbury, now known as DePauw, from 1872-75.

The First Catalogue

Dempster did little as Illinois Wesleyan president, but he may have had a hand in producing the first catalogue, which appeared in the fall of 1852, though it purported to describe the year 1851-52. It perhaps made Illinois Wesleyan look like more of a college than it was. For in the fall of 1852 there was a faculty of five (one of whom had left, another, the president, who almost never was there). Yet the catalogue could name eight students in the classical college course and 26 students in the scientific course. There was an astounding 101 students in the preparatory course and the catalogue goes on to outline the full course of study, text by text, for both levels. The library already numbered 1,000 books, but the big surprise was 1,700 scientific specimens, a collection that would grow to significant size in the 19th century. German was a modern language, not quite offered. The University had found a teacher, if any student was interested, but it appeared none had been so far. The catalogue reported that building would begin on a "New College Edifice" next year, while class work continued in the Methodist church, which could accommodate up to 150.

The First Commencement

Illinois Wesleyan was ready to have its first commencement on July 3, 1853. Two degrees were awarded that day. A bachelor of arts degree, generally regarded as the first, went to James Hugh Barger, son of the Methodist Episcopal minister who had played a major role in establishing the University. The other degree was a master of arts, *in cursu*, really an *ad eundem in cursu*. Daniel Wilkins, Jr. was "an alumnus of four years standing" from the University of Michigan. Normally in the 19th century an M.A. followed *in cursu*, that is in the normal course of things three years later. Virtually nothing other than receiving the degree needed to be done. Colleges also gave local residents their own degrees comparable to what recipients had earned elsewhere—the *ad eundem* degree. Wilkins, thus, got from Illinois Wesleyan the degree he would have earned for just showing up at Michigan.

Adlai E. Stevenson

Among the University's earliest students was a future vice president of the United States, Adlai E. Stevenson (1835-1914). Although official records of his attendance at the University are lost, he tells his story in a 1908 autobiography.

Stevenson was a lad, age 17, when he arrived in Bloomington in July, 1852, accompanied by his parents, aboard a horse-drawn wagon that had made the trek from Kentucky. Other sons had preceded Stevenson's parents to McLean county, setting the scene for a family reunion.

Education was a concern in the Stevenson family. " . . . the conclusion reached," according to the 1893 *[Illinois] Wesleyan Echo* was, "to send Adlai to the Illinois Wesleyan University." He stayed about a year and then he and his cousin went off to Centre College, where Stevenson married the president's daughter but did not graduate. He returned to Illinois, practiced law in Metamora and Bloomington, was elected to Congress in 1874 and 1878, served as first assistant postmaster general under President Grover

Adlai E. Stevenson

Courtesy of the McLean County Historical Society

Cleveland and in 1892 was elected vice president on the winning ticket with Cleveland, serving from 1893-97. In later years the former vice president taught in the University's law school.

The Board Revolution of December, 1852

Despite a happy first commencement in 1853, things were clearly rocky the previous December. The community spirit, which pervaded the early ideas for McLean College, had fallen apart in late 1852, when the board met at Goodfellow's house. Of 10 trustees who were up for reelection, only five were retained in office. The board voted thanks to their old president Dr. Hobbs and took two ballots to choose James Miller as his replacement. It took three ballots before James Allin was reelected vice president. These facts are not the traits of a happy board and a lot of questions remained unresolved.

Trustee Jesse Fell was clearly ascendant at that meeting, for he is the author of three consecutive motions that were adopted. Perhaps most interesting was the grand conception of the building which he led the board to adopt. There would be a "main edifice with two wings or subordinate buildings situated on either side and at convenient distances from the main structure." No plan survives, but clearly this was to be a symmetrical elegant college structure on an

Proposed early college plan. Only North Hall, with cupola, was built.

impressive scale. Work in 1853 would begin with one of the wings at a cost no greater than $6,000.

However, unanswered questions from that meeting were: Where would it be built and how would it be funded?

The December, 1852, meeting gave the illusion of progress on the building's location. The board had been talking about the location of a college since February, 1851. At that time two trustees, James Miller and James Allin, had each offered to donate 10 acres. The board thanked Miller and accepted Allin's proposal. Complications arose in May. Allin had insisted on some conditions respecting his gift. Barger moved to go ahead anyway, but his motions and Allin's conditions were voted down. Later that month the board started anew finding a site, and when it sorted multiple offers in August the trustees once more chose James Allin's proposition: 10 acres north of his house, which was north of the city.

In 1853 and 1854 the board struggled to find construction funds. Agents were appointed and pledges were made, yet ready funds were not

yet adequate. Nonetheless, the board dreamed in April, 1854, of adding a boarding house to plans for the college grounds.

The prime vehicle for funding in the planning of 1853 was selling scholarships. In a plan parallel to what McKendree had done earlier, Barger and his colleagues planned to build a $150,000 endowment by selling scholarships. A commitment of $25 brought four years of tuition for a student, $50 brought nine years, and $100 earned the right to send students for 25 student-years. The plan had not worked well at McKendree and fared no better in Bloomington. A year later Barger had sold 104 scholarships netting only $5,325.

In October, 1853, the board was either considering a new site or was told it ought to after a town picnic. In 1899 Mary Hoover's memories were distinct. Shortly after she had come to town, she and friends took basket suppers and like many others, walked up Center Street to a picnic "held in the grove that had been selected as the site for the Illinois Wesleyan University." She was unsure in 1899 whether the picnic itself was where Old North was built, or farther west and a little north. Forty-five years later she remembered the leaves of red, gold, and brown against the steel blue sky, an altogether brilliant outing.

Work actually began on the Allin site. Lumber and other materials were gathered for construction. Yet very strangely in June, 1854, the board raised anew the whole question of location. Once more there were three sites, in addition to Allin's, that remained live options. Linus Graves offered 10 acres on Grove Street, near the Illinois Central depot, Kersey Fell offered land near the two railroads, and finally nurseryman Franklin Kelsey Phoenix had a proposition.

Phoenix would sell Illinois Wesleyan 8.5 acres "including his fine grove situated a little east of Main Street and north of the city." If the trustees accepted the offer, he would give $1,000, half in cash to the University, the other half in trees and shrubs. Immediately the board learned that if the Phoenix site was accepted, there would be four pledges of $500, including ones from David Davis, William Allin, and James Allin. It was a proposition hard to resist and immediately the Allin site was given up. Illinois Wesleyan would rise on the Phoenix nursery grounds.

Bloomington as a College Town

In the summer of 1854 Bloomington surely saw itself as a college town, but Illinois Wesleyan was only marginally part of that scene. Daniel Wilkins, who received an M. A. at the first commencement, was now head of the Central Illinois Female College. After the University of Michigan, Wilkins had traveled about teaching landscape painting, settling in Bloomington in 1851. His college opened in 1853, and that first fall Wilkins had 221 pupils at the school and college levels in an old seminary building at Main and Olive. Many of his trustees were also on the Illinois Wesleyan board. If Illinois Wesleyan had one college graduate by 1854, so did the Central Illinois Female College,

which awarded Sarah Funk the degree Mistress of the Liberal Arts. The college lasted at least until 1857, when it seems to have migrated to Abingdon, Illinois, where Hedding took the official name Hedding Seminary and Central Illinois Female College.

Then there was the colorful Dr. J. R. Freeze, who built College Hall on Center Street, just west of the courthouse. There he hoped to open the Western Law and Medical College. Freeze wrote all about it in Bloomington's first city directory of which he was author and publisher in 1855. Chartered in 1853, the school listed a roster of eight on its medical faculty. Though its building was finished, "unavoidable circumstances" delayed regular course work. In the meantime College Hall was a veritable cultural center for Bloomington with public lectures on science and concerts by the Bloomington band.

College Life

Illinois Wesleyan was barely a functional college, but its students and faculty showed real signs of college life nonetheless. That the University's Philomathian, a literary society, gathered for a program in College Hall on December 5, 1854, is about the only record the group ever existed. Music brought together talent from many sources. Both Mr. and Mrs. Wilkins were quite musical, as was J.W. Sherfy, head of the preparatory program at Illinois Wesleyan, who for a time was conductor of the new Musical Association, which performed at College Hall. Vocal music was part of the program at the Female College, even though one business leader threatened to withdraw his support unless the institution stopped what he thought a "waste of time and energy."

Students went to political talks, too, some at College Hall, some at Major's Hall, others at the courthouse. Former U.S. President Millard Fillmore appeared in June, 1854, and Abraham Lincoln and U.S. Senator Stephen A. Douglas appeared on the Nebraska question—an event a youthful Adlai Stevenson remembered attending.

Probably more exciting to the students of Illinois Wesleyan and the Central Illinois Female College was the possibility of a joint outing. The Illinois Central Railroad started regular service to Bloomington on May 24, 1853, and within two weeks one group had mounted a special railway excursion to a grove 20 miles north along the Mackinaw River near Kappa. The next spring the professors of both colleges probably arranged for extra cars, for nearly 200 faculty, students, and friends gathered for picnics with fishing rods and swings. The 8 a.m. train was scheduled to take an hour and 17 minutes to run the 22 miles to Kappa, but that was part of the fun. All had a wonderful day in the country until the southbound train came through Kappa at 5 p.m.

Summer 1854

In 1853 and 1854 there had been wrangling over the University's site, funding seemed to lag, the board leadership was constantly changing, and Illinois Wesleyan was far from flourishing. Illinois Wesleyan President Dempster was very seldom present and in summer 1854 he chose to resign to work on his Bible institute in Evanston, Illinois. The board voted to "regret the loss of Dr. Dempster's presence," an odd phrase when some historians have thought he was never in Bloomington.

Things worsened in the fall of 1854 and the early winter of 1855. There was wrangling over costs of moving lumber from the old site to the new one and Goodfellow resigned, leaving the institution without a president or president pro tem. The board tried, unsuccessfully, to retain Andrus again and tried to make Peter Akers president. Akers, a trustee, was a Methodist presiding elder in another area. He would accept the post only if it was endowed with $15,000. Under the circumstances, that was another way of saying no. Later that month, the board debated suspending the school entirely. Andrus was invited to return to take charge of instruction, not quite offered the presidency. He declined. Contractors talked about liens on the college for unpaid bills

and the board even considered building on the old Allin site. Given all these circumstances, comparatively few students were enrolled and the board was way behind on paying the faculty.

Isaac Kenyon, a student during that period, kept a diary. On January 22, 1855, he wrote: "The Illinois Wesleyan University suspended operations this morning, the school not being sufficiently large to support the teachers." While Illinois Wesleyan wondered what might happen next, the boys acted. Twenty-seven of them went to the corner of Main and Olive and somehow signed up at the Female College. They were welcome there, at least until April 30 as Kenyon's diary continued: "The young men have been thrown out of the school on account of the dissatisfaction of some of its patrons, their wish being none but the ladies be permitted to attend."

The expulsion was fortuitous, for it offered at least a minimal enrollment for the plan being developed by Illinois Wesleyan's loyal Clinton Sears (1820-1863). Sears had appeared in Bloomington in two roles in 1852. He was professor of ancient languages and he was a fund raiser. Born in New York, he graduated from Wesleyan University in 1841, went to seminary in Cincinnati, and served several churches before becoming a professor.

When the board met in April, 1855. Sears offered a plan for the future, which was accepted in June now that there were at least 27 potential students. Sears spoke with vigor as he outlined details in August. He prescribed "efforts be made immediately and energetically in its behalf by opening the school, by providing for new buildings and perfecting the endowment."

His plan for the future revealed difficulties in the past. Earlier decisions made in one meeting had been overturned in later discussions and forward movement had been impeded by unending debate and continual reopening of old questions. Sears' plan: he would be president *and* head of the board. Board decisions were put in the hands of an executive committee of five with power to act on a continuing basis. Sears structured incentives to succeed: his annual salary would be $800 plus a percentage of donations raised, yet he aimed at finishing the college building, constructing a sidewalk to town, building a dormitory to cost no more than $12,000, and establishing an endowment of $50,000. The sidewalk was of critical importance. Bloomington's center may seem relatively close to the campus now, but it was then considered a long, muddy walk. Sears gave the board a mandate: if it wanted him to do all this, then the building and sidewalk must be finished by October. The board agreed and suddenly Illinois Wesleyan had a president, its first in residence.

Optimism was premature. The building and the sidewalk were completed after Sears provided part of the funds for the sidewalk himself. Yet fund-raising lagged, and at the board's meeting in July, 1855, the first ever in the "College Building," Sears had not raised the funds he had hoped. When the board saw the numbers, it realized the president had been paid a salary $60 less than Sears had spent himself on the sidewalk. Sears quit. After he left in October, 1856, Sears was pastor of Methodist churches in Springfield and Urbana, Illinois, and Cincinnati. He was a chaplain with the 95th Ohio Volunteers during the Civil War.

Once more Illinois Wesleyan had no president and a very uncertain future. It was a Methodist school in a town with many churches and two other colleges. In a word the school had a sectarian image, uncertain management, and no money. The board now hit on a new approach: if it was to be a Methodist school, could the local conference fund it? This had not been part of the original model. The Methodist Conference annual meetings in Peoria in 1856 were the place to ask. In the meantime, the board adopted this terse resolution: "that the school be suspended until a sufficient amount can be raised to pay off all the indebtedness of the Board of Trustees."

With an exiting president, an unpaid faculty,

an unfunded building, an ever-changing board, two alumni (another had graduated in 1854), and heavy debt, Illinois Wesleyan closed for the second time in six years. Most probably thought it would never reopen. High on that list was the board, which in August, 1856, voted to sell the fabled sidewalk and rent the building to "any one who will carry on a good school."

Peoria, 1856

The Peoria meetings of the Methodist Conference offered new hope. Changes will seem very subtle to those not versed in ecclesiastical politics. Illinois Wesleyan previously had been an independent institution whose rules required that a majority be members of the Methodist Episcopal church. Other than that, it was an independent corporation with a self-perpetuating board. The old board now offered to turn over control completely to the Illinois Conference in the south of the state and the new Peoria Conference. The conferences would choose trustees and the expectation was they would provide funds directly. The University would become a church agency "under their exclusive control."

Delegates to both conferences agreed to the proposition. Motions adopted stipulated a new charter reflecting the organizational changes and the name was to "be so changed as to be called a college." The preparatory department was to be reopened on a solid basis. Within the next few months as the conferences nominated their own trustees, some of the old community leaders who had worked for the dream of a non-sectarian college in their community disappeared from the roster.

Probably the best part of this new arrangement, however, was the arrival of the Munsell family.

The Munsell Brothers

There is no denying that Illinois Wesleyan University owes its existence to the three Munsell brothers: Oliver S., Charles W. C., and

Oliver S. Munsell

Charles W. C. Munsell

Edward. The University had halted operations in 1856 when perhaps any rational manager would have quit.

To be sure, the University had 10 acres of land, but resting on that property was a half finished, debt-ridden building. Efforts to raise endowments had foundered, enrollment was soft, assets were nil, and the trustees were obligated to pay 22-percent interest on a debt. Adding to these financial woes was the fact that 1857 turned out to be a notable depression year, when a financial panic struck New York.

Ohioan Oliver Munsell (1825-1905) had studied under private tutors and then attended Asbury College in Indiana, now DePauw University. With his father's encouragement, after Asbury, Munsell spent a year studying law and was admitted to the bar in 1846. "Though admitted to practice, he never followed the profession," according to *An Historical Sketch and Alumni Record, 1855-1896*, "as a revolution had taken place in his thoughts and plans. In September of the same year he was licensed to preach." From 1851 to 1854, when his health failed, Munsell was principal of Illinois' Danville Seminary. Somewhat recovered, he moved to Mount Morris, Illinois, in 1856, where he taught at the Rock River Seminary.

Munsell was elected president of Illinois Wesleyan in July, 1857. He recognized needs and possibilities, so he made a contract with the Board of Trustees very similar to what

Sears had sought. He would come to Illinois Wesleyan, if he had complete financial control and could select the faculty. Surely the most amazing part of this arrangement was his plan to run the University for three years at his own personal expense. Who could resist?

His brother Charles W. C. Munsell (1822-1915) was to be financial agent and trustee of the University. Also a native of Ohio, Charles Munsell came to Illinois in 1832 and was admitted to the Methodist ministry in 1846. He already had played a key role in raising funds for founding Illinois seminaries in Danville and Shelbyville.

The Munsell agenda aimed at improving finances by $75,000 to pay off debts, erecting additional facilities, and building an endowment. On July 31, 1857, the *Daily Pantagraph* reported on Munsell's progress, observing that "doubtless many of the citizens of Bloomington have been led to consider the Illinois Wesleyan University as defunct, to use a vulgar but expressive word." But, the newspaper added, "it is, perhaps, time that such a mistaken notion should be corrected." While Munsell had not raised all the money needed, the *Daily Pantagraph* reported that "the Trustees have made arrangements for the opening of the University this coming fall and are able to assure the public that the Institution, so far as the maintenance of the school for three years to come is concerned, is upon a reliable basis."

A vocal quintet from 1868 with Joseph Fifer,
Governor of Illinois 1870-74, middle, seated.

For three years a third Munsell brother, Edward B., was part of the University. From the fall of 1858 to 1861 he was professor of mental and moral science.

Back in Business

Oliver and Charles Munsell were undaunted by neither troubled finances nor the Panic of 1857. They got the University back in business. The Munsells found money to complete the building or "College Edifice" as it was then called. In September, 1857, 17 students started courses.

Within a week, however, six of these 17 had left school because, as Munsell in later years recalled, "They said it was so lonesome. The students advised the faculty to leave also, but we stayed."

Munsell even organized a second catalogue, which came out in the summer of 1858. One can count the improvements. The College Edifice was described as "new, spacious and convenient; beautifully located in a pleasant grove." It had recitation rooms and a chapel, the library was growing, and "philosophical and chemical apparatus" (a standard term for scientific equipment) had been bought from eastern cities.

Munsell cast a broad appeal for students. Though Illinois Wesleyan had Methodist support, it was not just for Methodists. Daily chapel was required, but students were allowed to attend any of the seven churches in town on Sundays. Students were prohibited from amusements on Sundays, as well as being absent from their rooms "at improper hours," they couldn't drink, write on furniture, wear firearms, contract debts, use profane language, or refuse compliance with any faculty requirement.

In the fall of 1858 Illinois Wesleyan still had a long way to go. The new edifice would house instruction facilities for 250 students. The catalogue listed three sophomores, four freshmen, and 40 in the preparatory department. For financial purposes Munsell must have been delighted to have 13 additional students even though they were "irregulars." The next two falls the composite enrollment hovered around 90 students. Gradually students came and stayed, regular catalogues appeared, and the roster of preparatory students, college students, and graduates grew.

In 1860 Oliver Munsell's three-year contract was up and financial control reverted to the Board of Trustees. However, Munsell insisted on financial discipline, and the Board of Trustees agreed.

The catalogue for 1857-58 shows a surprisingly interesting university for an institution that so recently was in a perilous condition. There was a faculty of five for a college-student population of 20 at most.

By the end of the 1850s, Illinois Wesleyan's financial complexion was brighter. The University's accounts in 1858-59 showed $11,700 in resources versus $12,584 in liabilities. The $25,000 endowment campaign was going well and by October 12, 1859, only $1,250 of the $25,000 remained to be raised. Ninety-two students enrolled for the 1860-61 school year on the eve of civil war, including two seniors, six juniors, eight sophomores, 16 freshmen, and 60 preparatory students.

The *Daily Pantagraph* reported on July 4, 1860, Independence Day, that the "Messrs. Munsell Bros. are laudably expending much money and labor to make their Institution what it ought to be and we trust their labors of love may early begin to meet their merited reward. They speak cheerfully of the prospects of the Institution and think the school will be large this fall, should the crops turn out favorably."

III. The Civil War to 1888
A College and University Become Reality

⌘

Abraham Lincoln's election as president of the United States crystallized the national political forces and the simmering debate over slavery that drove the nation to civil war in the early hours of April 12, 1861.

Confederate forces took Fort Sumter and every aspect of American culture was touched for the next four years. Paradoxically, compared to earlier years, Illinois Wesleyan flourished.

There is no record that Lincoln ever spoke at Illinois Wesleyan, but Adlai Stevenson, a future U.S. vice president, was one Illinois Wesleyan student who remembered hearing him and Stephen A. Douglas, a U.S. Senator from Illinois, speak in Bloomington. Members of Illinois Wesleyan's Board of Trustees played no small role in Lincoln's election to the White House. Trustee Kersey Fell first encouraged Lincoln to run for president, and trustee David Davis was a Lincoln confidante. The Munsells had known Lincoln since 1840, when the future U.S. president stayed in their house and the future Illinois Wesleyan president, Oliver Munsell, was a 15-year-old. Munsell was not forgotten in Washington, when Lincoln appointed him head of the Board of Visitors of the United States Military Academy at West Point in 1863. Ralph Waldo Emerson, the great man of American letters, served on the same panel.

Munsell set a new model, for he was president, professor, and scholar. In 1871 as the new building opened, Appleton in New York published his *Psychology, or, The Science of Mind,* a book that was to go through many editions as the century went on. Future Illinois Wesleyan faculty would henceforth be publishing scholars as well.

On the eve of the Civil War, Illinois Wesleyan with its 92 students was doing the things colleges normally did in the spring as the Belles Lettres Society had its first annual exhibition. Three months after the Fort Sumter battle, the University convened its first wartime graduation on July 3, 1861, as two more students received diplomas. One of the graduates that day, Harvey C. DeMotte (1838-1904), would join the faculty in September as professor of mathematics and librarian and spend the rest of his life coming and going at Illinois Wesleyan.

Kersey Fell

Born in Illinois Regiment, DeMotte found his way to Bloomington in 1856. Faculty would remember him as a colleague with a "special aptitude as a tutor and remarkable ability as a student in mathematics." After serving as a lieutenant with the 68th Illinois Regiment, DeMotte resumed his teaching of mathematics until 1884, when he accepted the presidency of Chaddock College in Quincy, Illinois. In 1877 DeMotte

◄ Old Main, later Hedding Hall, was the center of campus life from 1871 until its demolition in 1967.

Joseph (left) and George Fifer

had received a Ph.D. *in absentia* from Syracuse University.

The University's first two graduates—James H. Barger and W.F. Short—received master of arts degrees *in cursu* at the 1861 commencement. Alas, John Barger, the first alumnus, died four months later after a hunting accident.

When the 1861-62 academic year opened, enrollment stood at 96 students, including one graduate student and 45 students in the preparatory department. Ironically, University enrollment grew during the Civil War. And by 1864-65 the University could count 236 students, still all male, 57 in the Model School, 138 in the preparatory program, and 41 in the college.

The increased student body came from new programs, new funds, good marketing, and a burgeoning population base. However, students were not just local, but regularly came from Missouri, Arkansas, Kentucky, Indiana, Iowa, and Ohio, as well as Illinois. Even in the 1850s there had been students from Texas and New Jersey.

President Munsell announced new scientific developments in the catalogue of 1862. New chemical "apparatuses" were on the way and the state of Illinois had provided many new geological specimens for students to use. The State Natural History Society had located its collections in Bloomington. In 1858 the Illinois Natural History Society had brought these collections to Bloomington, where they were the basis of the first public museum in Illinois, located in the Phoenix block on Courthouse Square. For students science was not just books, it was also fully illustrated "in the museum and in the field," according to the 1862 catalogue.

Early in the Civil War the University's single building ran into some tough times when a windstorm blew off its roof. Repairs cost $1,000. "When the roof blew off," President Oliver Munsell said, "people thought it a misfortune, but I thought it a blessing. For the citizens of Bloomington came to our help and by their aid we got a new and better roof."

The University and the Civil War

In 1942 the *Argus* researched Illinois Wesleyan's role in the Civil War and found that many students found their way into a volunteer company of 200 that entered the conflict as a state militia guard unit. In time the company petitioned for regular status and became part of the 68th regiment stationed at Wheeling, West Virginia.

Sophomore George H. Fifer enlisted in the Union army on August 10, 1861. He died of wounds received during the attack on Fort Esperanza, Texas, in the winter of 1863, making him the first alumnus battlefield casualty.

George Fifer's younger brother, Joseph (1840-1938), also served in the Union army. He was a member of the class of 1868 and the 37th student to earn an Illinois Wesleyan diploma. On July 13, 1863—just days after Union victories at Vicksburg in the west and Gettysburg in the east— "Private Joe" was severely wounded on a Jackson, Mississippi, battlefield. He survived the war, entered law and politics, and in 1888, at age 48, he was elected the 19th governor of Illinois.

From his house on Bloomington's Franklin Square, he remained a loyal alumnus and led the citizens' committee of 1899, which raised enough money to clear a deficit that threatened to close the enterprise. Like Adlai Stevenson, he later taught in the law school.

Illinois Wesleyan in Wartime

Despite the ravages of war, the academic calendar continued. Three students received degrees at the 1862 commencement, including Henry W. Boyd of Bloomington, who enlisted as a hospital steward within a week of graduation and became a brigade surgeon. Later, he was professor of anatomy at Chicago's Rush Medical College.

When the 1862-63 school year opened, most of the students from the 68th regiment had returned to a campus continually improving under Oliver Munsell's leadership. The museum continued to grow with valuable collections of specimens in ornithology, geology, botany, entomology, mineralogy, and marine shells. And after Munsell visited Washington, D.C., a set of

Bloomington and Illinois Wesleyan gathering at the courthouse square to mourn the death of President Lincoln.

Smithsonian publications arrived for the library. More audible than visible was a new 750-pound bell to summon students to class.

Commencement 1863 graduated four students and one of them became a University legend. An honorary master of arts degree was awarded to Major John Wesley Powell. Powell had a good feeling for Bloomington, for he had become the Secretary of the Illinois Natural History Society in 1861, shortly after its collections were located on courthouse square.

Despite wartime conditions academic initiatives were vigorous. The University first offered vocal music in the collegiate department about the time it launched the Model School for Boys. Consequently, when the 1863-64 academic year began, the University had its first woman instructor as Sarah J. Kern began directing the Model School, which attracted an initial enrollment of 42 students. With confidence far different from the 1850s, the University built a wooden schoolhouse on the east side of campus just for this program.

Campus Atmosphere

The atmosphere in the midst of Civil War was described in an April 18, 1864, *Daily Pantagraph* account of campus activities:

"The young men of Illinois Wesleyan University will give a public exhibition in Phoenix Hall next Thursday evening of a decidedly unique character. It will be a representation of the present National House of Representatives, in which will be included a discussion upon a series of resolutions concerning the French occupation of Mexico, the President's Emancipation and Amnesty Proclamations and our relations toward England. This will be an interesting entertainment conducted by young gentlemen of ability and the friends of the school will be glad to witness it."

The 1864 commencement saw degrees awarded to five students, including Joseph H. Pancake, who became head of the Model School before practicing law in Bloomington until 1891,

when he moved to Kansas and became a member of that state's legislature.

As the end of the war neared, faculty met in January, 1865, "to consider the matter of raising a fund to provide for the free tuition of disabled young soldiers and the sons of needy or deceased soldiers." On April 3, 1865, the faculty minutes contain this terse comment: "Half holiday granted. Richmond captured."

An Assassin's Bullet

But, as peace emerged from war, a great tragedy took place on April 14, 1865—the assassination of Abraham Lincoln. Some 6,000 gathered at the courthouse square on the following Sunday as speakers expressed Bloomington's sense of horror at Lincoln's death. Most students were there.

One of the four students who received diplomas in 1865 had a gift for President Munsell—a silver-headed cane. And a distinguished Bloomington political figure, David Davis, received an honorary degree. Davis (1815-86) was a U.S. Supreme Court justice, appointed to the nation's highest judicial bench by his good friend, Abraham Lincoln. Davis served as a trustee from 1852-56. His encouragement and gifts had been instrumental in selecting the Phoenix nursery site for the University.

By the mid-1860s enrollment swelled to a new high, 198 students—57 in the collegiate and 141 in the preparatory department. There is some indication in University records that the soldiers-turned-students had some difficulty adjusting to civilian life, now freed from military discipline. Faculty meeting records find many entries along these lines: "punishment for willful violation of college rules."

1866 Commencement

Illinois Wesleyan's 1866 commencement has been described as a "brilliant affair." There were a record six graduates, but probably the best remembered part of the ceremony was the tree planted to symbolize the last four years of war and the prospect of future peace. A large ever-green tree was planted in front of the University hall, an initial living memorial to those who were killed in the Civil War.

John Wesley Powell

War's end not only brought former soldiers to the ranks of students—it brought new faculty. When a major from the Second Illinois Artillery joined the faculty, the University acquired its most colorful figure of the 19th century.

John Wesley Powell (1834-1902) was a

John Wesley Powell

natural academic. He was born in Mount Morris, New York, the son of an itinerant Methodist minister. Powell went to schools in Ohio, Wisconsin, and Illinois before attending college at Illinois College, Wheaton in Illinois, and Oberlin, without managing to graduate from any of them. He taught school in the 1850s, but his great passion was natural history and geology. He loved collecting specimens and taking notes. The Illinois State Natural History Society made him its secretary in 1861, an office which brought him to Bloomington, where the eager collector could deposit his best specimens.

During the war, Powell rose from private to major and he lost his right arm at Shiloh in April 1862. As soon as possible, he was back as chief of artillery for the 17th Army Corps. Never forgetting geology even during the war, he was

out collecting specimens near Vicksburg, a famous Mississippi battlefield. After many years in college, his honorary M.A. from Illinois Wesleyan was the only degree he had and at war's end he moved to Bloomington as professor of geology, and curator of the University collections and the Illinois Natural History Society Museum.

Powell stayed for only a year, or two, or three. Accounts vary. When the new building at Illinois State Normal University was completed it offered a far better home for the collections of the Illinois Natural History Society, which moved from the city's square to the Illinois State Normal University museum, thus, bringing Powell an association with ISNU. But in his short time at Illinois Wesleyan, he accomplished extraordinary things.

He gave the University a seal and a motto— *Scientia et Sapientia.* Knowledge is fundamentally facts, wisdom is reflective judgment on them, and a university education provides both, as his motto put it so succinctly. He designed a new diploma with his seal. Given his association with collections and museums and the great museum rooms in the new building of 1871, it is impossible to think he was not a continuing influence in both program and design. But most of all he infused the academic program with a sense of scientific mission which has never left it.

During his last two years in Bloomington, Powell became the grand embodiment of that phrase Munsell had put in the catalogue of 1862: science would be "fully illustrated . . . in the museum and in the field." Those years gave new meaning to "field." Powell took Bloomington students on the first expedition of its kind in the United States. In later years Illinois Governor Joseph Fifer remembered "my professor of science was Major John Wesley Powell, explorer, ethnologist, linguist and sociologist, a very great man." Those were just the traits needed to lead students off into the unknown of the Rocky Mountains and the frontier of the American West.

Powell at Harper's Ferry, Virgina, May 1873 with (from left to right) Sir Archibald Geikie, a renowned Scottish geologist, Powell, Charles Walcott, who succeeded Powell as director of the Geological Survey, and an unidentified individual.

A young John Wesley Powell.

Powell with a Paiute Chief 1873.

Exploring the West

Powell's first expedition was in 1867. He set out across the plains after acquiring assistance from the U.S. War Department. Among the adventurers were Leonidas H. Kerrick, principal of the Model School, and three Illinois Wesleyan students: senior Joseph C. Hartzell (later a Methodist Bishop of Africa), sophomore Francis Marion Bishop, and junior Martin Titterington. Kerrick served as mineralogist, Hartzell and Bishop were zoologists, and Titterington was a herpetologist.

Meeting at Council Bluffs, Iowa, the group deviated from its original plan to explore the Bad Lands because of an Indian threat. Instead, the party followed the Platte River across Nebraska and headed for Denver, where it arrived on July 1. It was a difficult trip on horseback and in mule-drawn wagons, but a profitable journey. The scientific team collected many specimens along the way. From Denver, the explorers went to the canyon of the South Platte, still adding to their collections and crossed a range of the Rocky Mountains to the base of Pike's Peak.

As the expedition unfolded, *Daily Pantagraph* readers followed their adventures in dispatches from Hartzell. One piece told the tale of climbing Pike's Peak, difficult under any circumstances, but the unstoppable Powell had lost an arm:

"But climbing nearly to the top of one of the peaks from which the main route could be reached, we encountered what had been a great slide of rocks, lying then upon the mountainside in rough, unstable irregularity. An attempt to cross, mules stepping or jumping from rock to rock like goats, falls and bruises for both man and beast, the snow was reached, but rocks continued, the attempt was abandoned and a perilous descent began, firm footing at length gained in comparative safety, and a new place selected for the ascent—all this consumed time and muscle."

The 1868 expedition west was larger and included five students: L.W. Keplinger, a recent

graduate and topographer; junior James B. Taylor, geologist; Edmund D. Poston, a second-year preparatory student, geologist; freshman Rhodes C. Allen, ornithologist, and Lyle H. Durley, a student in the scientific course and ornithologist.

A trip highlight was the ascent of Long's Peak. "There they took barometric observations, erected a small monument of rocks in which was placed a tin can containing data on the expedition," Elmo Scott Watson wrote in the centennial history. "After raising the American flag, the major made a short speech declaring that they had been successful in an 'undertaking in the material or physical field which had hitherto been deemed impossible' and predicted that their feat was 'but the augury of yet greater achievement in other fields' . . ."

Powell left an indelible stamp on U.S. higher education as the first professor to introduce field work on a grand scale into the undergraduate-college curriculum.

Powell's Legacy

Powell's expeditions to the western frontier produced a number of firsts: the climbing of Long's Peak, the exploration of the Continental Divide, a series of ethnological studies of Western Indian tribes, exploration of the Grand Canyon by white men, and maps of the Grand Canyon. In 1875 the Smithsonian Institution in Washington, D.C., published Powell's expedition reports about the geology of the Grand Canyon and the Utah Mountains.

Powell held many interesting posts throughout his career: a founder of the National Geographic Society (1888), second director of the U.S. Geologic Survey (1881-94), and first director of the Smithsonian's Bureau of American Ethnology (1897-1902). He was responsible for collecting and recording much of the language and lore of Native-American tribes.

Illinois Wesleyan continues to honor Powell with a campus monument, and the annual research conference, which keeps his spirit alive. Powell's connections continued long after he had gone to the Smithsonian. Based on his scholarly work, Illinois Wesleyan conferred a Ph.D. on him in 1877. This was not an honorary degree, but it was part of the external-degree program, which had begun in 1874. Powell continued to augment the University collections and the library today displays pieces of Native-American pottery, which he gave to Illinois Wesleyan.

Engaging Personalities

The years spanning the Civil War to the mid-1870s saw many engaging personalities attracted to Illinois Wesleyan. They were a diverse group of publishing scholars as well as memorable teachers.

For example, there was Bradford S. Potter, who was born in upstate New York in 1836. He went to Walworth Academy and then taught school before he entered Genesse Wesleyan, now Syracuse University. After two years as the principal of an academy, he moved around swiftly through Indiana and New York before he went to Baker University in Kansas as professor of mathematics. From that post, he was called to Illinois Wesleyan as the Isaac Funk Professor of Agriculture from 1867 to 1876. He also succeeded Powell as curator and was responsible for the major museum installation on the third floor of the new building constructed in the early 1870s. Potter left in 1876, but returned in 1884 as professor of mathematics and then professor of natural science until 1892.

For many years Potter and his colleague Harvey C. DeMotte published *The Alumni Journal*, an interesting vehicle for students as well as faculty. Potter also was co-author of surely the first book published by an Illinois Wesleyan student. After some time probably teaching, R. B. Welch ultimately graduated from Illinois Wesleyan in 1877 and became superintendent of schools in Pontiac, Illinois, and then president of the State Normal School of Kansas. He stayed on in Topeka as a lawyer. Yet, in 1871 he was a sophomore, when he and Potter published *Common Sense Applied to*

Numbers. Printed in Bloomington, it taught a system whereby those who learned it could eyeball a column of figures and announce the total. Another trick shows how to know—not guess—the day of the week for any historical event. Only one copy seems to survive, which turned up in a Bloomington flea market for $2, a reemergent monument to early student–faculty collaboration.

Jabez Jaques (1828-1892) was born in England. Like Potter, he too was a Syracuse alumnus, head of his class in 1854. He moved among schools and churches as a Methodist minister for several years until he was appointed professor of ancient languages at the University of Rochester. Jaques arrived at Illinois Wesleyan in 1865 to teach classics and, now for the first time in the curriculum, German. Ten years later, he left to become president of Albert College in Belleville, Canada and returned to Illinois in 1886 as president of Hedding College.

Lucien Marcus Underwood (1853-1907), a New Yorker with a Ph.D. from Syracuse, was the Isaac Funk Professor of Agriculture from 1880-84. Just like John Wesley Powell, Underwood was a scientist who went on to a national career. While Underwood was at Illinois Wesleyan, he wrote *Our Native Ferns and Their Allies*, which was first published in 1881.

Another faculty member from the early 1870s merits note. There from 1871 to 1873 at the bottom of the faculty list was Charles P. Merriman, who taught French, Spanish, and Italian. In 1849 when he was the newspaper editor, he had organized the first efforts for a Bloomington college. Now living in reduced circumstances, he found part-time employment at the venture he had launched. Everyone else was professor; he was instructor.

Academics in the 1860s

The 1865-66 catalogue reported that the scientific curriculum had been rearranged to meet the wants of students "whose time, means, and

The University
seal on McPherson
Theatre. The seal and
motto were designed by
John Wesley Powell.

other circumstances do not admit of their pursuing the regular Collegiate Course." The program
now took four years and included all the other
work of the "Regular Course" except the ancient
languages.

From the first, Illinois Wesleyan offered multiple undergraduate degrees. Even in the 1851-
52 catalogue the Scientific Department offered
the degree of Bachelor of Science in English
Literature. "It embraces," according to the catalogue, "all the studies of the collegiate course
except the Ancient Languages" and required two
years after the preparatory department.

Collegiate Study, however, led to the bachelor of arts degree, "the same as is pursued at the
oldest and best colleges in the United States,"
the catalogue declared. This program took four
years after preparatory work and with no hesi-
tancy at all the catalogue assured students, "This
course is the only reliable one for making sound,

practical, and accomplished scholars."

The 1866 catalogue carried another of those
provisions, which put Illinois Wesleyan in a
league with standard American, and English
practice. As is still the case at Oxford, the
degree of master of arts went to any "Bachelor of
Arts of three years standing, who in the interval
has sustained a good moral character," according
to the 1866 Illinois Wesleyan University catalogue. This practice was given up only in the
early 1890s with academic reforms enacted at
that time—and only applied to bachelor of arts
degrees, never bachelor of science degrees.

Admission of African-American Students

University trustees approved admission of
African-American students in 1867. In May,
1867, there was an exchange of letters in the
Daily Pantagraph between President Munsell and

Alfred O. Coffin

Hannah I. Shur

an individual dubbed, "Radical," focusing on the admission of African-Americans to the University.

The background for this exchange of correspondence is found in the minutes of the April 17, 1867, faculty meeting record: "Whereas 'an American citizen of African descent' has applied for admission to our institution; therefore . . . this question be submitted to the Executive Board for their decision." The June 18, 1867, minutes of the Board of Trustees' meeting said that the matter of admitting "Negroes to the college" was referred to a committee. Finally, the June 21, 1867, board minutes reported that the committee's favorable decision on admitting African-Americans was adopted. If, after all these discussions, the student in question enrolled, all record has been lost and this pioneer cannot be identified. Nonetheless the principle had been established and did not change.

The first African-American graduate of Illinois Wesleyan was Gus A. Hill, who received a law degree in 1880 and later became an attorney in Chicago.

Alfred O. Coffin was another early African-American graduate of the University. Coffin, who was born of slave parents in Mississippi in 1861, attended the mid-1880s, studying biology as part of a post-graduate course. Eventually, he became a teacher and college professor.

Clarence A. Johnson of Normal, Illinois, was another early African-American student.

A freshman in the 1909-10 academic year, Johnson was enrolled in the scientific course and served as treasurer of the Munsellian Literary Society. Johnson, who died in 1912 before graduating, was memorialized in a front page *Argus* article on October 29, 1912, which emotionally declared: "He commended the esteem and respect of all of his fellow students and these words from his pen will be treasured by many who knew him." The *Argus* editors printed a three-page piece Johnson had written, entitled, *"The American Negro."*

First Female Graduate

When Illinois Wesleyan held its commencement in 1872, the University marked a milestone. President Munsell, who bestowed a degree on his son, also "was for the first time called upon to confer the regular degree of the University upon a lady," according to historian Elmo Scott Watson. "The appearance of Hannah I. Shur upon the platform to receive her diploma was greeted with hearty applause by the audience, showing a genuine sympathy with the 'advance step' taken by the Institution." She was the 74th student to receive a diploma.

Shur (1838-1912), whose maiden name was Weatherby, was born in Chesterville, Ohio. She married Artemus O. Shur in March, 1863, and two years later moved to El Paso, Illinois, where she was active in the women's club and other organizations.

Henrietta Cramp

Charles Cramp

Mrs. Susannah M.D. Fry

Some trustees of Illinois Wesleyan had suggested admitting women to the University as early as 1851. In 1869 one trustee offered a resolution "asking for a change in the charter so as to admit Females to the University as students," triggering a "spicy debate" and the resolution was tabled.

Higher education was already more accessible to women with the emergence of new colleges for women: Vassar, Smith, Wellesley, and others. During the 1869-70 academic year, the board moved toward the admission of women and in June, 1870, the trustees and visitors convened in Bloomington. President Munsell delivered a faculty report:

"Your faculty would further recommend the consideration of the possibility of admitting ladies as students to the University and herewith beg leave to present a resolution adopted at their last regular meeting for the year, viz.

"Resolved, that we recommend to the joint Board of Trustees and Visitors of the University that the privileges of the University be extended to all regardless of sex."

The faculty recommendation was referred to a trustee-visitor committee, which reported to the board that they "unanimously and heartily concur with the recommendations of the faculty," triggering another debate over various resolutions and counter resolutions. Eventually, a

vote was taken. The recommendation that "classes of the University be opened to ladies" won on a 17-5 vote.

The Coeds

And so women were admitted in 1870. Twenty-two women entered the University that year, including Kate B. Ross, who was admitted as a sophomore, and Delia Henry and Rhoda M. Wiley, who were admitted as freshmen, while 19 women were admitted to the preparatory department. Ross and Martha Benjamin graduated in 1874. None of the discussions on admission of women turned on market expansion, but that was the net effect of opening the doors: by 1875 a third of the freshmen were women.

The Women's Educational Association was formed on June 3, 1874, by "several ladies," including Jennie F. Willing, professor of English language and literature, who was elected chairman of the meeting. Subsequently, the association—which survived until 1892—adopted a constitution that defined its goals: "the endowment of a Woman's Professorship, and secondly, the raising of a fund to provide a home, and assist young women who are struggling to educate themselves . . .," the 1874 catalogue explained.

In September, 1875, the association leased the building, known as Major's College and opened a ladies' boarding hall. Subsequently, the association purchased the Major's College property, located three blocks from the campus. For young ladies who wished to pay their boarding fees through their own labor, they could enjoy "the privilege of one hour domestic work per day," which would garner them "[t]en cents per hour . . . for satisfactory work." In 1884 Charles and Henrietta Cramp gave $4,000 to liquidate the indebtedness on the property. The hall, afterwards, was known as Henrietta Hall in honor of Mrs. Cramp.

Early Female Faculty

The first woman to hold a professorship was Jennie F. Willing. She was professor of English literature in the University from 1873-76. Born in 1834, Willing earned a master of arts degree from Northwestern. Mary Kuhl, instructor in German, also became one of the first female teachers in 1874.

Susannah M.D. Fry, who was the chair of belles lettres from 1876 to 1890, was for many years the only woman on the faculty. Additionally, she lived in Henrietta Hall, serving as matron. Fry had attended the Female Normal School at Oxford, Ohio, graduating in 1859. She was gifted in drawing, painting, music, and literature, which she taught in high schools, before she married James D. Fry, a Methodist minister, in 1868.

In 1873 she and her husband traveled and studied in Europe. A biographical sketch of Fry observed that "during her fourteen years of teaching she distinguished herself as a scholar and public speaker of great ability, being especially strong in literature, history, history of art and aesthetics," adding that she "exercised an influence second to but few who have been connected with the University at any time, and to her more than anyone else is due the successes of the Women's Educational Association." Fry received a master of arts degree from Ohio Wesleyan University in 1878 and a doctorate from Syracuse University in 1881.

A New Building

Oliver Munsell excelled at both vision and funding. Originally Illinois Wesleyan had planned a grand building with two flanking wings. In the 1850s trustees could barely manage building a diminished version of one of the wings. That and the school building were now the sum total of the facilities. Munsell and his colleagues imagined a solid future, an expanded university, and an appropriate building to house it.

Planning, architectural and financial, went forward. In June, 1868, architect O. S. Kenney of Chicago presented draft plans, and so did Rudolph Richter of Bloomington. The board opted for Richter's plan, which survives in the original.

The 1868 catalogue announced this "second University building" which would be a "model of taste and beauty." The building was to be five stories in brick and stone, measuring an impressive 70 by 140 feet. In late 1868, the catalogue continued, the foundations already had been laid, but construction did not go as fast as predicted. In early 1868 Munsell had $40,000 in pledges, and in June Professor DeMotte was given partial leave to act as development officer.

Yet only on September 9, 1870, could a cornerstone ceremony be scheduled. At that time President Munsell recounted the University's early history, reviewing the difficult conditions when he had arrived. However, despite difficulties and roadblocks, especially during the Civil War, Munsell was optimistic, seeing a growing university in the years ahead. Many documents and memorabilia were placed in the cornerstone before it was sealed. Estimates for the structure were $65,000, when the board voted to go ahead. At contract time it was clear the building would run $85,000, and when it was first illustrated on the cover of the 1870-71 catalogue the caption trumpeted "Cost $100,000." Dedication took place in June, 1871.

Oliver Munsell was not given over to naming buildings with monikers sure to warm old memories of distant years. Even in 1881 the

Sketch of Hedding Hall circa 1872.

catalogue talked of two campus buildings, the "large building" and the "other building." By 1881 the original building of the 1850s was simply the Preparatory Building, while the large building seemed to have no name at all. It was probably just "the University." By the 1890s it was called "the Main Building" and only in the 20th century would it become Hedding Hall.

But regardless of the name, the new building transformed what the University was and what it might be. Illinois Wesleyan now had offices, classrooms, laboratories, and even some room to grow. Catalogues, yearbooks, and the surviving original plans allow a fairly accurate tour.

There were two laboratories in operation by 1887, with a new biology lab to be developed the following year. Scientific equipment and study specimens were points of pride, giving students "the opportunities for original work."

In 1887 the John Wesley Powell Museum was finally installed in its special room on the top floor. Overall it measured a substantial 70 by 80 feet. Powell probably had a continuing role in stocking it, for "government surveyors" had contributed plants from Colorado and Utah. The Holder collection included 200 stuffed birds, there were thousands of shells, insects, skeletons, rocks, and fossils. And even in the 1800s Powell surely had seen to providing Zuni and Moqui pottery and costumes, together with many stone implements. For the curious, it must have been just the wonderland it was designed to be.

Amie Chapel, located in Old Main, served the campus' religious needs from 1872-1930, when Westbrook Auditorium became available. Amie Chapel was named for the mother of Colonel W.N. Coler of Champaign, Illinois, who gave $5,000 to finish the facility. Until the

Amie Chapel in Hedding Hall.

completion of Presser Hall in 1929-30, Amie Chapel was the place for lectures, concerts, all school meetings, and chapel services.

Other rooms in the building were devoted to literary societies. The basement had laboratory and work rooms. Overall Munsell's new building gave the University the notion that great things lay ahead.

Literary Societies

Literary societies sprang up as they did at most colleges during the 19th century. Most campuses supported multiple societies, sparking rivalries. The first appeared at Illinois Wesleyan in 1859. The 1862 catalogue called the Belles Lettres Society a "spirited association of energetic young men," and it must have been for it lasted until 1893 through an era of fast-changing clubs. Belles Lettres meant a lot to Joseph Fifer, a former Illinois governor, who graduated after the Civil War.

"When I was in college," Fifer remembered, "we had a Shakespeare Club that met once a

week. We studied the plays from end to end and that stored our minds with treasures for life. And, we had a Belles Lettres Society that met every Friday night when we held debates, declamations, and essays. There is where I first learned to talk on my feet. The result was that when I went into public life I never was afraid of an audience."

A rival appeared with The Munsellian, which was founded on May 23, 1863, and named after President Munsell. The society was given a large room in the new building, constructed in 1871, which had a stage, a piano, and at least 50 chairs. There also was a library collection. By 1908, however, the Munsellian had dwindled to three members, all of whom had graduated. But in 1911-12, it saw a rebirth with a membership of 11, including Clarence Johnson, an early African-American student, and V. E. Ilahi Baksh, a law student from Bombay, India, who also was active in the debate club. The 1911 *Wesleyana*, commenting on Baksh and his wide-ranging activities, said:

"... you haven't been around the campus if you don't know 'Vic.'"

The minutes from the October 1, 1875, meeting of the Munsellian describes the range of the group's activities, which included orations, instrumental solo performances, readings, vocal solos, instrumental duets, and debates.

Women wanted to join the debate societies. A bad idea the faculty thought in 1870, but by 1871 women were active in both groups. They staged a first in February, 1872 with a debate on women's suffrage, "the first attempt of the kind in the annals of the University," said *The Alumni Journal*.

It was in the Munsellian hall that a dozen students met in 1878 to start a third literary society, The Adelphic, named in honor of President William H. H. Adams' (1875-88) own Adelphic Society from his undergraduate days at Northwestern University. In 1894, female students campaigned for election to the board of the Adelphic Society, but failed. The 1908 *Wesleyana* offers a glimpse into what it was like at an Adelphic Society meeting: "For the great Adelphic meetings, [t]here are heard debates and readings, [s]tories, poems, and orations, [p]apers over which the wise men, [w]ould have pondered with amazement—[t]here great questions are brought forward, [a]re expounded and decided..."

Still another literary group appeared with the Amateurian Society, which was organized in May, 1890, by students in the preparatory department. One prominent member of the Amateurian, according to the 1908 *Wesleyana*, was Alan Barnes, son of President Francis G. Barnes (1905-08).

The Oratorical Association, a university-level program, was a group, according to the 1895 *Wesleyana*, "composed of the regular active members of the Adelphic and Munsellian literary societies." It sponsored an annual oratory and declamation contest between the association's Adelphic and Munsellian members, the winner of which was sent as the representative of the University to intercollegiate contests.

Literary Activity

In 1870 Professors DeMotte and Potter started and ran *The Alumni Journal*, a title which makes it sound like a magazine for graduates. It was and it was not. The advertisements show it had a heavy Bloomington circulation and at least one alumnus reader wrote that the magazine brought happy memories of his old college days. There also were announcements of weddings and new jobs. But the literary societies had their own pages and if professors wrote about the importance of the classics, students produced essays, poems, jokes, and gossip. It was a college magazine.

Other student publications were not long in coming. In 1872 *The Ventilator's* first issue was its last, for surely it defined the boundaries of the era by exceeding them. Even today it is hilarious. It would be issued "whenever the mental and moral atmosphere of Bloomington becomes noisome, and demands purification." The writers lacked the imagination to make up names. They just used real ones in explaining how commencement honors were handled: relatives of faculty and sons of Methodist ministers got priority in honors, so did students who did not play billiards and drink beer (with the exception of one, who did both, whom the faculty wanted to include). Candidates for high honors also were expected to affirm the "infallibility of the Faculty." As for President Munsell's new book *Psychology*, they suggested it should have been titled *Egoology*, "inasmuch as the strong personality of the learned author is visible on every page." They noted that he argued against genius being hereditary, a logical conclusion they thought given his own family.

Students of the literary societies took over *The Alumni Journal* in 1877, when the publication became *The Student Journal* and continued in the same format. Not without humor, it was much more staid and perhaps, therefore, more durable. It went on until 1884. Somewhat similar in style and format was the *Bee*, which ran from 1882 to 1887, a fraternity-based project.

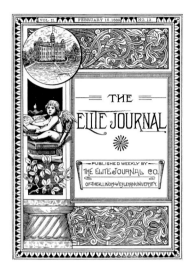

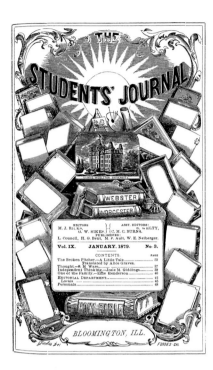

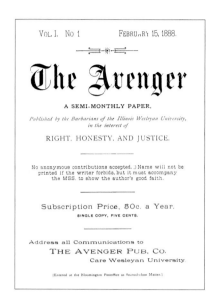

Things heated up in fall 1887, when the faculty ruled that student papers should be balanced, open to all, not partial to literary societies, fraternities, or independents. Ignoring the rule *The Elite Journal* (1887-1892) continued the style of the *Student Journal* with a literary society focus, which prompted Greek interests, as they called themselves, to launch *The Oracle*. Good students of Aristotle know he divided the world into Greeks and others, known collectively as Barbarians. Accordingly in February, 1888, "the Barbarians" produced *The Avenger*, still a third paper, printed anonymously on pink paper and scattered by town newsboys. For weeks the campus wondered who did it, as the papers questioned the propriety of professors showing fraternity favoritism amid "the clash and fury of hate and malice" surrounding Greek organizations.

The Avenger's greatest contribution was recording the roster of campus activities available to the students: three papers, five secret societies, three literary societies, two parliamentary societies, an Oratorical Association, a fire department (mostly faculty), an athletic association, a chess club, YMCA, YWCA, three quartets, a practicing orchestra, a Republican club, a Prohibition club, "and a janitor." Not bad for a college of only 147 students.

Lectures in Town

Debate was by no means limited to literary societies and students were surely drawn to the traveling lecturers and performers who appeared in College Hall, Durley Hall, and other spots near Bloomington's town square. Students were surely among the audience on the two nights when a Japanese dance troupe performed in Bloomington in 1868. And, Illinois Wesleyan often organized lectures for the community in the 1880s and 1890s. On March 9, 1882, Bloomington had a chance to see the great English writer Oscar Wilde on his American lecture tour. However, the *Daily Pantagraph* was not kind the next day. Perhaps he didn't fit in. Wilde wore a plum-colored plush suit with knee breeches, he had long uncouth hair, and he spoke in a monotone without regard to punctuation. The paper concluded that his talk on Art Decoration offered "nothing of the slightest importance to the American people." But at least his Bloomington crowd was bigger than he drew in Peoria the previous night.

Sports

Intercollegiate contests were not only in oratory as the post-Civil War years saw the first appearance of college sports.

Football team
from 1907.

Baseball started as early as 1869 and by 1874 a team was successful enough to win the state amateur championship, beating the Pontiac Athletics 13-8. By 1878 baseball was a regular organized sport, strong enough to take on and defeat the University of Illinois in 1886, 20-17.

Football appeared as a student sport in 1874, but there was no organized team until 1887, when the University colors were navy blue and light gray.

Charles Craig and the Birth of Football

A football team was organized by Charles C. Craig, who had learned the finer points of collegiate football while playing for Columbia in the mid-1880s. After transferring to the law school from Columbia in 1887, students discovered Craig had played football in the East. One day he returned a stray football to some students, using a long drop kick (which was apparently new to them), prompting a request for him to put together a football team, according to a 1940 letter Craig wrote to the *Daily Pantagraph* Sports Editor Fred Young, class of 1915.

"I informed the students," Craig wrote, "that the best way to learn the game would be to get up two elevens and mark off the bounds and erect goal posts, and start playing and I would help them all I could."

Craig recalled that Illinois Wesleyan played its first football game—"under inter-collegiate association football rules, and I believe it was the first game played between colleges in Illinois"— in April, 1887. Illinois Wesleyan played two games in the fall of 1887, with what is now known as Illinois State University, winning both games. However, "Normal" won the 1888 contest.

"We tried to get games with the University of Illinois," Craig recalled, "and other nearby colleges, but, . . . they were apparently not playing the game . . .," adding that, "In those days, we played a faster game, the side having the ball did not go into a huddle before each play."

A varsity football team was organized in 1890. During that season, Illinois Wesleyan defeated the University of Illinois, 16-0. Football was a rough game, even in the "Gay Nineties."

In an 1891 contest between Illinois Wesleyan and Eureka College it was reported that an Illinois Wesleyan player "lost some blood" and two Eureka players sustained broken fingers.

Student Housing

The University's second catalogue came out in 1858. The University had but 60 students. The catalogue informed those students about "the College Boarding House," offering food for $2.25 a week and an unfurnished room for an additional quarter. No record survives of this College Boarding House. And further, the same catalogue goes on to report yet another "new building has been erected on the College Campus"— a spot for "self-boarding," where a student could reduce living expenses to $1 a week. This facility also remains unidentified.

The special College Boarding House disappeared with the 1860-61 catalogue in which students were told they could board with "respectable private families" in the city for $2.50 to $3 a week. Self-boarding was still an option in the new building, again potentially running as little as $1 a week.

Fraternities and Sororities as Boarding Houses

Phi Gamma Delta became Illinois Wesleyan's first fraternity in 1866. Sororities followed with Kappa Kappa Gamma seven years later.

At first, fraternities and sororities seem quite logical on a campus without dormitories. Good theory, perhaps true on some campuses, but the first house came 33 years after Phi Gamma Delta was organized. Before that they were clubs. Tau

Kappa Kappa Gamma 1886

John Sterling

Thomas Sterling

Kappa Epsilon, founded at Illinois Wesleyan in 1899, was the first to have its own house.

In time fraternities became boarding houses, providing food, shelter, and hospitable cheer through four years of college life, but initially they seemed a combination of literary club and secret society. Chi Phi began at Princeton in 1824, but was abolished in 1830, when there was a reaction to secret societies. Kappa Alpha started at Union College in Schenectady, New York, in 1825. When Sigma Phi and Delta Phi appeared at Union in 1827, the pattern of multiple societies, and rivalries, was set. When Hamilton College started a Sigma Phi chapter in 1831, it established for these social groups the idea of a national brotherhood with branches on many campuses.

The first fraternity appeared at Illinois Wesleyan on December 4, 1866, when six men received a charter for the Alpha Deuteron chapter of Phi Gamma Delta. There is some tradition that the fraternity was a secret group for two years before its existence was generally known.

Sororities arrived in 1873, just two years after the first women enrolled. Millie Clark heard about Kappa Kappa Gamma through a cousin who attended Monmouth. Clark was actually a pledge at the Monmouth chapter, but opted to enroll at Illinois Wesleyan as a sophomore in 1872. Once here, she and two other women petitioned for an Illinois Wesleyan

chapter, which was granted November 24, 1873.

By 1879 the fraternity movement was widespread enough that William Raimond Baird could edit the *Manual of American College Fraternities*, with notes of chapters and histories. Illinois Wesleyan was among the schools tabulated. After Phi Gamma Delta and Kappa Kappa Gamma there followed another sorority, Kappa Alpha Theta, in 1875. Men were quick to respond with Delta Tau Delta in 1876 and then two more in 1878: Phi Delta Theta and Phi Delta Phi.

In 1880 all secret societies were excluded from the University building and one group at least was renting a room in Durley Hall on the town square. But, over time, things changed for the fraternities were meeting in recitation rooms again in 1883.

A pioneering 14-page newspaper, *The Oracle*, appeared in 1887-88, chronicling campus Greek life, the law school, and sports. Subsequently, *The Athenian* appeared, a fortnightly magazine "issued in the Literary interests of the Illinois Wesleyan University and its Greek-Letter Fraternities." This magazine was launched on January 17, 1890, with a two-page essay, "The Idea of the Fraternity." Much of *The Athenian's* coverage, according to *Through the Eyes of the Argus: 100 Years of Journalism at Illinois Wesleyan University*, argued against a rival publication, *The Elite Journal*, which it charged was "an anti-fraternity organization . . . that

College of Law
Class of 1914
with Scott Lucas,
future Senator from
Illinois (top row, shaded).

employs itself in creating a division in class and college politics and interests, much to the detriment of these rather than to the fraternities themselves."

Alumni Society Formed

One of the most endearing developments of Illinois Wesleyan's first 15 years was creation of an alumni association in the early 1860s. The purpose of the organization, according to an early constitution, was: "To perpetuate the pleasant memories of college days to strengthen the bonds of fraternal feelings and to advance the interest of our Alma Mater." At this time, the

University had 11 living alumni. However, pride in the University was such that Harvey C. DeMotte, class of 1861, was moved to start an alumni association just two years after his own graduation.

DeMotte, professor of mathematics, organized the gathering on the evening of July 1, 1863. He was quite naturally the group's secretary, while his classmate of 1861, Peter Warner, was named president. W.F. Short, class of 1854, then "the oldest living graduate" delivered an address. When the commencement of 1863 was finished, the historic roster of B.A.s stood at 12.

5 1914.

Munsell Resigns

With little anticipation or expectation, Oliver Munsell resigned as president in the spring of 1873 and near suddenly the man who had taken a project and made it a college was gone. If Charles Merriman had the initial idea for a college, and John Barger made it an ongoing organization, it was Oliver Munsell who in 16 faithful years had made it a well-housed educational and fiscal success.

Fallows and the University

Samuel Fallows succeeded Oliver Munsell as president of Illinois Wesleyan in 1873. Two years

later he was gone. Yet, in that short time he had made Munsell's successful college into an operating university. And he did it despite the Panic of 1873, one of the periodic depressions that swept the United States.

The panic deeply affected the University. It "depreciated values, prostrated business and indirectly added greatly to the indebtedness of the institution for its main building," what would become Hedding Hall, according to *An Historical Sketch and Alumni Record, 1853-1896.*

Fallows, who was born in England, came to the United States with his parents as a youngster. After graduating from the University of

Wisconsin, he was vice president of Galesville University in Wisconsin, where he also taught for two years. Fallows entered the Methodist ministry, and during the Civil War was chaplain of a Wisconsin infantry unit. In 1871 Wisconsin's governor appointed him state super-intendent of public instruction, a post to which he was then elected twice.

He resigned from Illinois Wesleyan to become Bishop of the Reformed Episcopal Church and Rector of St. Paul's Church in Chicago.

Samuel Fallows

College of Law

The College of Law was organized by Judge R.M. Benjamin and Owen T. Reeves. The first class graduated in June, 1875, consisting of seven members. By the mid-1890s, nearly 300 students had graduated from the law department. Benjamin served as law dean from the school's inception until June, 1891. He was succeeded by Reeves, who kept the office until his death in 1912. Charles Laban Capen followed Reeves as dean, serving until 1924.

A history of the University, published in the mid-1890s, observed: "In this department, the method of teaching law mainly by daily recita-tions from approved text-books, accompanied by familiar expositions and pertinent references to reported cases and the statutes of the State, was first introduced. This method of instruction proved highly satisfactory in its results and attracted marked attention, to such an extent that now in most if not all the law schools of the country the method has come into partial use."

It is interesting to note that efforts at co-edi-fication also reached the law school in the 1870s. Marietta Brown Reed Shay, class of 1879, was the first female graduate of the law school and was the sixth women admitted to practice in Illinois. She authored one of the first U.S. law books written by a woman, *A Student's Guide to Common Law Pleading: Consisting of Questions on Stephen, Gould, and Chitty*, published in 1881. Shay, who was enrolled in 1877-79 and died in 1939, won a $50 first prize for the best final exam.

Law-school enrollment had dropped to 16 in 1884, but surged to 133 by 1923. However, it usually averaged about 60 students. The law cur-riculum, lengthened from two to three years in 1897, combined professional, university-affiliated law teaching with the apprenticeship method. The faculty included local judges and practicing attorneys.

Classes typically met in the basement of the Main Building, constructed in the 1870s, except for a time when the school rented classrooms on the east side of Bloomington's Courthouse Square to accommodate attorneys who didn't feel they had the time to go to campus to teach their classes.

By the early 1890s, Illinois Wesleyan's law school had built a solid reputation. The June, 1893, edition of the [*Illinois*] *Wesleyan Echo* observed: "The reputation of this college is as broad as the whole west. From all parts of the land students come to enjoy the privileges here afforded. The judges of the supreme court of Illinois have recommended it and have backed up their words by sending their own sons to Bloomington."

The law school operated from April, 1874, until June, 1927, when it was forced to close due to its inability to comply with regulations set by

J. Byron McCormick

Sigmund Livingston

Scott Lucas

the North Central Association of Colleges and Secondary Schools. Much of the law school's history was lost with other University records in a 1943 fire.

The death of the law school contrasted sharply with its prior success. During its 53-year existence, the law school graduated nearly 1,000 lawyers, including: Idaho Governor H. Clarence Baldridge; Wyoming Governor Lester Hunt; and University of Arizona President J. Byron McCormick. Unusual for the time, the law school also graduated women, including Antoinette Funk, class of 1898, who practiced law in Chicago and in the public land division of the U.S. Department of the Interior.

Another notable law school graduate was Sigmund Livingston, class of 1894, who in 1913 founded the Anti-Defamation League of B'nai B'rith—an organization dedicated to the social, educational, and cultural betterment of the Jewish people. He also authored the book, *Must Men Hate?* (1944).

U.S. Senate Majority Leader Scott Lucas

Perhaps the most famous law-school graduate was Scott Lucas (D-Ill.), class of 1914, who served in the U.S. House of Representatives from 1935-39 and the U.S. Senate from 1939-51. Lucas rose through the Senate ranks and was Majority Leader in 1949-51. He helped to organize the American Legion, was a staunch New Dealer, and was a stern critic of U.S. Senator Joseph McCarthy's (R-Wis.) tactics in his anti-communism crusade. Lucas was a civil-rights advocate, supporting legislation for the Fair Employment Practices Commission, abolition of the poll tax, and anti-lynching laws.

When Lucas first ran for the U.S. Senate in 1938, Hugh Darling, president of the class of 1925, wrote alumni: "[Illinois] Wesleyan, the students and alumni, will receive added recognition by sending Alumnus Lucas to the U.S. Senate from down state Illinois. He will not break faith with the friends of good government."

The School of Music

Another major addition of the 1870s was the School of Music. Music instruction had started during the Civil War, when H. C. DeMotte was made vocal instructor in addition to his regular duties as professor of mathematics. His task was to teach basic music to a chorus that met twice weekly.

Few subjects are more complex than the early history of the School of Music, for it goes back and forth between University connections and private groups. Even the location varied over the years and until 1929 practically the last place music would be taught at Illinois Wesleyan was on the main campus, although DeMotte started out in one of the recitation rooms in Old North. He used a violin to lead the chorus, the University having no piano, organ, or orchestra.

F. A. Parker joined the faculty of the Northwestern Academy of Music in 1871 and in the following year he had an Illinois Wesleyan appointment as well. The Northwestern Academy was at 318 North Main Street and offered instrumental work as well as voice. In 1877 the Northwestern Academy fundamentally was acquired as the new School of Music. Parker became its first dean, while two women and another man taught piano and voice to an enrollment of about 100 students. Coeducation had real implications for music, for it was assumed it was a subject women would want to study. The college awarded its first diploma in 1879.

Change was afoot in the late 19th century. The *Wesleyana* of 1895 caught the vibrations: Parker was out as dean and J. F. Fargo, who had been at the Northwestern Academy since the 1860s, took his place. Laura B. Humphreys became head of voice, when enrollment dropped to 90, while "the standard gradually increased." Humphreys, according to a history of the School of Music written in 1932, had returned from a course in Europe to take charge of the voice department "and to her is the credit for having had much influence in developing the great voice of Marie Litta, afterwards famous as one of the leading opera singers of America."

Non-Resident and Graduate Department

The other major creation of 1874 was the non-resident and graduate department, all largely the work of President Fallows and Professor Jabez R. Jaques.

The non-resident program was designed for academics and clergy who could not study in residence on campus. The 1874 catalogue described the program this way: "The Illinois Wesleyan University in being the first to adopt the *non-resident* plan of the world-renowned London University in the United States, has met an urgent want of the American people, hitherto unrecognized in our collegiate system of instruction."

In October, 1874, the Reverend G. G. Roberts of Mohawk Valley, Ohio, was the first to enroll in the program. The department moved along, but only with five or six students a year. Professor C. M. Moss is credited with transforming the program. He was a Syracuse University alumnus, who had a Ph.D. from there as well—a degree that was taken while he was teaching at Illinois Wesleyan. Moss built just such a program in Bloomington. Enrollments grew directly with Moss' advertising efforts.

Alumni rosters show a great many Canadian alumni of this graduate program, largely explained through Moss' Canadian offices. The entrepreneurial Moss even recruited an English agent, Joseph Fennemore. Relatively few English students showed interest, but in 1895 the count was 60 Canadians doing degree work.

Moss left in 1891 to be followed by Professor Robert O. Graham, professor of chemistry and geology, who built the program still further. Graham, an 1877 Amherst graduate, was elected professor of science at Monson Academy, a New England prep school, before he completed his undergraduate work. Eschewing a medical career, he became professor of chemistry at Pennsylvania's Westminster College, where he occupied the chair for eight years. He received a Ph.D. from Johns Hopkins University in 1888, arriving that fall, and remaining until 1911. A multitalented individual, Graham also found time along the way to serve as a consultant to Funk Seeds and the Chicago and Alton Railroad. By 1895 more than 400 men and women were taking systematic courses of study at home, knowing that "rigid examinations will test the thoroughness of their work," according to Watson's centennial history.

Far smaller, but still active in its own way, was the resident graduate program, which offered the M.A. and Ph.D. degrees.

The 1875 catalogue lists the offerings of the resident graduate program. The degree of A.B. was given and could be obtained "by pursuing a course of study for one year after graduation, in any one of the following subjects: Philosophy, philology, history, political science, mathematics, physics, chemistry, natural history, and pedagogics—and passing a thorough examination therein. Candidates for this degree must present a satisfactory thesis." The University also gave "the degree of Master of Arts, *in cursu,* to, "all Bachelors of Arts of three years' standing, who, in the meantime, have sustained a good moral character, and give satisfactory evidence that they have successfully prosecuted advanced studies, whether professional, scientific, or literary." Illinois Wesleyan awarded Ph.D's to those "who shall pursue as residents for at least two years, and as non-resident students for at least three years after graduation, any one of the subjects specified for the degree of A.M., shall pass a satisfactory thesis on some subject in the department chosen by the candidates. The thesis must embody the result of original research, and shall consist of not less than three thousand words."

Fallows Leaves

Like Munsell, Fallows resignation was completely unexpected when it came in 1875. Fallows departed to become Rector of St. Paul's Church in Chicago. He was soon the Rt. Rev. Samuel Fallows as a bishop of the Reformed Episcopal Church, but the general public probably knew him best in his later years as a writer. There were the books on the Bible and theology one might expect of a bishop, but there were also books on science and travel, and he became something of a specialist on heroes and disasters, as he wrote about patriots, the assassination of President William McKinley, and the 1906 San Francisco earthquake.

Finding a successor to Fallows was not easy, but the board finally persuaded William Henry Harrison Adams to accept their offer. If Munsell built a college and Fallows a university, it was Adams we may thank for saving the whole from the brink of disaster one more time, and putting all on a firm financial setting.

President William Henry Harrison Adams

Born in Effingham County, Illinois, in 1840, William Henry Harrison Adams joined the 111th Regiment at the outset of the Civil War. Like Powell he was a major by war's end. After the conflict he finished Northwestern in 1870 and went directly into the Methodist Episcopal ministry at churches near Bloomington. From the Methodist church in Clinton, the young major was elected president of Illinois Wesleyan in 1875.

W. H. H. Adams

Adams inherited the strengths and weaknesses of the previous decades. Universities are built on funds. Pledges portend future strength, but current expenses require ready cash, and many of Munsell's initiatives were financed with loans. Cash was always marginal and even as the great new building of the early 1870s was planned, faculty members were asking quietly to be paid their regular salaries.

The University surely had an ominous lesson in finance when Illinois Wesleyan became heir to a failed college. Finance at Chaddock College in Quincy, Illinois, faltered and though the buildings might continue as a school, collegiate efforts were given up in 1878, their loyalty transferred, at least officially, to Illinois Wesleyan. Henceforth, even into the 1920s,

Faculty and students in 1893. The faculty are seated in the front row with President Wilder (fourth from the right) and Owen T. Reeves, President of the Board of Trustees, and Dean of the Law School, (fifth from the right).

Chaddock alumni were listed in Illinois Wesleyan rosters, even though they may never have been in Bloomington.

The Chaddock case was all but a portent. It was complex then, near inscrutable now in a short history, but in the late 1880s a series of pledges, notes, financial panics, estate complications, deadlines, and balances due led the *Daily Pantagraph* to announce "A College for Sale." Adams had labored mightily on finance and lit-

tle else for his first five years, but adequate totals seemed elusive. Real resources did not match balances due. The end of the University seemed at hand for the third time, when those who had loaned the money against the collateral of the buildings now would foreclose and sell the buildings "to the highest bidder for cash in hand" on January 1, 1881.

Supporters rallied. Others took over Adams' duties on campus and he became a full-time

fund-raiser. The trustees arranged to have the sale postponed and Adams' strenuous financial efforts, which then entered a sixth year, met with success in March, when adequate cash in hand finally ended the uncertainties that had plagued Illinois Wesleyan from the 1850s. Having gone so far, there was no stopping Adams. He continued to work on finance, and by 1887 he was exhausted, but the university now had a real endowment worth more than $100,000. But, Adams' health was wreaked.

Rather than accept a resignation in 1887, the trustees gave Adams a leave of absence. In 1888 he resigned due to continuing health problems and survived only until March, 1890. He is surely one of the heroes in the university's history, allowing every development that came later to operate on a new plane of fiscal solidity.

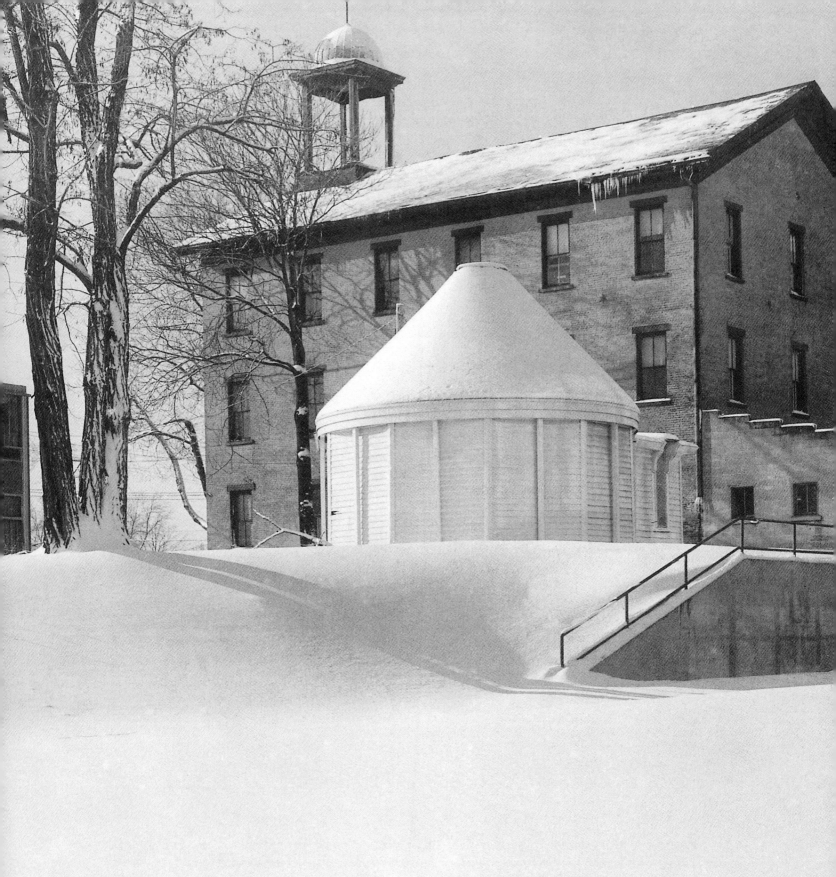

IV. Wilder and Beyond

W illiam Wilder and Edgar Smith, the next presidents of Illinois Wesleyan, continued the tradition of building a university organized around the liberal arts. However, the presidency of Francis G. Barnes, the chief executive who followed Smith, marked a brief flirtation with the polytechnic mode then gaining favor on other campuses.

President William Henry Wilder

William Henry Wilder (1849-1920), class of 1873, followed his friend William Henry Harrison Adams as campus chief executive, becoming the first alumnus president of Illinois Wesleyan. In his nine years in office Wilder advanced the cause of serious science and "serious" fun, while Illinois Wesleyan reached new maturity as an American college.

Born near Greenfield, Illinois, in 1849, Wilder worked on a farm as a youngster. He graduated from Illinois Wesleyan in 1873 and moved among nearby towns as a Methodist minister, a role that saw him elected to the University's Board of Trustees.

Wilder's presidency was marked by extraordinary vigor: the curriculum was completely revised, electives were introduced, the faculty was expanded, foreign students arrived, a significant astronomical observatory was opened, an athletic field and gymnasium were set up, the endowment reached new levels, a women's dormitory was designed (though not funded and built), and the first yearbook appeared, as did a companion history of the University in 1895. The library grew significantly, a university press appeared, and the first endowed scholarships were established also during Wilder's tenure.

Wilder was a prodigious fund-raiser, who rose to a challenge. Shortly before his death Hiram Buck gave the University a farm valued at $15,000, with the stipulation that double that amount be raised as a match by January 1, 1893.

Wilder and his staff not only secured the necessary $30,000 in subscriptions, but found an additional $7,500 they could put toward expenses. A university going somewhere found resources. By July 1, 1895, the endowment was valued at about $188,000.

William Wilder

Wilder also took important steps to improve campus facilities. About $15,000 was spent upgrading buildings and grounds, $2,000 was paid for an athletic park, and $1,900 for two city lots, which were earmarked as sites for a new gymnasium and a janitor's house. Henrietta Hall was purchased by the trustees from the Woman's Educational Association and remodeled for use as a women's residence hall. To supplement the library, the Wilder Reading Room Association also was organized.

◄ Behr Observatory with Old North in the background.

President Edgar M. Smith

The June 11, 1897, edition of the *Daily Pantagraph* reported that President Wilder was about to tender his resignation to the Board of Trustees and return to pastoral work. His resignation was effective on August 31, 1897, and Professor Robert O. Graham was appointed acting president.

Edgar Smith

Edgar Moncena Smith (1845-1924) became the next president of Illinois Wesleyan in 1898, a time when America's victory in the Spanish-American War made the United States a nation with global interests. In May, 1898, the *Argus* reported that "war fever" had broken out in the literary college and that "a number of young men have formed themselves into a military company. About 70 have said they would attend drill and the company is one of which the school may be proud." Later, the newspaper told of some students enlisting in a regiment.

When Smith was inaugurated during commencement week, 1898, Professor Robert Graham welcomed him on behalf of the faculty and students, while Joseph C. Hartzell, now Methodist Bishop of Africa and a veteran of one of John Wesley Powell's expeditions west, spoke on behalf of the alumni.

Smith was a New Englander. Born in Livermore, Maine, he graduated from Wesleyan University in 1871, then moved back and forth between Methodist churches in Rhode Island and teaching at Wesleyan. Later assignments took him to New York and Maine, before he was chosen president Montpelier Seminary in Vermont in 1895. From that post, three years later, he was elected president of Illinois Wesleyan.

Despite taking the helm of an institution with property valued at almost $400,000, Smith found the University $36,000 in debt. The difficult times were caused, in part, by the growing quality of local high schools, which diminished enrollment in the preparatory program. Illinois Wesleyan needed more money and a campaign was designed in 1903. Smith resigned the presidency in 1904.

First Scholarships

Efforts to secure private financial support of Illinois Wesleyan date to the University's 19th-century birth. The 1877 *Illinois Wesleyan University Catalogue*, for example, has a section headlined, "Benefactions Solicited," which mentions "the need of a library fund; a fund for the assistance of worthy young men and women who are struggling with poverty to educate themselves for future usefulness." And, this was at a time when tuition varied from $12 to $14 depending on attendance during the fall, winter, or spring terms.

Only in 1895 did scholarships finally appear when the catalogue announced the first two. Mrs. Martha E. Cameron gave $1,000 in memory of her daughter and the Anderson family set up the William W. Anderson Scholarship in a like amount. Interest from each fund could then cover the tuition at $39 a year.

A Distinguished Faculty

The Wilder presidency also saw many scholars join the faculty who would leave their mark on the University.

Melvin P. Lackland was professor of mathematics and astronomy in the early 1890s. He had entered the preparatory school in 1872 and graduated from the college of letters in 1878, serving as president of his class. He completed religious studies at Garrett Biblical Institute in 1881. He did special work in mathematics at John Hopkins University in 1888, subsequently teaching mathematics at Chaddock College in Quincy, Illinois, where he also served as president. Chaddock was acquired by Illinois Wesleyan in 1878.

Wilbert Ferguson, an 1879 graduate of Ohio Wesleyan University, arrived in 1894 as acting professor of Greek. He was elected professor the next year and went on to become one of the University's most beloved faculty members. Ferguson (1857-1944), who was born in Ohio, worked at times as a schoolteacher and a newspaperman. He was elected assistant professor of ancient languages at Adrian College in Michigan in 1882, assuming the post of chair of Greek the next year, where he remained until 1894. During that time, however, he spent two years studying in Germany.

Robert Benson Steele, who was born on a Wisconsin farm, joined the faculty as professor of Latin in 1891. Steele, an 1883 University of Wisconsin graduate, taught school for two years before entering John Hopkins University for graduate work. In 1886 he was elected professor of Latin at Ohio's Antioch College, but reentered Hopkins in 1888, receiving a master's degree in 1889 and a Ph.D. in 1890, when he was elected professor of Latin at St. Olaf College in Northfield, Minnesota.

Steele had a reputation as a wide-ranging scholar, a precursor to the multitalented liberal-arts philosophy of the 1990s and beyond. He "is not only a master of his own department," a biography pointed out, "but is perfectly at home in history, English literature, Greek and philosophy. For several years he has had charge of the English classics in the preparatory school and directed the study and composition required." He published widely on Latin authors.

Martha Luella Denman was named Charles Cramp Professor of Belles Lettres in 1894. A McLean County native and an orphan, Denman traveled widely as an undergraduate studying at the State Normal School in Normal, Illinois and Smith College before she graduated from the University of Michigan in 1893.

Morton J. Elrod was a worthy successor to John Wesley Powell. Elrod, who was born in Pennsylvania in 1863, but spent his childhood in Iowa, graduated from Simpson College in 1887 and worked as a schoolteacher. President Wilder hired Elrod in 1888 as an assistant teacher in the science department. He was appointed an adjunct professor of natural science the next year and was elected professor of biology and physics in 1891. He also was curator of the museum and like Powell he led student explorations to the Rocky Mountains in 1894 and to Yellowstone Park in 1895. Professor Denman of English also went on the Yellowstone trip. Elrod was a prodigious writer, from studies of the butterflies and shells of Montana to guidebooks to Glacier National Park.

The First International Students

Life at Illinois Wesleyan changed in August, 1889, when the first international students arrived. Tokyo residents Y. Osawa and K. Tanaka, ages 25 and 24, respectively, came to Illinois Wesleyan to study law. The *Daily Pantagraph* on August 23, 1889, described the two as "exceptionally smart," adding: "They studied five years in a law college at Tokyo and were then admitted to the bar and practiced law two years. A year and a half ago they came to San Francisco and have been studying the English language." They graduated in 1890. On the eve of Osawa's departure from Bloomington, he wrote a letter to the editor, which the *Daily Pantagraph* printed on September 23, 1890. Osawa expressed regret at leaving Bloomington and appreciation for many kindnesses. "For my *alma mater,"* he wrote, "the [Illinois] Wesleyan Law School, I shall always cherish with the most sacred affection and shall regard the year passed within its walls one of the happiest of my life."

By 1909 Keizo Mitamura, a student from Tukuiken, Japan, attended Illinois Wesleyan and in 1915 two more Japanese students were on campus: Michio A. Nakamura and Keihoku Chugakuko.

Henrietta Hall

Henrietta Hall had been renovated as a residence for women in 1884. Rather than apologize for the distance from Henrietta Hall to the main building, catalogues pointed out that the three-block walk was a way of guaranteeing healthful exercise. Fees for residents ran from $2.50 a week, with an hour's work per day, to $3.50 per week, with no work expected. As part of necessary equipment, women residents were told to bring an umbrella and a small and large spoon each marked with their names. Men could dine there for $3 a week, but residence was limited to women.

Deferred maintenance was a problem in the 1890s. Needed repairs demanded a budget the dwindling number of resident women could not support and the women's association finally gave up in 1892, prompting the University to buy the building. However, renovations were scuttled and the building was torn down. But the University history of 1895, again with a brave and bold stroke, illustrated a beautiful projected hall for women. Four stories of elegant architecture, designed by Reeves and Baillie of Peoria. It was to be built for $15,000 and opened for the fall of 1896. Nothing happened, alas.

Living Options for Students

In the mid-1890s students had various living options beyond boarding houses and other facilities. The first yearbook in 1895 described three clubs: The Ross (established 1889), Bundy (1894), and Henrietta.

The Ross Club, 911 Prairie, was started by J.P. Edgar, class of 1890, in 1889 during his senior year. By 1895, judging from a yearbook

Henrietta Hall

photo, 12 men and 11 women ate and lived there. It was called the Ross Club because of Mrs. Ross and her daughters, who cooked and served food to the students. Students at one table often spoke French, students at another table conversed in German.

The Library

The library is central in any academic era and Wilder had the main collection, which had grown to 7,000 volumes, moved from the main building to the third floor of the preparatory building in 1891. An indoor picket fence provided colorful separation from the readers and the open stacks. In addition the University developed the Wilder Reading Room for newspapers and magazines, but the library collections paled in comparison to the attention given the museum. Indeed, museum expansion had been the reason for moving the library.

The University Museums

The museums with its two large rooms on the second floor of the college building was clearly the glory of the University. The library got three pages in the 1895 University history, while the museum received seven pages. George W. Lichtenthaler died in San Francisco in 1893, leaving Illinois Wesleyan his collection of 10,000 species of shells, 1,000 species of marine algae, and 500 species of ferns, fittingly all displayed in the Lichtenthaler Museum. Another room was the Cunningham Museum, where students and townspeople alike could see Zuni and Moqui utensils, pottery, articles of dress, and other items from John Wesley Powell, a collection of about 1,000 insects from Dr. Benjamin Walsh, and a miscellaneous collection of birds, reptiles, and mammals from Idaho.

George Vasey, a botanist at the U.S. Department of Agriculture, donated a large collection of plant specimens. The herbarium in the museum, thus, had most of the plants of Illinois and a great number from Colorado and Utah. Another donor had given 200 specimens of birds, plus some preserved mammals and reptiles, while President William Adams had given a collection of fossils from the Cincinnati area.

Behr Observatory

The Observatory

C. A. Behr of Chicago presented the University with an 18.5-inch diameter telescope in 1895. The instrument was made in England and the observatory rose with its distinctive cone-shaped roof to become the third building on the main campus block. The observatory, named for Behr, also included a visual and photographic spectroscope, a duplicate of one used in an observatory in Potsdam, Germany. Once complete, this installation was capable of serious research and accounts at the time ranked the new telescope as the eighth largest in the United States.

Undergraduate Curriculum

The 1890s brought considerable revision to the undergraduate curriculum, as electives arrived at Illinois Wesleyan.

Through these reforms there were now four undergraduate degrees. All required 47 term-length courses, with most of the work specified just as in the old curriculum. Students, however, were given the option of filling out the required number of courses with anything they might choose to elect themselves.

There was no major involved in any of these degree programs. Majors came only in 1932. By choosing one of the four degrees students selected an area of vague specialization, but one far from what we would call a major today.

Whether there were majors or not, science remained a curricular focus. In addition to the observatory and museum collections, there was the new Shellabarger Laboratory for advanced work in chemistry. In addition, the Henry S. Swayne Private Laboratory, a new facility first described in the 1894 University catalogue, was called a "thoroughly equipped and highly expensive laboratory" suited for special and research work, offering students "unexcelled advantages."

The Fine Arts

President Wilder was ready to build programs in the fine arts basically through corporate takeover. The 1890 annual meeting of the Board of Trustees added an art school and a music school to the University brand. Both already were flourishing independently in Bloomington.

Music at Illinois Wesleyan

Bloomington was a musical town. There were many concerts and music stores, and commercial music teachers flourished together along Bloomington's Main Street.

The School of Music had grown continually since 1877, despite unstable leadership. C. Morris Campbell became dean in 1877, the fourth in six years to begin the task. Yet, there were 150 students from Colorado, Kentucky, Missouri, and Florida as well as Illinois, studying piano, violin, organ, clarinet, voice, harmony, and music theory. John R. Gray became the sixth dean in 1889 and he and Wilder moved boldly. The success of the University programs did not preclude other independent music schools, even in a town of 10,000. The Bloomington Conservatory of Music was doing well and it was now merged with the Illinois Wesleyan school. The next catalogue touted the new College of Music as "one of the largest and best equipped musical schools in the West."

Like a merged corporation, the new school had two co-directors. John R. Gray had run the University programs, while Oliver Ross Skinner had been head of the conservatory. Born in Lake Zurich, Illinois, in 1864, Skinner had studied piano, organ, and theory in Berlin before coming to Bloomington in 1887 to run the conservatory. However, Mrs. Gray was waiting in the wings.

The new music faculty consisted of eight, who taught piano, organ, violin, and vocal music to students of many ages, most of them not otherwise students at the University. The new Hoblit Building was erected on North Main Street in Bloomington in 1897 and the University's College of Music occupied the entire second floor and part of the third floor. In terms of the number of students enrolled, it was the University's largest enterprise. In 1888 before the merger, the University had counted 110 music students in all categories. After the merger the number was never under 500 through the 1890s.

John Gray died of measles in 1893, whereupon the College of Music had a new co-director, Mrs. John R. Gray. She, too, was a musician, who had studied in Leipzig before coming to Bloomington with her husband. She comes through as a formidable figure, determined to be Mrs. John R. Gray, even after her husband's death. She even signed diplomas "Mrs. John R. Gray." She and Skinner led the school together until 1907 and she remained another year.

The Wilson School of Art

Oscar L. Wilson had a school of art in Bloomington. He was transformed into a professor at the Wilson School of Arts, when it affiliated with Illinois Wesleyan. Wilson led a faculty of 14, offering instruction in 16 subjects to 162 students.

The art faculty specialized in subjects ranging from crayon drawing, painting of landscapes and still lifes in oil, and water-colors, to china painting, flower painting in oils, architectural drawing, and photography. The close relationship between students and instructors was emphasized with this statement in the 1891 catalogue: "Students are taught individually and allowed to advance as rapidly as their ability permits—*but no more so.*"

The 1895 yearbook described the Wilson College as having "won a foremost position among the art schools of the West." The 1897 Illinois Wesleyan catalogue describes the college, noting there was a short course, which in 18 months qualified "amateurs to teach." The two-year course brought a certificate, the three-year course a diploma, a five-year course resulted in an artist's diploma, and a six-year course yielded a teacher's diploma.

Like the School of Music, the art program was in town at 516 North Main Street. The art program never kept up with music in strength. If there were 162 students in art in 1891, even with the interesting offerings enrollment fell gradually to 50 by September, 1897.

Delmar Darrah

College of Oratory

The decade of the 1890s was an era of oratory. Political legend William Jennings Bryan, for example, captivated a public wherever he spoke and shops were filled with books on oratory. Catching this enthusiasm in 1893 Illinois Wesleyan opened a College of Oratory, attracting an astounding 134 students in its inaugural year. Delmar Darrah, who had received a Ph.B. degree from in 1890, was the college's guiding spirit.

Born in Tolono, Illinois in 1868, Darrah was described as having "a splendid voice, is most polished and graceful in delivery, clear and forcible in thought, and is a ready and apt teacher in his profession." He moved to Bloomington at age 15 and was an alumnus of the preparatory department and college before he returned to his alma mater to teach.

The College of Oratory taught speaking, voice culture, gesture, action, physical culture, Shakespeare, and acting. "The aim of the school," the 1895-96 catalogue said, is, "to develop the individuality of the pupil and to create expressive readers and efficient teachers."

By the end of the decade, the University's catalogue spoke of a School of Oratory then enjoying "a season of unparalleled prosperity." Darrah remains an annual presence in Bloomington for he devised and wrote the Passion Play, still performed annually as a community venture. The first commencement of the School of Oratory was in 1895.

The Wilson
School of Art.

Summer School Inaugurated

The University offered a summer school for the first time in the mid-1890s as an experiment. Classes for the summer of 1896 were planned in preparatory Latin, Greek, history, mathematics, German, rhetoric, English grammar, civil government, physics, botany, zoology, and physiology. Collegiate classes were anticipated in Latin, Greek, German, mathematics, biology, and physics, "provided three or more persons desire to take the same study."

The organizers were surprised by how many students signed up for summer work, a sad commentary because it was designed for students whose "irregularity in attendance or deficient preparation" may have thrown them behind their class, as well as to give college students the opportunity to do extra work.

End of the Non-Resident Program

The move to end the non-resident department seems, in part, driven by concerns about similar programs nationally and their ability to adequately monitor students' progress. When the non-resident program began, most Americans who aspired to a scholarly career went to Germany for a Ph.D., which fast became the degree for a professor to have. Princeton in the 1860s was giving the Ph.D. as an honorary degree for professors and only in the late 1870s did Princeton set up a program for earned doctorates, just as Illinois Wesleyan had awarded the first earned doctorates in its own program.

By 1905 there were many American graduate schools offering regular, resident graduate work, and the market for advanced degrees through distance learning was drying up. After many years of interesting success, the non-resident department of the University was abolished under Edgar Smith's administration. In June, 1905, the Board of Trustees voted that enrollment in these programs should cease in July, 1906, but that those already working would be allowed to finish their degrees. The last non-resident degrees were awarded in 1910. But just because the non-resident program closed does not mean regular graduate work ended. Not all Illinois Wesleyan Ph.D.s were non-resident. In 1909, after the non-resident program was abolished, the catalogue roster of students was headed by Rabbi George Fox as a resident graduate student for the Ph.D., and in 1910 Amos Arthur Griffes received a Ph.D. in sociology. After that graduate students remained in residence, but few degrees were given until the World War I era, when a number of master's degrees were awarded. But the days of Illinois Wesleyan as a graduate-school power were over.

Days of Glory

Illinois Wesleyan thrived in the 1890s, probably beyond the imagination of any of its founders. There were two steady elements between 1885 and 1900. The enrollment of the college always was between 90 and 130 students, and there were usually around 450 students on the books, not in Bloomington, as part of the non-resident degree program. Yet, the preparatory program enrollment jumped from 120 to 220, the law school grew from 29 students in 1885 to 77 students in 1895, and where there had been 854 students on the books in 1885 there were 1,566 in 1895.

Campus Life in the Early 20th Century

In the early 1900s, there were only 120 college students, but they were the lively center of a real college life. Law students sometimes took part in student organizations too, and the preparatory students had their own activities. The literary societies continued with their rivalries adding competitive spice to intellectual investigation. Publications added more competition, as did debate.

There also were service groups. The Young Women's and Young Men's Christian Association (YW and YMCA) were popular organizations in the early 1900s. The YWCA at Illinois Wesleyan was organized in April, 1884, and the group's object was to "work for young women by young women." The YMCA at Illinois Wesleyan preceded the YWCA by three years. The Oxford Club, founded in the spring of 1906, was organized in order to bring divinity students into closer fellowship with one another and to enrich campus religious life.

Uprising of the Mules

The "Gay Nineties" at Illinois Wesleyan was an era remembered for some elaborate pranks and high jinks clearly illustrating that students weren't always attending class or studying.

One such incident was the Uprising of the Mules, recorded in detail much later by Ralph M. Green of the class of 1904. The uprising, according to Green's tale, took place in the late 1890s and was sparked initially by a celebration marking an important football victory—a nighttime campus romp marked by a "big bonfire, college yells, songs, and speeches."

After the crowd dispersed, a small group of male students lingered, trying to think up an "exciting stunt." One lad recalled that a man who lived nearby had a team of mules. As the prank unfolded, the idea was to sneak the mules from the barn to the chapel, located on the second floor of Old Main. The mules were secured and in the early morning hours were taken to the steep steps leading to the chapel.

"Now the uprising began," according to Green. The mules were stubborn creatures and the "boys had a tough time pulling and boosting, but finally succeeded in getting the mules to the top of the stairs and into Amie Chapel."

Now the plot thickened. The lads decided to paint the mules with black and white stripes, making them appear Zebra-like. "Paint was found," Green wrote, "and the job accomplished."

The culprits left the mules-cum-Zebras tied to the seats for a janitor to discover the next morning. Word spread quickly around campus about the episode and most students, according to Green, "came to see Operation Downgrade, backing the Zebras down the steps, as they refused to go down head first. Then came the fun of cleaning up the Chapel, unpainting the mules, and collecting a fund in settlement with the mules' owner.

"There were plenty of volunteers . . . for these jobs," Green recalled, "and after a lecture from the [Illinois] Wesleyan President to the whole student body, all went back to normal life on and off campus."

The Birth of the *Argus*

Collegiate journalism took a major step at Illinois Wesleyan in 1894 with the birth of the *Argus* on September 17, 1894, a newspaper still publishing weekly 106 years later. Poetry and oration adorned the newspaper's inaugural front page—not hard news.

There was no way to know initially whether the *Argus* was just another in the changing panoply of student publications. For five years, beginning in 1887, there was an anti-fraternity paper, *The Elite Journal*. It provoked a pro-fraternity press, *The Athenian*, of 1890, which became the [Illinois] *Wesleyan Echo*.

These rivalries apparently led the faculty to support establishing a newspaper representing the entire University and student body. Consequently, seven students from the incoming junior and senior classes were invited to publish such a paper. The enterprise, according to the 1895 *Wesleyana*, met the hearty endorsement and support of the Board of Trustees and Visitors.

The *Argus* was printed by Illinois Wesleyan's own press from 1894-1903, under the direction of Wilbert T. Ferguson, professor of German and Greek. The early *Argus* staff consisted of five junior and senior editors—an editor-in-chief, a literary editor, two local editors, who covered campus news, and an exchange editor to gather news from other colleges. A business manager and subscription agent rounded out the staff. Until 1912, college credit was given for sufficient work on the *Argus*.

A Yearbook

As the years unfolded, Illinois Wesleyan began to look more and more like the standard American college. Other colleges had yearbooks and in 1886, J. H. Shaw, editor of *The Bee*, produced Illinois Wesleyan's first yearbook, the *Wesleyana*. When another appeared in 1895, the first was forgotten or ignored, and the new one called itself Volume I. Only after another decade would "Volume II" appear in 1905. Production has been consistent ever since, though editors mid-year have not always bristled with confidence.

Tau Kappa Epsilon
Fraternity House
circa 1902.

A New Fraternity

On January 10, 1899, five students organized a society under the name, "Knights of Classic Lore." Their avowed purpose was "to aid college men in mental, moral, and social development" and from this nucleus the Tau Kappa Epsilon fraternity began to grow. There were then two other fraternities—Phi Gamma Delta and Sigma Chi, plus two fraternities with inactive chapters: Phi Delta Theta, which existed at Illinois Wesleyan from 1878-97, and Delta Tau Delta, which operated from 1877-80.

The five students who founded the Tau Kappa Epsilon fraternity in 1899 were Joseph L. Settles (1871-1943), a 1902 graduate who became a Methodist minister; Owen I. Truitt (1868-1929), a 1902 graduate of the academy who became a clergyman in Burma and the United States; C. Roy Atkinson (1877-1930), an alumnus of the class of 1900 who had a keen interest in music; Clarence A. Mayer (1879-1960), a 1902 graduate who taught music here after studying in Germany and went on to found the Springfield College of Music and Allied Arts; and James C. McNutt (1878-1962), a 1901 graduate who was a medical doctor. They are among Illinois Wesleyan's best known alumni for their names are memorized by each year's pledge class. From these origins, TKE has grown to 300 active chapters and colonies with more than 9,000 undergraduate members and 155,000 alumni.

On the women's side two sororities also appeared. The Eta chapter of Sigma Kappa started at Illinois Wesleyan in 1906, the organization having begun at Colby College in 1874. The Omicron chapter of Kappa Delta was established at Illinois Wesleyan in 1908, only 11 years after the sorority started at Longwood College in Farmville, Virginia. By 1910 there were five sororities at Illinois Wesleyan, enough to start a Panhellenic Council to coordinate sorority activities and rules.

Athletics Take Shape

Both academics and fun moved forward with President Wilder's enthusiasm: teams got a proper field and there was a new gym for men and women, perhaps more for women, at first.

Spirits and facilities were high when Edgar M. Smith became president in 1898. He was, he said, "heartily in favor of manly sports of all kinds and would encourage their propagation to a reasonable and well-defined limit." However, Smith also offered a warning that "an excess of athletics to a degree where it worked injury to the studies would not be tolerated." It fell to his era to build regulations as well as fields.

Teams often supported themselves. On June 23, 1898, the *Daily Pantagraph* reported that before school had closed for the summer Smith had gone "among the scholars with the leaders of athletics and succeeded in raising $200 by subscription. Early in the season last year, the boys raised $125 but it was not used, leaving a balance in the treasury on the next term, with the exception of money expended for football suits. With nearly $300 to start on and lots of interest, [Illinois] Wesleyan is bound to come to the front in the athletic world."

In the fall of 1898, C. D. Enoch was hired to coach football. Enoch, a former University of Illinois player, led Illinois Wesleyan to a 12-6 victory over his alma mater. The October 14, 1898, edition of the *Daily Pantagraph* said: "The University of Illinois boys were unmercifully dragged in the dust by the lighter but much more scientific players of [Illinois] Wesleyan . . ." Incidentally, this newspaper report is credited as the first mention of green and white as Illinois Wesleyan's colors. In 1887 the University's colors were navy blue and light gray and in 1892 the colors adopted for a baseball tournament in Urbana, Illinois, were purple and steel. No one would hear of Titans until the late 1920s, but the "Green and White" had fun developing an enthusiastic following.

Wilder Field

The same year basketball debuted, $2,000 was earmarked to purchase what became known as Wilder Field. Students raised $500 toward purchase of the "athletic park," located on the present site of the [Illinois] Wesleyan Stadium. "These grounds," the 1894 catalogue pointed out, "have been fenced, thoroughly tiled, and put in first-class condition for all legitimate college sports which have the encouragement of the faculty." By 1907 Wilder Field had stands able to seat about 400.

Football was the fall sport and later yearbooks gave each player and game full coverage. Around 1900 President Smith may have found money for the "football suits," but the team was still somewhat intermittent. The College Conference of Illinois and Wisconsin (CCIW) was formed in 1903 with Illinois Wesleyan and a dozen other campuses as members. The next year, football took the field again after a two-year hiatus.

Baseball

Baseball was the senior sport, but that had little to do with winning seasons. The University lost the 1890 championship game to the University of Illinois, 5-4. Three years later accounts were different. The June, 1893, edition of the [Illinois] *Wesleyan Echo* made this assessment of the baseball team: "The lethargy that has characterized [Illinois] Wesleyan athletics for some time past has been cast off in the enthusiasm and success that is attending this spring's baseball team. The purchase of an excellent park for their games inspired the [Illinois] Wesleyan boys to do their best."

Track

In the 1895 yearbook only football and baseball teams appear, but by 1905 track got equal billing with an 18-member team. By 1908 there was an indoor meet with four other schools, and a series of five outdoor spring events.

Ringers

Sports had their ups-and-downs in the 1890s and were more exciting for it. Lack of rules allowed all shenanigans. Two football games in 1896-97, for example, were played with "ringers"—non-students. A history of athletics, written by long-time coach and professor Fred Muhl, reported:

An early track race at Wilder Field.

Baseball team
circa 1900.

"Dwight Funk again captained the football team. Two games were played and the faculty stepped in and threatened to expel the captain and manager if any more ringers or non-students played. The team was disbanded." Funk never claimed to be an Illinois Wesleyan student. He was a local Yale alumnus who simply liked to play the game.

And, in 1897-98, the Bloomington City Council tried to outlaw football. "Dr. Graham of our faculty," Muhl wrote, "who also was city alderman, had a successful fight in the local city council against an attempt to abolish football in the town of Bloomington."

Funk was an amateur. Old Hoss Radbourn wasn't. As a major-league player on his way to the Baseball Hall of Fame, Radbourn (1854-1897) invented the curve ball. He won 60 games one year and when his arm gave out he came back to Bloomington and ran a saloon and billiard parlor, except for those great afternoons when he went out to pitch for the Illinois Wesleyan team.

The issue of "ringers" evidently still was alive after the turn of the 20th century. The 1908 catalogue explicitly prohibits "ringers" from playing, declaring: "The following eligibility rules have been approved and will be in operation in the future. No student shall be eligible to take part in any contest, who is not a *bona fide student,* carrying his work at a grade not lower than 70." Baseball must have had a particular problem, for baseball players had to have been enrolled in the previous term, as well—current status wasn't enough.

Law students played on the teams too, and in 1908 the captains of baseball and track were in the law school.

A Gymnasium

Suggestions that the University needed a gymnasium appeared in student publications in 1888, and in 1894 President William Wilder produced one, though its details have faded into mystery. Far from the great athletic complex of today, the Shirk Center, the University built a 40-foot by 40-foot brick building at 405 E. Phoenix. This was the first gymnasium, under the direction of Delmar D. Darrah, professor of elocution and director of physical culture.

Basketball Takes Center Court

Basketball first appeared in 1894 with a women's game. Elocution Professor Delmar Darrah, class of 1890, who doubled as director of physical culture, brought basketball to campus. The story of Darrah's basketball team was recounted by Fred L. Muhl, long-time athletic director and mathematics professor, in a piece chronicling University sports from 1870 to 1930. "A gymnasium was provided for the use of the [Illinois] Wesleyan students during the year 1894," Muhl wrote. "Here basketball was introduced by D. D. Darrah who was the faculty director of physical education. The college girls played many games. The girls' home games were played in the ING [Illinois National Guard] armory at Center and North . . . The girls continued to play inter-city basketball, but lost most of the games that season . . ." Evidently, a few years later, women's basketball was halted, according to Muhl, "as the mothers of the girls stepped in and said 'enough is enough.'"

No sport has been introduced for the "first" time more than women's basketball at Illinois Wesleyan. The 1908 yearbook would write: "This is the first year that the girls have had any part in the athletics of Illinois Wesleyan." Twelve women rented the YWCA gym for two hours a week, found a coach, played the Y team four times, won 1, lost 2, and tied 1. But the big victory: for the first time a women's team got a picture in the yearbook.

Perhaps the men were jealous, for in the very next season the women disappear from the yearbook and the first men's team is there in 1910-11 with a 2-3 season, completely unsure whether the game will continue as an intercollegiate venture. Both women's and men's teams concurred: they were handicapped by the lack of a gymnasium. The 1894 building had been phased out and nothing replaced it.

The Preparatory Department

The preparatory department, an important part of Illinois Wesleyan since its founding, had been under the general direction of the faculty except for a brief two-year period. However, in 1883, it was organized into a distinct school and the Reverend Hyre D. Clark was chosen as principal.

The preparatory department continued until 1919. At first it taught high-school age students at a time—in the 1860s and 1870s—when there were still few good regional high schools. Consequently, enrollment in the preparatory department climbed steadily from 71 in 1863-64 to 280 in 1877-78, but rosters fell as the number of community high schools began to multiply after 1900.

By the mid-1890s its curricula comprised four year's work and several courses leading to corresponding courses in the College of Letters and Science. An 1895 profile of the preparatory program observed "that it now ranks among the foremost preparatory schools of the country."

50th Anniversary

As the 20th century dawned, Illinois Wesleyan turned 50 years old. This milestone prompted reflection on the accomplishments of a half century.

The University had awarded degrees to 1,121 graduates during those first 50 years and had somewhere between 25,000 and 30,000 students. The 26 resident graduates in the 1900 graduating class in the College of Letters set a record. This era saw the College of Letters offering 118 courses of which more than half were elective. The endowment was valued at nearly $200,000 and more than another $100,000 would be earmarked for the University from legacies.

President Edgar M. Smith (1898-1905) made this assessment of the University in a letter he wrote to the *Daily Pantagraph* on May 2, 1901: "It has been the chief factor in the higher education of the young people of the city and county and adjoining counties . . . It has added much to the material prosperity of Bloomington and contributed largely toward the production of that intellectual, social and moral atmosphere, for which the city is justly distinguished. In this respect, the more thoroughly the influence of the University is studied the more highly it will be estimated."

Smith drew this conclusion about the University: "Its degrees are recognized and its work taken for full value by the best colleges and universities of the country."

President Francis G. Barnes

Francis George Barnes (1866-1910), an Englishman, became president of Illinois Wesleyan in 1905, serving until 1908. He came to America with his parents at age 4 and by age 19 he was doing missionary work on the way to becoming a Methodist minister in North Dakota. He was a minister before he was a college student, and thus he finished Hamline University at age 31 where senior status did not preclude his being captain of the football team. Immediately on graduation he became principal

Francis Barnes

of Epworth Seminary in Iowa. He received a Doctor of Divinity degree from Upper Iowa University in 1900.

Barnes became president of Grand Prairie Seminary in Onarga, Illinois, in 1901. A leave-of-absence allowed graduate work at Harvard, and at age 39, while still at Harvard, he was chosen president of Illinois Wesleyan.

Barnes' presidency began on July 1, 1905. Two days later he told the *Daily Pantagraph*: "This is an age of publicity. I am going to adopt some of the methods of the commercial traveler in presenting the claims of [Illinois] Wesleyan to the young people of this and other states who ought to be students here."

"The one important need of the University at present," Barnes added, "is students and larger attendance. I believe that the chief way and the best way to get students is to let the young people who are preparing to enter college know what . . . [Illinois] Wesleyan has to offer, and they will do the rest . . . I will go up and down this state telling the communities that Illinois Wesleyan University is in running order at Bloomington and that we await students and will give them the best there is in educational training."

That is just what he did. Over the next five months, Barnes visited more than 160 towns, giving an average of five speeches a week. The

Domestic Science
class in Old Main.

enrollment of 1,068 students in 1904-05 had been its lowest in nine years. However, by 1905-06, enrollment had climbed to 1,350 students.

Barnes also championed a revamped curriculum designed to be more attractive to prospective students. While his goal was not to diminish Greek, Latin, and other classical studies, he was convinced that the college of the future had to respect the era's demand for practical education.

The Annual Banquet had become a feature on the yearly Illinois Wesleyan calendar. The fifth such banquet was held on February 20, 1906. The event was an opportunity for faculty and alumni to dine and cheer together. The 1908 yearbook reported that 250 gathered at the new Illinois House to enjoy "the dainty menu and witty toasts." The tasty menu featured baked halibut, fillet of beef, snow flake potatoes, chicken salad, Neapolitan ice cream, casino cake, and cafe noir.

Despite this gaiety, within a year of taking office, Barnes' health began to fail, a situation some have credited to the "strenuous program" he had undertaken. He took a six weeks' vacation in the "wilds" of New Mexico, returning to campus in December, 1906. As a result of rapidly declining health, he eventually settled in

Pasadena, California, where he died after a brief illness on October 14, 1910.

Commerce Program Launched

Wilder and Smith had organized the University around a liberal-arts model, but Barnes flirted with the polytechnic approach to attract more students. New courses would attract more students even if they did not fit the liberal-arts pattern. Commerce came first, followed by domestic science.

A new program in commerce began in June, 1906, with the goal of preparing women, as well as men, for "the higher walks of business life." The Department of Commerce, as it was first called, had two programs: a one-year course in stenography and a one-year course in business. One of its stranger assets was an "extended and rare collection of cereals and manufactures" gathered for illustrative purposes.

The stenography course covered shorthand, with special attention to the "science and art of phrase making." All stenographers also took typing—two hours a day. Business-course students studied bookkeeping, penmanship, commercial law, arithmetic, and geography. They learned how to write advertisements and the basics of

English without which "no good paying position" would be conceivable. In 1909-10, business students became part of the School of Commerce.

Domestic Science Program

The Domestic Science program was launched in 1906. First in the hands of Hettie M. Anthony and then Clara G. Pett, the program was a two-year course on housekeeping, which could lead to a bachelor of domestic science degree, if two additional years of college work were added. The 1910 catalogue detailed a program, combining many fields to train women to run homes. The scientific pursuits of chemistry, physiology, bacteriology, economics, hygiene, and art were translated into cookery, dietetics, home nursing, and household management.

Enrollment had grown from 38 women in the first year to 49 three years later. The 1909 yearbook had 15 graduates in caps and gowns and the freshman class dressed in a costume, which appears to be a cross between a maid and a nurse.

However, changes were coming. Ina Pitner took over the program in 1909 to be followed by Mabel Campbell in 1910. Pitner added domestic art as a field, fundamental sewing and the use of fabrics for decoration. Campbell abolished the two-year program completely and substituted a four-year bachelor of science degree instead. Whether a school or a college, both terms were used, there were three degree candidates for bachelors of science in household economics at the 1910 commencement. The home-economics major was dropped at Illinois Wesleyan in 1971.

Women's University Guild

Since its earliest decades, the University has found strength in assistance from the community. The Women's University Guild, an example of community support, first appeared in the records of 1906.

In the first decade of the 20th century, the guild backed the move toward domestic science, and it funded and ran the first year of the program. Having demonstrated it could be done, the guild essentially gave the whole thing to the University as a gift, according to the 1908 yearbook.

Having created the domestic science program, the women of the community then turned to the library, which needed help. They had it repapered and repainted, and had its furniture and bookcases refinished.

The Women's University Guild also supported a new "cottage dormitory system." The 1908 yearbook reported that it was ready to rent and furnish two cottages near the University, which the head of domestic science would then supervise as dormitories for women.

The February 7, 1911, *Daily Pantagraph* reported that until 1910 the guild operated two houses on Chestnut Street. Subsequently, the former residence of a doctor, located on East Washington Street, was leased. The house contained room for a dozen girls, while about 25 others roomed in the neighborhood and took their meals at the dormitory. The girls paid $3.50 a week for board and the rooms rented for $10-$12 a month.

The Woman's University Guild grew to 516 members in its first year with Mrs. Chalmers C. Marquis as president. Membership included leading women from Bloomington and Normal, as well as the wives of faculty members and trustees. A major guild undertaking was the Carnival, a fund-raising event that was a notable resource for renovating buildings and beautifying the campus. The Carnival, an elaborate community fair, was first held in April, 1906, in the Coliseum, which was decorated in green and white and filled with booths offering refreshments, art, books, and college goods of all sorts. Plays and shows were given by University and high-school students, and there was a Merchant's Parade on two nights. The parade included 150 young ladies in costumes appropriate to the businesses they represented. The Carnival promoted town-and-gown unity and provided $4,000 for use in beautifying the campus and buildings in preparation for Barnes' inauguration during commencement week, 1906.

Winifred Kates

The real excitement of the Carnival came unexpectedly on Saturday morning, April 21, 1906, when a letter arrived from industrialist and steel maker Andrew Carnegie, a philanthropist. Barnes had hoped to build a new science building and on that Saturday morning came a letter from Carnegie, pledging $30,000 toward the project. "With this gift and the leadership of our new President," the 1906 *Wesleyana* commented, "a new era is dawning for the [Illinois] Wesleyan."

Masquers

Winifred Kates, who taught elocution and dramatic arts, was surely the direct stimulus for Masquers, the drama organization that began in 1914. The group's first play, *Contrary Mary,* was staged on December 17, 1914. The students had the option of presenting their plays in the Chatterton Theatre in downtown Bloomington, which opened in 1912. The 1922 yearbook says Kates, whose married name was James, directed the Masquers' plays for the first four seasons. In January, 1918, the Masquers presented, *Our Children,* for the benefit of French and Belgian relief funds during World War I. However, the group disbanded in 1918 due to the war, but in 1920-21 it was back with strength.

Changes in the Library

The early years of the 20th century saw many changes in the University's library. By 1904-05 the library was situated in Old North and housed a collection of about 10,000 volumes. Electric lights were installed in the summer of 1912, enabling students to use the room after dark.

In 1913 Kathleen Hargrave was appointed full-time librarian and in 1914-15 she organized the library's holdings, classifying books according to the Dewey Decimal System.

An interesting tradition emerged in 1915-16—a custom that lasted for nearly two decades—when students in the English-literature department began levying a 50-cent assessment on their peers and presented 100 books to the library as a Thanksgiving offering.

During the World War I era, funds flowed to the library from several sources—for example, $1,000 from University of Illinois President Edmund Janes James whose father had been an Illinois Wesleyan trustee—and interest from these various accounts was used to build the library's holdings, which reached 12,000 volumes by 1918.

Household Economics and Art

By 1910 Illinois Wesleyan had two more constituent schools. Household Economics had a four-year course, offering the degree of bachelor of science in household economics. The program taught cooking and sewing. The 1912 yearbook commented that the students learned "the highest calling of women—the making of a happy home."

Over the decades many programs have come and gone and one was refounded as a new venture—the School of Art. The University made another go at art in 1907 with the University Guild as the prime motivator. Guild members who were interested in art suggested the courses and the guild installed the instructor, Abigail Rees. When the Wilson School of Art flourished in the 1890s, it had about 10 people teaching a wide variety of subjects, but in 1908 virtually the

Freshmen Women
in 1916.

same offerings were in the catalogue, all taught by Rees. She covered freehand drawing, architectural history, water color, oil painting, and china painting. Each year about a half-dozen students majored in oil painting. The 1908 yearbook tabulated 15 students enrolled in art—all but one were women.

Women's Residence Halls

In 1911 there were two halls for women—East Hall and West Hall. Men's housing was provided in several fraternity chapter houses: Phi Gamma Delta, Sigma Chi, Tau Kappa Epsilon, and Phi Alpha Delta. Other housing options, circa 1917, included boarding with "private families" for $4-$6 per week, or boarding in "clubs, thus reducing the expense of table board from $3.50 - $4.50 a week. Rooms heated and lighted cost from $1 to $1.50 per week," according to the 1917 catalogue.

The Women's University Guild in 1910 was leasing two "modern homes" a few blocks away from campus for the women of the University. The matrons there gave families the feeling that their daughters were "in safekeeping" rather than just "rooming and boarding at will around the city."

The 1912 catalogue was full of enthusiasm about a new combination hall for women and the president's residence. It was the seven-year-old house built by A. E. DeMange, three stories, brick with stone trim, so wonderfully furnished with wood finishes that "it is the admiration of Bloomington." It should have been, for Antoine DeMange had built it in 1906 for $80,000. It had a tile roof, once had an elevator and ballroom on the top floor, and was located one block from campus. President and Mrs. Kemp had a suite of rooms there and oversaw the facility.

The University could not afford to buy the house, so Kemp purchased it himself in 1910. Not until 1917 did the University buy the building, which would henceforth be known as Kemp Hall. The 1919 yearbook reports that 42 women lived there and 72 women dined there. In about 1923 the University purchased another Main Street house—dubbed Kemp Lodge—for about $40,000 to accommodate still more female students.

V. Kemp and the Collegiate University

Even a decade after he had left office, the *Daily Pantagraph* characterized Theodore Kemp (1868-1937) as "the greatest president Illinois Wesleyan had yet had."

Kemp finished DePauw in 1893, but only after Garrett Biblical Institute, and, thus, entered the Methodist ministry immediately. He served churches in southern Illinois before he was called to Grace Church in Bloomington in 1905. On the side, he taught English, the Bible, and ethics at Illinois Wesleyan during the 1906-7 academic year. Thus, many already knew him when he was chosen as Francis Barnes' successor as president in 1908. Kemp remained until 1922. He knew what a college was, he was a dreamer, and he had a magnetic-like attraction for finding support.

Theodore Kemp

William Wallis, who joined the faculty in 1912, knew Kemp well. Years later he wrote recollections of what Kemp had done: faculty salaries increased from $1,000 to $2,500 a year, the faculty grew from 14 to 30, the student body doubled, and the University was accredited by the North Central Association of Colleges and Secondary Schools. Even more impressive Kemp paid off $120,000 in debts, some acquired while he was president. During Kemp's term of office, University assets grew from $327,000 to more than $2 million.

"Five times as much money was secured for the University during this period," Wallis wrote, "as was obtained in all the 58 years of previous history of Illinois Wesleyan. Such were the achievements of Theodore Kemp."

Campus Finances

That finances always were a problem for the University was never a surprise to administrators or trustees. In 1911 Illinois Wesleyan launched an effort to raise an endowment, $500,000 if it could. Kemp worked closely with the Bloomington Commercial Club, which organized 10 teams to help.

What might happen if University funds grew was no mystery. Kemp had the courage to know that Illinois Wesleyan needed a library, a law building, a gymnasium, and a hall of languages, details Fred Muhl, assistant professor of mathematics and director of athletics, translated into a plan which the 1914 yearbook published with pride. It bears great similarity to what architect Arthur Pillsbury would conceive in more elaborate detail within the decade.

Fundraising and Theodore Kemp

Kemp inherited Barnes' campaign to raise $60,000 to guarantee the $30,000 from the Carnegie Foundation for the new Science Hall.

Setting the cornerstone of Memorial Gymnasium.

Science Hall circa 1912.

In July, 1908, the campaign was $18,000 short of the mark, but within a year, Kemp found the money, even increased the total to $100,000 to provide for the building and its equipment. And, so on March 10, 1910, ground was broken for the new science building, which today is known as Stevenson Hall. It was ready for occupancy for the beginning of the 1911-12 academic year. By June, 1915, additional efforts increased University assets by $379,000.

Mathematics Professor Cliff Guild—who also served as registrar, bursar, board secretary, and bookstore manager between 1905 and the 1940s—wrote: "Thus ended the first major financial campaign for [Illinois] Wesleyan. It had paid for itself, added nearly $200,000 to permanent funds, paid off all indebtedness and annual deficits, and had a small balance to spare."

As early as November, 1910, Kemp had included among the University's construction needs a women's dormitory (which became Kemp Hall) and a gymnasium. However, only toward the end of Kemp's administration did Memorial Gymnasium rise at a cost of $200,000. The result, according to Wallis again, was "an increased interest in intercollegiate athletics and an increased solidarity of the student body. Regular classes in swimming, gymnasium work and organized games under trained instructors for both men and women with a system of intramural competition" began a new era in campus athletics.

Women's University Guild

The Women's University Guild continued as a source of community support. It had planned a "cottage dormitory system," and in 1911 the

Women of Kemp Hall
circa 1920s.

View of Kemp Hall from
Main Street.

guild was running two houses on Chestnut Street—East Hall and West Hall. The next year this housing moved to a house on East Washington, which housed a dozen women, but welcomed 25 others for meals. The students paid $3.50 a week for board and the rooms rented for $10-$12 a month.

Male students lived at home, boarded in town, or lived in the houses that were now becoming an expected part of each fraternity chapter. Phi Gamma Delta, Sigma Chi, Tau Kappa Epsilon, and Phi Alpha Delta all had houses, but the sororities did not. The University sensed a special responsibility for women students.

A Great Academic Transformation

Kemp and his colleagues recovered the liberal-arts tradition and did much to transform the University. In the 1910-11 academic year, for example, there was a major reorganization, affecting the School of Commerce and the colleges of Home Economics, Law, and Fine Arts. (No one was ever sure from month to month whether those segments were colleges, schools, or departments.)

Curricular revisions taught students to speak of majors, minors, and distribution requirements. The catalogue announced a philosophy that put specialization in one field in the context of broad learning in four general disciplines.

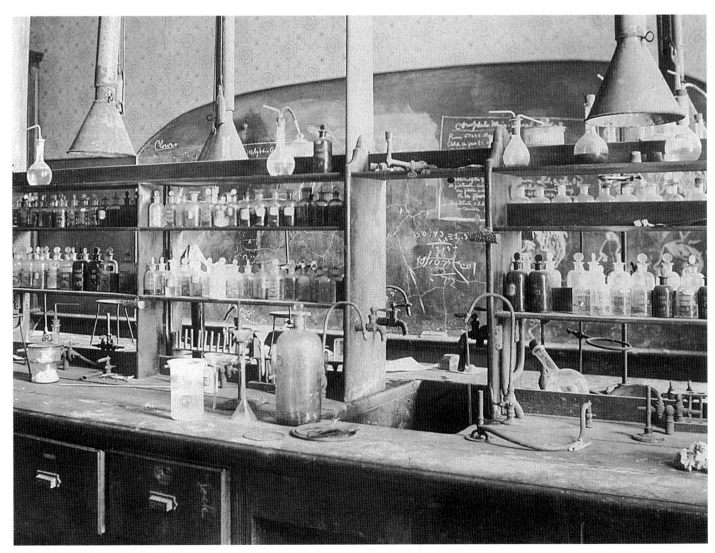

Chemistry laboratory in the Science Hall.

Students had to take a major, plus course work in four areas: languages (French, German, Greek, Latin); science or mathematics; English, speaking, religion, or philosophy; and history or social sciences.

Students and registrars now learned to count in hours as well, another national currency making its way to Bloomington markets. Degrees required 128 hours, a major 24, a minor 14. And for the first time grades would determine Latin Honors, a distinction first bestowed during the 1903-4 school year. *Summa cum laude* was to be given rarely and for special excellence only. *Magna cum laude* went only to those who had no grade lower than B, and no more than 15 percent of the class. *Cum laude* recognized students with no grade lower than B, and not more than 25 percent of the class. Then there was also the now extinct Honorable Mention, which recognized "successful and sustained work in one or more departments of study." When first given in 1910, there were no *summas*, four *magnas*, 12 *cum laudes*, and one Honorable Mention.

With the reorganization, the bachelor of philosophy degree was dropped, and henceforth the normal undergraduate degrees were bachelor of arts and bachelor of science.

A Distinguished Chemist

The fact that Carl S. Marvel (1894-1988) received bachelor's and master's degrees at 1915's commencement revealed his future promise and at least minimal life in the resident graduate program. Marvel grew up on a farm 25 miles from Bloomington and had studied Greek at the Waynesville Academy preparing for admission. When Marvel enrolled in 1911—joining his older sister Edith, already in the home-economics course—tuition was $56, but the family got a discount, as did others, who had more than one student attending. In 1912, 14 of the 39 sophomores were chemistry students.

Marvel launched his studies in the new science building under Alfred W. Homberger, the Isaac Funk Professor of Chemistry. Homberger, a

Carl S. Marvel

cosmopolitan sort who had studied in Germany, had revamped the chemistry curriculum to offer a broad range of 18 courses.

Eighty years later, Homberger's work was the subject of a careful study in the *Journal of Chemical Education,* in part because of the achievements of his students. All chemistry was taught by Homberger with three undergraduate assistants. Yet those early years in the new science building were wondrous times for chemistry students, five of whom went on to receive Ph.D.s. and four of them eventually listed in *American Men in Science*.

After receiving a Ph.D. at the University of Illinois, Carl Marvel was the founding father of polymer chemistry, which led to the development of plastics and other synthetic materials. He helped develop aviation fuel, synthetic rubber, and fire-retardant synthetic fibers used in space suits and in industrial applications as substitutes for asbestos. President Ronald Reagan honored Marvel in 1986 with the National Medal of Science.

The 91-year-old Marvel—who taught at the University of Illinois and the University of Arizona—received Illinois Wesleyan's 1987 Distinguished Alumnus Award for his contributions to chemical research and teaching.

School of Music Flourishes

The School of Music was flourishing around 1910. From its city headquarters, its 13 teachers

Charles F. Sindlinger

At a time when college tuition was $36-a-year, Gunn could command $6 for an hour lesson. Born in Kansas in 1874, Gunn went to Leipzig for piano studies at age 19 and remained in Germany and Austria studying and performing. In 1900 he returned to Chicago to teach at the American Conservatory, the Chicago Musical College, and the University of Chicago, while he also toured extensively. Paradoxically, given his completely European training, he was founding conductor of the American Symphony Orchestra, which was dedicated to the performance of American works with American soloists.

The director of the School of Music from 1913 to 1919 was equally distinguished. Henry Purmont Eames was a Chicago native, who spent three years at Cornell College before taking a law degree at Northwestern University. Music triumphed over law and he went on to study piano with famed Polish musician Ignace Paderewski. Though officially teaching in Lincoln, Nebraska, from 1898 to 1908, Eames spent much of that decade touring America, Britain, and continental Europe. Eames, who also was a composer, came to Bloomington in 1913.

trained preparatory and college students and operated a far-flung network of alumni, who were teaching in small towns who in turn sent their students to Bloomington.

There had been a complete reorganization of the school in 1909. This action presumably was a none-too-happy event for Mrs. John Gray, who had co-directed the school, since she decamped. Oddly President Theodore Kemp also became dean of the School of Music, at least for one catalogue. Not to be outdone, Mrs. Gray simply opened her own school, called, for her logically enough, Mrs. John R. Gray's College of Music. Never subtle, she even took a full-page advertisement in the University yearbook.

Bloomington music has long cast itself in a national context. There were great performers on the faculty and promotional rhetoric was not mere hype. Glenn Dillard Gunn was "one of America's foremost pianists," while A. F. McCarrell was "one of the most prominent organists in the west." Charles F. Sindlinger was a singer and conductor "known throughout the country." L. E. Hersey was a gifted teacher of violin, who in some seasons migrated off to Mrs. Gray's school, but usually returned to Illinois Wesleyan. These artists—plus the offerings of the Amateur Music Club and occasional appearances by grand opera companies—made Bloomington an interesting place for music.

The School of Law Prospers

The law school prospered under Judge Owen T. Reeves, who was dean until his death on March 2, 1911. Illinois Wesleyan owed him a great debt for 58 years of constant service. He was surely no opponent to multiple titles. Just before his death, he was president of the board and dean of the law school, yet to courthouse colleagues he was Judge Reeves, unless they were his old soldier-friends who perhaps called him colonel. At Ohio Wesleyan he was Dr. Reeves, from the LL.D. that institution had given him.

Law classes were taught in the basement of the Main Building, except for the moot-court sessions in the Courthouse. However, in Reeves' last years he was hoping a separate law building might emerge. After his death, the new dean, Charles Laben Capen, inherited the same futile hope.

Sigma Chi House, Homecoming 1922.

In 1917 the law school lost its other founder with the death of its first dean, Judge Reuben M. Benjamin. The *Argus* ran an appreciation of him. He had arrived in Bloomington in 1856 in time to hear Abraham Lincoln's famous "Lost Speech" in Major's Hall. "Lincoln was one of the three lawyers to examine this young candidate for the Illinois bar," the *Argus* reported. "The certificate to the effect that Mr. Benjamin had passed the examination was written by Lincoln himself."

Kemp and Making a University into a College

Theodore Kemp's leadership reversed some of the trends of the Barnes' years in creating separate centers of educational programs. The College of Liberal Arts reemerged as the central educational focus.

Schools are sometimes associated with individuals, and when Delmar Darrah resigned as head of the School of Oratory in 1910, the school split into a Department of Elocution and Dramatic Art, led by Winifred Kates, and a Department of Oratory run by Pearl Cliffe Somerville. The School of Oratory, thus, faded with its founder, though for 1911-12 there was the School of Music and Oratory. Oratory disappeared, as did the College of Home Economics, demoted to a department within a liberal-arts context. A college in 1909, Commerce was gone even as a department in the following year.

Campus Life, Traditions, and Spirit

Yearbooks could hardly be more buoyant than those produced while Kemp was president. The yearbooks record a campus full of lively joy. The YMCA, YWCA, and Oxford Club activities of a few years ago were now loosing ground to bands, plays, ukulele clubs, and an annual outburst of new organizations. Witty comment and well-captioned yearbook photos allow readers to see just how much fun students were having on campus.

Airplane Float,
Homecoming
circa 1920s.

Student Government Emerges

Premonitions of student government had come
in 1906 when President Barnes, as the yearbook
said, sought a "system and unity in the cheering
done by students" at athletic games. Consequently a student organization started with no
purpose but to coordinate cheers and songs.

Toward the end of 1914-15, Kemp went further. Perhaps an overall student organization
would improve communication, but when he
asked whether there should be a student government, the campus actually split on the issue.
Kemp and the faculty moved ahead, and "The
Student Council" was organized that spring,
charged with making "sane" student opinions
effective through helpful cooperation. It has
worked ever since.

Among later Student Council activities was
the parade associated with the Bradley football
game in the fall of 1919. Special railroad cars
were arranged to take spectators to Decatur, Ill.,

and an all-school banquet was held for the football team at the Hills Hotel during which they
were given "W" sweaters. The student government reminded freshmen that they were
required to wear green caps, "which they did
very meekly," according to the 1921 yearbook.

The Student Council's name was changed to
the Student Union in 1933 and in 1957 it
became the Student Senate, the name by which
it still flourishes.

Student Life

The 1911-12 school year brought a new series of
convocations. These were not chapels, but
weekly assemblies of all students in liberal arts,
home economics, and the academy to hear
speakers, musical performances, or discussions of
University life, which could be in the form of
debates, oratory, or discussions of student publications or athletics.

A happy sequence of growing traditions took the students through the academic year in the early 20th century.

The year began with The Grind, known as the "get acquainted" dance and "one of the big events" of the college year, according to the 1915 *Wesleyana*. Even in the 1970s this tradition was still grinding away.

College falls brought programmed competition between freshmen and sophomores across America. Illinois Wesleyan joined the trend with an annual ritual, which involved attempts by sophomores to cut the hair of freshmen, if the freshmen tried to throw a class party. The 1913 *Wesleyana* chronicles this escapade in an article, "The Freshman Party, From a Sophomore's Pen."

Fall now meant football and a new

Ralph Freese

sports mania swept the country. Normally staid weekly convocations were now sometimes transformed into "Enthusiasm Meetings" or in later terms, pep rallies. In October, 1911, Coach Fred Muhl's football team had just beaten Northwestern, and, accordingly, the team was called to the front of the chapel to talk about the next game against Lake Forest. As Ralph S. Freese, class of 1911, finished off the session with his "vigorous yells," "the enthusiasm reached a higher point than it has for some time," according to the 1912 *Wesleyana*. Freese was filled with school spirit for during the 1910-11 school year, he wrote the music to *The Cheer Song*, still played at every home football and men's basketball game. Chalmers H. Marquis, class of 1910, wrote the words.

Cheerleaders appear in the yearbooks of the first decade of the 20th century. However they were not called cheerleaders then, they were "yellmasters." They were men in light colored "W" sweaters, sometimes wearing hats and showing a great deal of confident enthusiasm. Their "yells" are recorded in the yearbooks, but by 1919, however, they had become "cheer leaders."

October brought the first of two carnivals. The women of the YWCA threw the Halloween Carnival in the science building's basement every October 30. In 1912 the event raised funds to furnish a YWCA room in the new science building. The Halloween Carnival had a fortune teller's booth, a candy booth, stunts, and a bootblacking service administered by the freshmen for their "elders."

The Alumni Association went back to 1866, but Homecoming was a new idea on November 10, 1917. It started full blown with fully decorated fraternity houses and residence halls, an elaborate parade down Main Street to the Courthouse Square, returning to Wilder Field, where the football team delighted returning alumni by defeating Bradley, 14-0.

Homecoming was not over. The night brought stunt shows and a program in Amie Chapel, where military themes predominated in the acts sponsored by fraternities and sororities. The whole thing had been organized in about a week.

Homecoming was an instant tradition. The 1919 *Wesleyana* commented: "Homecoming was a complete success . . . Old-fashioned football reigned and the boys played well." The yearbook continued: "The old grads began pouring back the night before, and by Saturday morning

Memorial Gymnasium

interest was tense." The festivities included a parade down Main Street highlighted by the band and cheerleaders.

Swing Out Day, which originated in the 1910s, came toward the end of March. Then seniors entering chapel "appeared for the first time in all the dignity of Senior apparel." The event was described by the yearbook as an engaging mixture of comedy and slight trauma. After Swing Out Day, seniors wore their caps and gowns to chapel every Friday for the balance of the school year.

Similarly appearing in the 1910s was Wesleyana Day, an event typically occurring in May and centering around students receiving copies of the yearbook. Far more than just handing out books to be read while ignoring the convocation in Amie Chapel, there was an inter-fraternity tennis match, a baseball game, a picnic lunch, and an evening program.

The seniors of 1913 revived what they took to be the custom of producing a play before commencement. The production that year was *The House Next Door* by J. Hartley Manners and it was directed by Winifred Kates of the elocution and dramatic arts programs.

By 1914 the May Carnival was a few years old. It was a junior-class party, which began with singing and an address by a professor. Afternoon activities, included a baseball game at Wilder Field, with a "parade in which the small children from all schools were given an opportunity to exhibit their individuality in decorating their bicycles and doll buggies." There was a May pole dance and spectators watched a stunt show in Amie Chapel.

By 1915 Piker's Day was among the most anticipated events on the annual calendar, even though it was a movable feast. Piker's Day usually took place in the spring—but the seniors in

1915 had theirs in the fall. Piker's Day amounted to a "Senior Party," when members of the graduating class skipped a day of school (an approved action) and took a trip to the country, where they had a picnic. They would spend the rest of the day, according to the 1915 *Wesleyana*, "roaming over the hills, gathering cat tails, or boating on the lake."

Clean Up Day came on a rainy April 25th in 1916. With rakes, hoes, knives, and baskets, students covered the campus tidying up the grounds. Freshman boys raked the grass, girls dug up dandelions, juniors raked the tennis courts, while seniors lined walks with stone. Faculty helped, too. Domestic-science students made a wonderful lunch for everyone, and that afternoon the seniors planted a tree.

Memorial Gymnasium Constructed

Athletics took on greater emphasis with completion of Memorial Gymnasium. As part of the agreement to keep the University in town, the Bloomington Association of Commerce helped raise $600,000 for the land and building, and the cornerstone for Memorial Gymnasium was laid in November, 1921.

The building was part of Pillsbury's architectural plan for the entire campus, in fact the only building actually built from the original conception.

The *Wesleyana* offered a tour: "When one enters the front doors of the new building he will be in a great hall, memorializing the soldiers of the world war . . . the gym floor will be 90 by 120 feet. The clear space in the middle will be 50 by 85, ample for basket-ball. Bleachers will be constructed around the sides. At one end there will be a gallery . . . An important feature of the gymnasium will be a large stage where oratorios, festivals and large meetings may be accommodated . . . The swimming pool will be in the basement under the stage." The facility also included offices for men's and women's physical education directors, storage for athletic equipment, and locker rooms.

The Legendary Frederick L. Muhl

Tom W. Scott, Illinois Wesleyan's first athletic director, left the University in 1910 to be followed by **Frederick Lewis Muhl** as director of athletics and instructor in mathematics. Muhl was a fixture on campus for decades. In football his record was 44-40-11, while in basketball he tallied a 139-62 record.

The 1912 yearbook reported on Muhl's influence in starting tennis. "With the advent of Coach Muhl," the yearbook noted, "came tennis, that is, an interest in it, because he is interested in it." There was an interest but no tennis courts and during the 1911-12 school year Coach Muhl started collecting contributions for courts, which eventually were built, only to be completely obliterated by the new science building. Two new courts were ready by spring, 1914, behind the new science building.

Muhl became a legend for his longevity and range of talent. In 1933, for example, he still was coaching track and was an assistant professor of mathematics. In 1939-40 he returned to his old role as athletic director. And, in the 1952 yearbook, 42 years after his arrival, he's no longer coaching day-to-day, but still serves as an assistant mathematics professor. A gauge of just how beloved a character this faculty member had become is seen in the 1951 *Wesleyana*, where he is shown in a Homecoming photo with 11 of his players from his 1910 football team, all in formation four decades after the fact.

Golden Age of Athletics

Overall, the Kemp years were a "golden age" of athletics at Illinois Wesleyan, in part because of Fred Muhl, who became football coach in 1909. That year, the team held rival Northwestern University to a scoreless tie, a precursor to a widely heralded 3-0 victory over Northwestern in 1910. That team, under Captain Theodore Fieker, class of 1912, went on to win the state championship, while the spring's track team won the intercollegiate meet in Peoria.

The men's basketball team emerged in 1911. Fred Young, class of 1915, was captain of the squad that won the 1912 Illinois small-college basketball tournament. And, a few years later, the baseball team won the Little Nineteen championship.

Regional athletic groups were in constant flux and opponents vary widely from the local small colleges, to schools, to YMCAs, to Northwestern, Illinois, the Little Nineteen, or the College Conference of Illinois and Wisconsin.

The decade spanning 1910 to 1920 boasted many athletic stars, including J. Norman Elliott, class of 1916, twice captain of the basketball team and a future football coach, and Scott Lucas, class of 1914, a left end on the 1912 football team and future Majority Leader of the U.S. Senate.

Get the Goat: Athletic Rivalries

Sports thrive on classic rivalries and for decades the motto, GET THE GOAT, decorated floats and events surrounding the Millikin game. To get one's goat is a normal enough idiom, but around 1912 there was an actual object, a stuffed goat, connected to a charming toy cart. Pictured in the 1912 yearbook, the trophy moved back and forth between Bloomington and Decatur after each appropriate contest—football, basketball, baseball, track, or debate. Travel started in 1905 and by 1912 the symbol of prowess had moved back and forth 31 times.

◄ Coach Hill on Wilder Field.

Intercollegiate Play for Women

The 1919 yearbook reports a first—intercollegiate play for women. The women's tennis team played Millikin on May 19, 1917, in what the editors said was the first year of a women's tournament. Illinois Wesleyan won, but everybody got a souvenir trophy.

Coach Muhl also revived women's basketball. Elaine Strayer was director of women's athletics and the 1921 yearbook reported the "first girls' basket-ball team." The new women's coach teamed up with visiting French student Elaine Thiebaut, who had led a team in France. Together they had a 13-player team, which competed with high schools and other local teams.

The 1921 yearbook cited Muhl's accomplishments, noting he had a record surpassing any other in the conference—one football, one track, one baseball, and three basketball championships. He even had faculty playing. The 1920 tennis Conference Faculty Championship was won by Professor Ralph Clayton Hartsough. Only students, however, were members of the "W" Club, having won an official letter in a major sport.

Social Clubs

The Xi chapter of Alpha Gamma Delta was established in 1914 at a time when women's groups had chapter rooms, rather than residences. Their room was located on the third floor of the Academy Building. Later the chapter room moved to Old Main and to a rented house, with ownership of a house on Main Street coming in 1930. Alpha Gamma Delta was founded in 1904 by 11 women at Syracuse University.

Greek-Life Pranks

Fraternity and sorority high jinks are part of the era's remembered lore. A "pajama parade," reported in the June 10, 1913, edition of the *Argus* is a case in point. It seems that in the wee hours of Tuesday morning, June 3, after the year's last fraternity meetings, a group of venturesome spirits "donned their garb for retiring" to raid various dormitories. ". . . the sleepers

"Pajama Games" Homecoming 1928.

[were] dislodged by feet, arms, legs and otherwise and pressed into line," the newspaper reported. The parade included 43 pairs of pajamas, 18 night shirts, two bath robes, and two men 'otherwise attired.'"

The paraders sang and offered University cheers, despite threats of police action, prompting "a few Juliets" to push aside the curtains and appear at upstairs' windows. The revelers traipsed through Bloomington's streets accompanied by the "steady tramp of bath room slippers," waking residents. They even visited the homes of a few drowsy professors, encouraging the scholars to "sally forth and deliver their best lectures which they did with the best grace possible."

World War I Comes to Campus

A chauffeur's wrong turn down a Sarajevo street in 1914 and two gunshots, killing Archduke Franz Ferdinand—heir apparent to the Viennese throne—and his wife, Sophie, triggered World War I. The clash, which lasted 1,567 days, killed 15- million soldiers and civilians, toppled four monarchies, and cost about $337.9 billion.

Illinois Wesleyan President Theodore Kemp called World War I, 1914-18, "the holiest cause ever undertaken by the country." The conflict deeply affected the University. Some faculty were caught in Europe when hostilities broke out. At the start of the 1917-18 academic year, enrollment dropped 15 percent, to 262 students, with women outnumbering men on campus 141-121. Only a half dozen men graduated in the spring of 1918, and the *Daily Pantagraph* observed: "The fraternity houses at [Illinois] Wesleyan are all but deserted now and as long as the war continues the same condition is very likely to exist

. . . Nearly every fraternity at [Illinois] Wesleyan has a service flag from 30 to 50 stars on it."

On the home front, sororities like Sigma Kappa held a "French market" in a hotel, which raised $500 for the Belgian Relief Fund. During the influenza epidemic that swept the United States during the war years, a fraternity offered its house as a temporary hospital for flu victims. Among those hardest hit by the epidemic were the campus's own soldier-students, the boys in the Student Army Training Corps (SATC).

The United States had entered the "war to end all wars" in April, 1917. Subsequently the University was among 300 campuses nationally with SATC units offering students military instruction.

As overall enrollment fell, President Kemp advertised the new government program to find federal dollars to replace local tuition: "Go to College. Free Tuition. Free Board and Room. Free Gymnasium. Free Swimming Pool. $30.00 per month from the Government." There was nothing about making the world safe for democracy in this advertisement and only the "Free Uniform" and a few details in fine print showed this was anything more than free college. As military drill became compulsory for all male students, there soon were three units training on University grounds.

The SATC was part of a government program to subsidize colleges for loss of their male students because of the draft law. On September 16, 1918, Illinois Wesleyan signed contracts to take 300 military students and provide housing and instruction. The fall program was to begin on October 1, therefore, the beginning of the regular semester was pushed back to September 30.

But all of this was very perplexing for Kemp and his colleagues as each messenger brought telegrams with different plans. A commanding officer did not arrive until October 8, though the University was quite happy to have Captain H. M. Wheaton, a Yale alumnus and former football coach at the U.S. Naval Academy at Annapolis.

The Bloomington Association of Commerce joined with the University in helping finance and construct a combination barracks and mess hall on the future site of Memorial Gymnasium. A large building project, the wooden structure was nonetheless finished and occupied by November 9 just in time for the war's end on November 11, 1918.

What to do now? At first, the plan was that the men would continue in residence, with their drillmasters, for the rest of year, spending by government directive more time on college studies than military pursuits. But new orders were forthcoming and everyone was sent home on December 13, 1918.

Shortly thereafter, the barracks were sold off and removed and by 1920 there was virtually no sign of the program. In fact, the 1920 yearbook commented boldly that the SATC was "a huge joke and costly experiment."

French Students Escaped the War

In the fall of 1918, 133 French college students came to the United States, sent overseas by the French government to continue their education. Three of those exchange students enrolled at Illinois Wesleyan. Two of these students were the Baron sisters—Idellette and Annette—from Lyons, who lived in Kemp Hall. One of the women "expressed wonder and surprise at the richness of America and its comparative freedom from the pinch of war, as compared with her own country," according to an article in *McLean County and the World War*.

The third exchange student from Belfort, Alsace, was Jeanne Seigneur. She is mentioned in the 1920 *Wesleyana* in a piece headlined, "Our French Girls," which commented: "Our love and admiration for France and her noble people have been strengthened by having in our midst such fine types of French womanhood." Seigneur and Annette Baron graduated in 1920, while Idellette was a member of the class of 1921.

"War Fever"

The wartime mood on campus was captured in the book, *Through the Eyes of the Argus: 100*

Years of Journalism at Illinois Wesleyan University, which reported: "The first active-duty issue [of the *Argus*], which appeared on October 17, 1917, complete with a patriotic front-cover graphic, told how 'war fever' had set in at [Illinois] Wesleyan. Even the peace orators who had been preaching international cooperation just one year before were now 'devoting all their energies to the study of how to fight successfully for Uncle Sam,' according to an editorial."

April 18, 1917, was Flag Raising Day, timed to commemorate Paul Revere's famous ride through the Massachusetts' countryside warning the colonists that the "British are coming" during the Revolutionary War. Earlier that spring workmen had finished putting up a 75-foot-tall flagpole and April 18 was set for its inauguration. There were Coach Muhl's cadets, the Daughters of the American Revolution, and the Grand Army of the Republic—the local Civil War veterans—who had marched to the campus from the courthouse with their own flags.

This "war fever" may have contributed to sparking a new spirit on campus, especially among female students. One manifestation of

this was the [Illinois] Wesleyan Girls' Training Camp, an effort apart from sororities or the YWCA which united the women "with the idea of service in every way possible to the school," according to the November 28, 1917, *Argus.*

"Over There"

By the war's end, about 200 students and alumni had served in the military. Though records are sketchy and at times contradictory about 15 alumni died during the war: five on battlefields and 10 from illnesses. Memorial Gymnasium was dedicated on December 14, 1922, in memory of the University's World War I dead.

Army Private Paul Martin, class of 1918, was among the first of 1.3-million U.S. troops to face the Germans in October, 1917. Martin, a member of a medical detachment with the Army's 26th Infantry Division, got a feel for combat by talking to English veterans. Martin wrote in an October 8, 1917, letter that, "There is something about the rough soldiers' life that gets into a man's blood and holds him."

In June, 1918, U.S. Marines, including Sergeant Gerald Thomas, class of 1919 and a

Athlete to Sportswriter

Fred Young, class of 1915, was an early 20th-century sports standout in basketball, baseball, and tennis. To those who knew him, he was always "Brick" Young. By any standards he was basketball's key star in its first four seasons, sometimes making as many as 25 points a game. He was an outstanding baseball pitcher. A career highlight came for him when he pitched a no-hitter against future Chicago Cubs' pitcher Joe Cook in a semi-pro league and drove in the game's only run.

After a brief tour of duty in semi-professional basketball and baseball, Young became a reporter for Bloomington's *Daily Pantagraph* in 1918. He was named the newspaper's sports editor in 1922, a post he held for decades. Over the years, Young organized baseball road trips and for 40 years helped recruit athletes for the University. He died in 1980 at age 88, after having attended many games in a field house named for him.

Bloomington men preparing to go off to World War I.

chemistry student, were rushed from their rest camp on an hour's notice to face a German drive at Chateau-Thierry, where U.S. troops quashed the enemy advance less than 50 miles northeast of Paris. For days, Thomas wrote, they faced withering artillery and machine-gun fire without provisions, water, or sleep.

"We stopped the 'Boche,'" Thomas wrote his family, "and recaptured a number of positions. Many of my comrades of the last year are gone. Among them my first 'bunkie.'"

Commenting on Thomas' exploits at Chateau-Thierry, a newspaper article reported, "The commanding officers of the 'fighting sixth' [Thomas' unit] were killed and Thomas . . . took command of their company and brought them through the fight in first class shape . . . Over five-sixths of Thomas' company were killed or wounded in action."

Army Lieutenant George E. Butler, class of 1914 and a lawyer, was captain of Coach Fred Muhl's 1914 football squad. In April, 1918, he was in No Man's Land, the deadly territory separating Allied and German trenches on the Western Front in France. "I swore at the moon the night I was out in No Man's Land with a patrol . . . ," Butler wrote. "It came out so brightly that I could see the barbs on the German soldiers' wires from a distance of 100 yards." Butler faced two German machine-gun nests. They were playing target practice with his unit.

Jesse S. Dancy, an 1899 graduate wrote letters to the *Argus* from wartime France. Dancy, a hospital chaplain, offered this description of life near the front in an article published in the November 14, 1917, edition of the newspaper: "It is a great experience to see convoys of wounded coming in, worn to the limit with sleepless nights, days and nights of fighting, and weakened with loss of blood, but exhilarated with the flush of battle and the confidence of victory . . . At the time, the loss of a leg, or an arm, or an eye seems of no importance when compared with the fact that the Germans are crumbling before their attacks."

Infantryman Howard Bolin was the first alumnus to die in France. He enlisted in the Army when he was a sophomore in the academy. Bolin received nine weeks of military training at Camp Green in North Carolina before shipping out to France. He died of battle-field wounds on July 20, 1918, one day short of his 23rd birthday.

Another fatality was Army Lieutenant Elmer Doocy, a 1916 law-school graduate, who received the Distinguished Service Cross for "repeated acts of extraordinary heroism," accord-ing to a communiqué from General John J. Pershing, commander-in-chief of the American Expeditionary Force in France.

The armistice came on November 11, 1918. Army Captain Ivan Elliott, a 1916 law-school graduate, recorded his reaction to peace: "I had a hard time getting away from Paris that night. They nearly upset the taxicab I was in to get at me. Seven French girls and an old woman did get me and hugged me."

Armistice

When news of the armistice arrived at Illinois Wesleyan, the November 22, 1918, *Argus* reported that, "As the parade passed the University and Kemp Hall, the girls [who made up the majority of the student body] throwing books and lessons to the wind, joined in the ranks."

The joy of victory, however, was tempered by the grief of parents and others for the University's fallen heroes. These men "who gave their lives for Liberty and Justice in the Great World War" were honored at a May 30, 1919, memorial service at Amie Chapel. Among those listed in the program for the service was George

Herman Anna who "fought like a hero, killing two of the three Germans who had concentrated their fire on him, but was wounded by the third."

Mildred Ralston of Vermont, Illinois, was too grief-stricken to attend the memorial serv-ice. She lost her son, Corporal William Ralston, a law-school student in 1914, when the steamer *Otranto* was torpedoed by the Germans on October 6, 1918, off the Scottish coast. His body was recovered three days later and buried with full military honors in a 17th-century church-yard on the Isle of Islay.

Before sailing for France, Ralston's 22-year-old son had written his mother, expressing an optimistic sentiment reflective of the World War I era: " . . . the war will be over some day and I will follow the flag back home . . . with the supreme satisfaction of knowing that my duty toward my country was well and faithfully done and that this world will be safer and better for women and children."

Post World War I Era

The Roaring Twenties was an age of speakeasies, the Charleston, the "return to normalcy" under President Warren G. Harding, and Charles Lindbergh's heroic flight to Paris aboard *The Spirit of St. Louis*. Some of the decade's free spirit was captured at Illinois Wesleyan in events like the Freshman Party.

Remember the ritual? The sophomores cut the freshmen's hair if they caught them having a party, which of course made them want to have a party.

Freshmen took to Lexington, Illinois, where they set up a camp site near the railroad station water tower and "so gathering around the fire and roasting their wieners, they ate their evening meal," the 1920 *Wesleyana* recounted. Games followed until it was time to catch the train back to Normal. Back home, the yearbook reported: " . . . the boys armed themselves with clubs and anything available that they could find and, fearing a sudden attack of the Sophs, they marched with the girls in the center of the group to Kemp Hall, and then on to Bloomington. The Sophs were out, but they fled from the unconquerable Freshmen. And so this indomitable class of '22 can always say: 'We had our party without any Sophs!'"

On another night, after a rainy three weeks in the spring, a progressive party was planned for May 8. As the crowd assembled, it was divided in two. One delegation headed to Kemp Hall, where a half-dozen fortune tellers were encamped "and each one was eager to lift the veil of mystery and disclose the secrets of the future," the 1920 *Wesleyana* reported.

Other party stops were the Sigma Chi fraternity house, where popcorn and candy were served and a pianist played tunes, including "Have a Smile for Everyone You Meet." The jolly group also invaded the Tau Kappa Epsilon fraternity house, where, according to the *Wesleyana*, "Loren Lewis, at the piano, and Rex Howard with his clarinet, gave a number of fine selections to an appreciative audience." Punch was served at the Phi Gamma Delta house.

The crowd eventually returned to campus, where the air rang with "Dear Old [Illinois] Wesleyan." The editors of the yearbook, concluded with this observation: "The crowning glory of the party was the ample lunch served by the committee near the hour of midnight, the college doors opened and out came a host of young people decorated in pink, yellow, blue and white streamers, and in their mouths—would you believe it—all day suckers!"

A 6.6-Ounce Gold Medal

In 1978 Illinois Wesleyan received a 6.6-ounce, solid gold medal, measuring 63 millimeters in diameter. The momento, the Acheson Medal, had been awarded to John Wesley Marden, class of 1909, in 1952 by the Electrochemical Society for his outstanding contributions in the science and technology of rare metals. The medal, turned over to the University by one of Marden's daughters, was established in 1928 to honor Edward Goodrich Acheson, one of the men who helped Thomas Edison develop the incandescent lamp.

Behind the history of the medal is the tale of an interesting and pioneering alumnus, who was present at the creation of atomic energy. Marden, who received master's and doctor's degrees from New York

University, had taught at the universities of Minnesota and Missouri from 1912-20. He was tapped by Washington during World War I to probe the properties of zirconium, fearing the Germans were using the substance or a derivative in their Big Bertha cannons, sparking his interest in rare metals.

In 1920 he joined Westinghouse Research Laboratories and remained there until his retirement in the early 1950s. He studied uranium as a possible replacement for tungsten in lamp filaments, learning much about production of pure uranium that would play a pivotal role in World War II's atomic-bomb project. Subsequently, as part of Manhattan Project, Marden and his associates were called on to produce 60 tons of uranium, receiving War Department and presidential citations for the work.

Marden was a charter member of Illinois Wesleyan's Science Advisory Committee, formed in 1954 to help guide development of academic programs, equipment, facilities, and graduate-school contacts.

VI. Realizing the Pillsbury Plan

The end of World War I brought an unexpected proposal, which upset local loyalists, but in the end consolidated great strength and vision—and in many senses put the University in the position it occupies today.

If other leaders of the University had been oriented toward frugal survival, President Theodore Kemp was the exact opposite. He knew the necessities of balanced current budgets, yet he saw clearly that future success was based on visionary and therefore solid, long-term planning.

Efforts around 1910 had sparked vision and Kemp's list of needs was well honed: a library, a law building, a gymnasium, and a hall of languages. Coach Fred Muhl showed additional talents by reducing the vision to a drawing for the 1914 yearbook, while basketball captain Fred Young, class of 1915, did his own parody plan in the same volume.

Kemp's Vision

There is perhaps no more glorious moment in the University's history than Kemp's talk to the Board of Trustees on December 9, 1916. Trustee minutes record it verbatim, with the copyist adding some subheads. Whether Kemp's or not, one of the subheads speaks for the whole: "Larger Plan Necessary."

Kemp scanned the environment. State universities were gathering thousands of students nearby. "What kind of school do we want Illinois Wesleyan to be?" he asked the board. His answer—a selective college of high achievement.

With the enthusiasm of the past years, undergraduate enrollments were increasing. How far should they go? Illinois Wesleyan had grown, too, but wisely capped its enrollment at 500. As pressure for admission increased—driven by competition and the ever-present search for quality students—universities were taking only the best-prepared students. Kemp suggested an undergraduate enrollment of 500. With more than 500 students, a college was no longer small and personal friendships among teachers and students were diminished.

As he spoke, there were 246 students in the college, gathering in four buildings on six acres. Law and music were in town. And, Kemp insisted on planning for the years ahead—12 years, 25 years, and even 50 years—even though that might not be adequate given the changes and developments in learning sure to follow.

Two questions were key: the nature of the University and its location. Kemp did a quick estimate of the buildings Illinois Wesleyan should have. He was brave as he listed them unflinchingly complete with estimated costs. As a comparison, he estimated costs of moving to some larger site and building completely anew.

Rather than thinking the man insane as he suggested abandoning a campus where the science building was only six years old, the board was mesmerized. Immediately it named a site committee, which consulted with Kemp and scoured local real estate for options. The board gathered again on February 7. It had quick estimates on 10 buildings, either organized on the present site or another. When expenses of grounds and construction were factored together, the present site could be developed for $570,000, a new site $580,000. Kemp then had the courage to say an additional $500,000 dollars was needed for the endowment.

The committee had worked hard. It had details and prices on 10 sites, ranging in size from 250 acres to only 20. Kemp and the board

Buck Memorial ➤
Library

debated size and concluded 80 acres was a minimum. The committee disbanded ready to relocate Illinois Wesleyan University on the grounds of the Bloomington Country Club, then owned not by the club but by the heirs of an estate.

Kemp's vision was hardly a secret. The February 15, 1917, *Argus* described the effort: "A new movement is now afoot at IWU the object of which is to provide for the development and expansion of the University; it is a movement which is heartily approved by all who are interested in [Illinois] Wesleyan for it had long been felt that the school was hampered and cramped by its small campus and few buildings. This new movement, which is being watched with much interest, will either provide for the enlargement of the present campus and the erection of several new buildings or for the securing of an entirely new site for the University on which to erect the various department buildings . . . The tendency and general sentiment seems to be for the obtaining of a new site and a new site of not less than eighty acres. Public opinion leans towards the changing of [Illinois] Wesleyan's situation."

Sad news came in June. Within 24 hours of the University's completing arrangements to buy the country-club grounds, the club had pulled itself together and made a deal with the owners. But the University's site remained an open issue, as the board wavered. Should the University buy adjacent properties or consider a completely new site?

The Springfield Fracas

Once the option to move was taken as real, multiple possibilities followed. By January, 1918, the board had begun very quiet discussions with backers, who wanted to move the entire University to Springfield. This was no theoretical option and there are printed plans with maps showing two potential Springfield locations.

News of the Springfield option leaked in early 1919, just after the armistice ending World War I. What amounted to a protest meeting gathered in April, 1919, as alumni and local business leaders made it very clear they had not supported Illinois Wesleyan on the assumption it would be anywhere but in Bloomington. Kemp and his colleagues mastered the growing hubbub for the glory of their ongoing plan. Judge Sain Welty (1853-1920), class of 1881 and a graduate of Yale law, had been head of the board during talks with the Springfield interests. He now assumed the public role of leading Bloomington support to keep the University in town. Six hundred and sixty thousand dollars later the "New Illinois Wesleyan Campaign" had done just that. Included in that pledge was funding for a gymnasium, the first of the many buildings, now destined to rise around the old campus.

With these commitments in hand, Kemp turned to local architect Arthur A. Pillsbury to render in new detail what Fred Muhl had sketched in 1914: a real architectural plan of the new vision. Soon he had plans for each of the buildings and above all a birds-eye rendering in color of the completed whole. It was breathtaking.

Architect's Vision

Arthur Pillsbury had been designing fashionable buildings and houses in Bloomington for some time. His legacy included the Schroeder building (1903), Ensenberger building (1926), Bloomington High School, and the building at Miller Park Zoo. Pillsbury was commissioned to do a complete renovation of the University. Had the era been able to afford it, Illinois Wesleyan would have had the potential to move to an entirely different level.

An April, 1920, Executive Committee report sketched the broad outlines of what might be called the "Pillsbury Plan"—an ambitious $1.1-million construction scheme. Laid out on expanded grounds was the "new" Illinois Wesleyan with an administration building (the Main Building completely refurbished), a men's dormitory group, four science halls, gymnasium, chapel, women's dormitory, and a library.

The Executive Committee report concluded the library "should be erected as soon as possible.

The Pillsbury Campus Master Plan 1920.

The needs of the students fairly cry out for a Library." The report added that, "The increased income necessary to support such equipment would require an addition of $1,320,000.00 to the present endowment." If the plan was executed, according to the report, the physical plant would be valued at nearly $2 million with an endowment of $2.25 million.

Fund-raising initially was in the hands of President Kemp and Albert G. Carnine, University field secretary and business manager. Carnine wrote a page-long essay for the 1922 yearbook, detailing his philosophy. "Our business is to turn out moral giants, well balanced morally, physically, and mentally, and in the degree that we do this on a larger scale because of an increased number of students, can we hope to become a 'Greater [Illinois] Wesleyan.'"

President Kemp was optimistic about prospects in June, 1921, as he told the board that the University had an "increasing number of prospective students knocking at our doors" and that "a million dollar endowment fund [had been] raised." Kemp predicted that program, architecture, and endowment would put Illinois among "the foremost colleges . . . in this or any land."

First Steps

That fall marked the first steps toward realizing the grand design. The gateway on Main Street was completed just as Pillsbury designed it. When local committees finished working on funds, the University was in a position to begin the gymnasium, which would rise as a memorial to those who had fought in World War I. Kemp and others laid the cornerstone on November 5, 1921. The gymnasium was finished by June 1, 1922, and by that time so too was Kemp. He had announced his intent to retire on April 18.

Martha Buck

Kemp wrote then that he had contemplated leaving for three or four years, waiting for a moment of stability to hand duties on to others. He felt some frustration in fundraising. Methodist conferences often grouped associated institutions for proportional parts of larger campaigns, therefore, the development officer Illinois Wesleyan had hired was often seconded for larger Methodist interests. The implicit lesson was that the University needed its own development efforts and its own roster of supporters. Kemp mused on things as Memorial Gym was finished and he decided the moment to leave Illinois Wesleyan had come. On July 1 he was gone. Among Kemp's activities in later life was two years at Hollywood Methodist Episcopal Church in Los Angeles and retirement. He died on May 20, 1937, in Los Angeles.

However, there were three more days of glory for Kemp as his departure neared. He gave a valedictory on June 12, telling the Board of Trustees that "these eventful years are to me more pleasure than all the gold of the world." The next day the community paid tribute to him at a luncheon at the Bloomington Consistory, an event far more than a valedictory. It fell to Kemp on that day to announce yet another great benefaction of which he had worked. Illinois Wesleyan would receive a $250,000 bequest from Martha Buck, trustee and widow of Hiram Buck, a long-time trustee and benefactor. Her gift was to go for the library,

that great building which evoked so much of Kemp's energy.

His last commencement followed on June 14. Kemp presented diplomas to 56 seniors and then moved to laying the cornerstone of the new Buck Library.

After Kemp's departure, administration of the campus was in the hands of Vice President Wilbert Ferguson and Dean William Wallis. The board did not search long, however, to find a successor. Indeed, the trustees never left the boardroom and made the president of the Board of Trustees the president of the University.

William Davidson

William J. Davidson

William J. Davidson (1869-1968) was a logical choice as the next president of Illinois Wesleyan. After graduating from Chaddock in 1893, he earned another B.A. from Illinois Wesleyan in 1894. Davidson studied divinity at Garrett and then alternated between teaching at Garrett and serving Methodist churches in Illinois, at least until he was chancellor of Nebraska Wesleyan for two years. He then returned to Garrett, where he had been professor of religious education. After Judge Sain Welty died in 1920, he became head of the board. Davidson was a logical choice to be president since he was an alumnus, he had led a college, and he had served on the Board of Trustees. He inherited the Kemp legacy in September, 1922.

When Davidson became president, the University had a faculty of 51 with 961 students. The "Roaring Twenties" saw student numbers grow to more than 1,300 with the addition of schools of speech and nursing. Despite declines in the music school and a 50-percent reduction in the number of law students as the law school neared closure in the 1920s, the overall student population grew as did facilities to accommodate their needs.

Under Davidson, the loyal and elegant Wilbert Ferguson, a fixture at the University since 1894, remained vice president. He had been on the faculty longer than anyone, serving as professor of modern languages.

William Wallis was dean of the College of Liberal Arts. A native of southern Illinois, Wallis began his higher-education experience at Southern Illinois State Normal School before finishing at Ohio Wesleyan in 1894. He had earned an additional A.M. from the University of Illinois in 1920. He was a school principal in several Illinois cities before taking on welfare work in the Army's 32nd Division during World War I. Wallis returned to Bloomington in 1921 and was appointed dean the following year, succeeding Ferguson.

Alumni Efforts

The 1922 yearbook reported alumni clubs in Chicago and New York. The secretary of the New York group was Sukeshige Yanagiwara, class of 1900, one of the University's Japanese alumni, illustrating the University's international reach.

Buck Library

Martha Buck's gift gave new vision and new direction to the Pillsbury Plan. Illinois Wesleyan would indeed have a new library, just where Kemp and Pillsbury had imagined it, but Pillsbury would not design it. The building was designed in the collegiate gothic style,

The reading room of Buck Memorial Library.

championed by architect Ralph Adams Cram, and easily visible on any trip to Yale, Princeton, or the University of Chicago.

For nearly 75 years, the library had shifted among cramped quarters in various buildings. Buck Memorial Library was constructed in 1922 and dedicated in 1923. The 1925 yearbook commented that the new library was "undoubtedly the most artistic building on campus," and even today careful inspection uncovers gargoyles missed without a lingering look. Its original reading room was particularly elegant.

Fund-Raising in the Roaring Twenties

Three months into his tenure as president, William Davidson reported that he and business manager Albert Carnine were spending "every day that it was possible . . . in the field . . . cultivating men and women," who were interested in the University. He added: "We have met cordial response in each instance. At no point have we met with any antagonism to our institution or our plans."

However, Davidson realized the daunting task faced by the University to raise sufficient funds to support the University's bold plans. Consequently, he cautioned: " . . . great patience is required not only in the doing of the work but in the attitude of the Board toward the men who are doing it. It requires a number of visits as a usual thing to convince a careful and able man that he ought to make a large gift to an educational institution or an educational cause. When the gift is made, however, it becomes clear at once that the time has not been misspent." More specifically, Davidson pointed out, "We are still in the process of financing the gymnasium. About $25,000 worth of bonds remain unsold."

By the end of Davidson's first year in office, he reported in June, 1923, that, "There are indications that our work was done not entirely without success." He also expressed his appreciation to the faculty, noting: ". . . I believe it would be very hard to find a faculty anywhere

Powell Monument

moved by a greater spirit of loyalty than is the faculty of the Illinois Wesleyan University."

However, University finances still weighed heavily on Davidson's mind, especially the debt incurred by construction of Memorial Gymnasium. He conceded in a 1923 Board of Trustees' report that it would be difficult to gain Carnegie Corporation support for a new science building because of the debt. And, of course, a new science building was a key element of the ill-fated Pillsbury Plan.

Collections and the Powell Monument

Explorer-professor John Wesley Powell was not forgotten and the class of 1923 took special pride in creating the monument that still stands along the sidewalk on what is now known as the Eckley Quadrangle.

The Aldrich collection, received in 1923, was considered to be "probably the most valuable art collection in this part of the country," according to the *Daily Pantagraph* on February 20, 1926. The collection contained original works by the noted English artist, Gainsborough, and Tintoretto, a 16th-century Venetian artist. Alas, they all disappeared with the Hedding Hall fire of 1943.

Academic Programs

The 1920s were somewhat paradoxical. Kemp's vision of a strong, selective school of national excellence was bearing fruit. Enrollment was up and new honorary societies appeared. Phi Kappa Phi became the senior honorary for overall excellence in any field. But specialized societies recognized outstanding work in particular areas. Theta Alpha Pi, in drama; Phi Mu Alpha, in music; Sigma Alpha Iota and Delta Omicron were music sororities; and a Women's Athletic Association. Yet, the appearance of oratory and nursing revert to Kemp's model of diversifying with programs offering regional usefulness.

Twilight of the Law School

Illinois Wesleyan University's law school first changed and then disappeared in the 1920s as the bar association placed new requirements on legal education. The first students in the 1870s had completed the law course in one year and might enter law school straight from high school. No undergraduate work was required. Illinois Bar Association rules later mandated a three-year course and in the 1920s the state legislature demanded first one and then two years of college before law school.

Charles Laban Capen (1845-1927) followed Owen T. Reeves as law-school dean in 1912. Another of the many natives of upstate New York on the early University staff, Capen had come to Bloomington at age 11 and graduated from Harvard in 1869. He spent two years in graduate work at Harvard before returning to Bloomington, where he was admitted to the Illinois bar in 1871. In 1899 he joined the Illinois Wesleyan law faculty.

Paradoxically the decade that saw the law school's demise began with dreams of its expansion. In 1922 the administration could brag quietly to the yearbook writers than an enrollment of 50 had seemed amazing in the 1890s,

College fun on Friday the 13th, 1927, in Old North.

Groundbreaking for Presser Hall October 13, 1927.

but in the early 1920s it stood at a solid 90 students. And if the University had succeeded in its development efforts and the general campus plan, then the dean hoped that one of the new buildings would house the law school.

Since its inception the McLean County Courthouse had doubled as the Illinois Wesleyan law school. Indeed, in the early 1920s there was considerable thought of expansion and among the Pillsbury Plan for the University was a law library, which would have been the first law building constructed on the main campus.

In 1924 the law school celebrated its 50th anniversary. The next year there were 107 law students enrolled and things seemed to be going well, but the school was a memory by 1930.

The decision to close the law school was made in 1925, but the faculty decided to graduate the remaining students. The last law-school class graduated on June 7, 1927.

The beginning of the end for the law school came in 1923 with a ruling by the North Central Association of Colleges and Secondary Schools. That organization declared that for a liberal-arts college to have an accredited law school, it also must be accredited by the American Association of Law Schools (AALS). Among its accreditation mandates, AALS required that law schools have a law library of no less than 5,000 volumes and at least three full-time professors. Illinois Wesleyan was a Class A college by the standards of the North Central Association and it lacked the funds to meet the AALS requirements. The faculty came to the reluctant conclusion that they could only graduate the current students and close.

Dean Capen resigned in 1923 and by 1926-27 enrollment had logically dwindled to 26 students. Almost as a celebration at the very end, the McLean County Bar Association gave a dinner on May 21, 1927, the very day Lindbergh landed in Paris. It was a last gathering of alumni while the school still endured. They all knew that when classes finished that spring, so did the Illinois Wesleyan School of Law.

College Dance in the Memorial Gym 1927.

The School of Music Prospers

While the law school disappeared, the School of Music prospered. In the fall of 1919 a building directly opposite the campus at University Avenue and East Street was purchased and its studios were equipped with grand pianos while the practice rooms were provided with upright pianos. It was a half-way measure, for students still divided their time between the new house and the buildings downtown. The program still grew, and in 1925, it was occupying two more buildings.

In retrospect Dean Arthur Westbrook brought magic when he arrived in 1922, as the college merged with the Bloomington School of Music. The roster soared to 300 students.

Arthur Lovejoy who brought the Jazz Age to the School of Music, marches through Illinois Wesleyan University's yearbooks like the golden youth of F. Scott Fitzgerald. He organized a jazz band—the Illinois Wesleyan Collegiates—and got them booked as the talent on a French

ocean liner bound from New York to France in the summer of 1928. The February 10, 1928, *Daily Pantagraph* reported that the group had "a six week's engagement in a Paris hotel or cafe and a trip through central Europe before they play their way back to New York again." Lovejoy organized the Apollo Club and bought them lots of train tickets to Chicago to broadcast, sometimes nationally, on WGN and NBC radio. The Apollo Quartet continued as heir of that club decades after Lovejoy left the faculty. Vera Pearl Kemp, however, brought the classics to lunch. Students knew her as professor of organ, but shoppers remembered her for organizing string quartets to play in local department tea rooms. She also is credited with sending the yearbook the most artistic of faculty photographs.

Construction of Presser Hall

The already robust music program advanced further with construction of Presser Hall in 1928-30, the last stand of the Pillsbury Plan. The building

Hedding College Building in Abingdon, Illinois. The columns for the Sesquicentennial Gateway came from this building.

was made possible by a conditional pledge of $75,000 from the Presser Foundation, established by the well-known Philadelphia music publisher, Theodore Presser (1848-1925).

The $190,000 facility contained 24 studios, plus recital halls, classrooms, practice rooms, and offices, according to the 1931 catalogue account, which added: "It is equipped with five pipe organs and 58 pianos. Its sound proof construction and convenient appointments remove the more serious handicaps under which the work of this growing school was for several years conducted. Presser Hall was dedicated on February 3, 1930." No one knew it at the time, but Presser Hall was the last building constructed that followed the program and design developed by Pillsbury and Kemp.

Schools of Speech and Nursing

Two new schools appeared in the academic year 1924-25. The first development of 1924-25 seems odd—the creation of a School of Oratory,

exactly what Delmar Darrah had been running in the 1890s. The school offered a course of study leading to a reintroduced degree: the bachelor of oratory. From one short description, it seemed more oriented toward producing actors than stump speakers. Yet one assessment said the course "was organized to meet the ever-increasing demand of students for an opportunity to specialize in the field of public speaking from a professional standpoint."

That same year the University joined Brokaw Hospital in creating a School of Nursing. As originally planned, it was a five-year program leading to a bachelor of science degree and a graduate nurse's diploma. The first two years were spent at the University, the third year split, and the last two at the hospital.

Home economics remained but placed less emphasis on cookery and more on textiles and design, though dietetics still was an important component.

Hedding Hall with Old North in the background.

A Memorable Debate

It was February 23, 1922—the day after a snowy Washington's Birthday holiday—when the Ripon College debate team visited Bloomington. Ripon defeated Illinois Wesleyan, 2-1. However, this contest is remembered because of the later fame of a Ripon debater.

Spencer Tracy, later the Academy Award-winning actor, was a Ripon team member. The debate was recalled during a 1977 visit to Illinois Wesleyan by Curtis MacDougall, the famed journalism professor-emeritus at Northwestern University, who was among the Ripon debaters and one of Tracy's fraternity brothers.

"We went to the Auditorium Theatre in Chicago the night before our debate at [Illinois] Wesleyan and saw Lionel Barrymore in *The Claw*," MacDougall recalled. "'Spence' came out of the movie and said, 'That settles it I'm going to be an actor.' He later appeared with Barrymore in movies."

Campus Life in the Jazz Age

The Jazz Age at Illinois Wesleyan was summed up by the *Argus* 15 years after the fact. On April 4, 1939, an article headlined "Traditionally Yours" revealed "approximately fifteen years ago, dances were an occasion to be hushed up. If the authorities got wind of a dance, it was just too bad. Sororities gave their dances in the names of private individuals. The alumni sometimes succeeded in giving it for them. On certain occasions, students had to have written permits from their parents in order to attend a dance."

Traditional rigidity of Illinois Wesleyan social rules got publicity without perhaps changing student behavior. Even in 1904 the *Argus* for example cited a *Chicago Maroon* article reporting that the IWU faculty had "prohibited dancing, card-playing, and theatre-going." However, enforcement seemed to be lax. A 1912 *Argus* editorial noted: "These regulations, however, have not been observed as judiciously as they might have been and a great deal of advantage

Overleaf:
North side of
Presser Hall shortly
after it opened
in 1930.

has been taken." In 1916 dances were going on, though the board reaffirmed its prohibition.

The Legacies of Chaddock and Hedding

The roster of Illinois Wesleyan alumni increased dramatically in 1928 without a single additional graduate walking across a stage to receive a diploma. Even before the Great Depression cast a dark shadow across the country, Illinois Wesleyan became heir to Hedding College of Abingdon, Illinois, a victim of economic troubles.

Illinois Wesleyan had absorbed Chaddock College in 1878, which fell to poor management, and Hedding, too, faced economic pressures. Hedding Collegiate Seminary had opened in a Methodist Church in the 1850s. A charter was obtained in February, 1857, incorporating the institution under the name of Hedding Seminary and Central Illinois Female College. Hedding's first building also was constructed in 1857 and another structure was occupied in 1874. In August, 1875, articles of incorporation were granted by the state of Illinois under the name of Hedding College. Jabez R. Jaques, professor of languages, had served as Hedding College president for three years in the 1880s.

Merger discussions started around 1920. Hedding ceased to be a degree-granting college in 1922, but continued to operate as a junior college until 1926. In June, 1928, Hedding alumni were formally adopted by action of the trustees. In December, 1930, the trustees entered into a contract with Hedding's trustees by which the endowment and annuities of that college were transferred to Bloomington The following March the Illinois Wesleyan board renamed "Old Main" to "Hedding Hall."

There is an interesting story associated with the Hedding Bell, now a campus fixture near Presser Hall. The bell was used to announce classes at Hedding from 1885 to 1918. For its first three years in Bloomington, it was inside Hedding Hall. Some wanted to put it in the belfry of Old North, since the University's original bell had been given away. But, what to do with the Hedding Bell?

A special monument seemed appropriate, but there was a lack of funds for construction. As often happened, the Student Union took over. Under the direction of Student Union President Richard Postlethwait, class of 1936, students contributed nickels and dimes as they entered the chapel. Enough money was collected to build the monument, which was dedicated during a downpour at Homecoming, 1934.

The First Rhodes Scholar: Reuben Borsch

Reuben Borsch, class of 1925, had a page-long profile in the 1925 yearbook. It could have been in any section, for the first Rhodes Scholar from Illinois Wesleyan was active in virtually everything. He majored in social science, was president of his class as a sophomore, the same year he was editor of the *Argus*. He was on the baseball team four years, captain as a senior, yet he was also in

Masquers, the drama club and he was active in debate his last two years.

As a Rhodes Scholar, Borsch studied at Oxford University in England, where he received a bachelor of civil laws degree. He joined the Chicago firm of Winston, Strawn & Shaw in 1928, where he practiced law for the next 48 years. Borsch also was a long-time trustee.

President Davidson and
John Phillip Sousa.

President Holmes and
Adlai E. Stevenson III.

VII. The Depression Years

President Herbert Hoover was bullish over the U.S. economy early in 1929. "A twelve month of unprecedented advance," he declared. However, beneath the surface, cracks were growing in the nation's economy and Illinois Wesleyan was not immune to the collapse which followed.

Wild speculation sent stock prices to their zenith on September 3, 1929, followed by a slow, measured decline toward a slump on October 24. Five days later, on October 29, 16.4-million shares were traded as huge blocks of stock were dumped by investors. That cataclysmic day went down in history as "Black Tuesday." By December 1, securities on the New York Stock Exchange had plummeted in value by $26 billion.

The Great Depression had begun. More than 1,300 banks shut their doors by the end of 1930. By 1932 the decline into economic oblivion resulted in 13-million jobless workers.

The Depression Hits
The financial affect of the 1929 stock-market crash on Illinois Wesleyan was not immediately apparent. However, a "Safety Fund Campaign" was launched in 1930, operating from February 20 to December 30. President William Davidson headed the campaign, which had a target of raising $750,000. Ultimately, the effort amassed $843,333.

By this time, the University had accumulated a deficit of more than $200,000 in operating expenses. To cover that debt—and the financial pressures triggered by the Great Depression—the trustees issued bonds totaling $250,000.

A Resignation
President Davidson resigned two years later on March 16, 1932. It was hardly a surprise because he had been talking with the board about quitting for months. Brushing aside concerns about his health, the board urged him to remain. The Pillsbury Plan was far from realized, but

Davidson, the trustees, and faculty could look back with real satisfaction to construction of Presser Hall, a substantial endowment, and other advances.

The 1933 yearbook called Davidson a "beloved leader and friend" of all students. Despite worries about his health, Davidson did not retire. In truth, he succeeded his successor. Davidson became pastor of the First Methodist Church in Springfield, Illinois, when that post became vacant as Harry W. McPherson moved north to become president of Illinois Wesleyan.

Harry McPherson Named President
Harry Wright McPherson (1879-1957), a 1906 graduate, became the third alumnus president when he took office in 1932. Born in Cumberland County, Illinois, McPherson had first come to the campus as a student in the academy. He knew student activities from having done them. In his own college years he had been a member of the Student Council, as well as editor of the *Argus* and the *Wesleyana*. He also had been in the Oratorical Society, male quartet, glee club, track team, Oxford Club, and YMCA. After graduation, he went to Boston University for divinity school before he was ordained to the Methodist ministry. As a Methodist minister in Springfield, he had given a Founders' Day talk and now he was chosen president of the University, an institution he already knew otherwise from the inside as a 16-year veteran member of the Board of Trustees.

When McPherson took office, America was in the depths of the Great Depression. Franklin Roosevelt was elected president of the United

Paint Day during the Depression years saw faculty and staff help to maintain the campus facilities. Here the faculty gets ready to paint rooms in Hedding Hall.

Harry W. McPherson

States the same year McPherson assumed the presidency. Wages had dropped 60 percent since 1929, white-collar salaries were down 40 percent, the jobless rate had tripled since 1930, reaching 24 percent in 1932, and the Federal Reserve Board's production index had plummeted 55 percent since 1929. The popular 1932 tune "Brother, Can You Spare a Dime!" captured the spirit of the economic quagmire in which McPherson was now to run a university.

Dismal Financial Outlook

Illinois Wesleyan's financial outlook was bleak with accumulated debt of $266,000, the product of a decade of deficit spending. Creditors were threatening lawsuits and foreclosures, arguments the University understood well since it had about 450 overdue accounts, ranging from 50 cents to $17,000. University salaries shared in the problem and the success of the time. Staff were kept, but with salary cuts of 30 percent or more, while continued loans were nudging permissible loan limits.

In writing the centennial history in 1950, Professor Elmo Scott Watson spoke to McPherson. As a trustee, McPherson had worried about piling up debt. "I often think this attitude," McPherson said, "had something to do with my being thrown into the midst of the stream and left to swim or else!" as IWU president.

When rumors abounded that the University might not open for 1932-33, McPherson released a statement of brisk confidence: "On September 9 Illinois Wesleyan will go into another year with the best and most modern college curriculum it has ever had to offer students."

That optimism was justified, for enrollments in the fall of 1932 showed a paradoxical 8-percent increase over the previous year. Other campuses found their count 13-percent down.

A New Tuition Plan

If he did not plan it as a publicity stunt, he should have. In September, 1932, McPherson announced the "Farm Produce for Tuition" plan. As early as September 9, the *Argus* reported: "Much excitement has been created by the recent announcement that [Illinois] Wesleyan is accepting farm goods for tuition." McPherson and business manager Nate Crabtree recognized that farmers had produce, maybe not cash. Crabtree even offered the appeal of a premium beyond market price.

The plan generated many deliveries and national and international news coverage. *The Chicago Tribune* reported on the IWU initiative, sparking newspaper accounts coast-to-coast. Paramount filmed "Farm Products for Tuition" as a "scoop" for its newsreel, *Eyes and Ears of the World*. The cameras recorded Justin Alikonis, class of 1935, chasing a pig and after catching it telling business manager Nate Crabtree that he wished to have the barnyard animal applied to his tuition. His request was granted. (By the way, Alikonis, a chemistry graduate, maintained his interest in food. He went on to become a brilliant scientist who revolutionized candy and other foods. His ration and survival bars went into battle with U.S. soldiers in three wars and astronauts took his candy—loaded with calories and vitamins—into space as part of their survival gear.) News of the produce-for-tuition gambit even went as far as London, where a *Daily Express* headline read "Back to Barter at an American University: Cattle Accepted."

The Faculty 1930.

McPherson and Crabtree still had other money-saving ploys with cooperative houses as components of a "work for part of tuition" program. In January, 1933, the University announced room rates at $1.10 a week, board at $2.75 or $3.

Faculty dedication also helped keep operating costs low during these lean years. In January, 1933, McPherson reported to the board that a portion of faculty salaries was being paid in "scrip" rather than currency. That the overall operating budget was $40,000 below the previous year helped, too.

Student Life in the Depression Era

The 1933 yearbook gives a good outline of student activities during these tough years, tales which appear perhaps more dreary in the recounting than they were at the time. Some photographs of the period would give no clue that an economic crisis was underway.

The *Argus* flourished under the editorship of Virgil Martin, class of 1932, who would go on

to be chairman of Carson Pirie Scott, the department-store chain. Martin made school spirit and appearance a bit of a cause. The fence at Wilder Field had not been painted for some time. The University treasury lacked funds, so Martin organized a collection at the chapel of September 30, 1931, to buy the paint, and the entire University took a day off on October 1, when faculty and students redecorated Wilder Field. It was shabby no more.

Homecoming in 1931 was November 6, with about 100 cars in the parade and a huge pep rally at Bloomington's Courthouse. It was even better when the football team beat Bradley and Herbie Kay and the WGN radio orchestra from Chicago played for the first Homecoming dance.

Tales of the economically depressed 1930s as a time of taut seriousness seem dubious compared to the record of Homecoming, 1932. The police were not as pleased at the students, when George Withey, class of 1932, led a snake dance of students from campus to Bloomington's Courthouse. The rest of the morning was spent dancing in the gym. There were more festivities on Monday. The Majestic Theatre—the vaudeville house built on the site of the Methodist church where classes were in 1851—admitted the students free that afternoon and at night they were back in the gym for more dancing. The seniors missed it all because they were having Piker's Day at Lake Bloomington.

On December 9 De Wolfe Hopper appeared on the Majestic Theatre stage to perform excerpts from the *Mikado* by Gilbert and Sullivan. Since the turn-of-the-century Hopper had been one of the biggest names in American musical comedy. On a more sober note, that same day, there was the annual Phi Kappa Phi address by University of Illinois Professor E. L. Bogart on "The Place of the United States in the World of Depression." Despite the bleakness of the times, the Carnival Dance took place in the gym on December 12.

The Titans, the moniker now carried by Illinois Wesleyan's athletic teams, celebrated New Year's Eve 1932 in the gym by beating Cornell University 33-22 in a basketball contest and within days the Apollo Club left on a singing tour aimed at recruiting new students.

Just as exams were about to begin in January, 1932, President Davidson announced that the faculty had changed the grading system from A, B, C, and D to H, S, and P. This change triggered some student complaints. An editorial in the January 17, 1933, *Argus* commented: "What are the advantages of our grading system over the methods more commonly used? When the new grading system was put into operation here, it was ostensibly for the purpose of eliminating as nearly as possible the tendency of the students to work for grades. It was thought that good grades should not take the place of desire for knowledge as a motive for studying . . . However, there are students who have been accustomed to consider good grades the only motive for hard work during twelve years previous to matriculation and who will allow inborn laziness to influence them if they are not spurred by the desire of the esteem of their fellow students . . . "

While the rest of the school was on semester break, the Apollo Club performed on two Chicago radio stations, WMAQ and WGN, and sang over the national NBC radio network as well. With the help of Alumni Secretary Nathan Lewis Crabtree, class of 1929, in making these connections, they were sure they had entertained about 12-million people during the year.

The campus was moved by Paul Harris, a return visitor from the National Council for the Prevention of War. He was on the campus February 15-17, 1932, and the excitement of his visit spurred creation of a student Committee on International Peace, which began formulating decided opinions on the Manchurian situation in the aftermath of Japan's 1931 occupation of that Chinese province.

January and February of 1932 brought other intercollegiate contests as the debate team took on regional colleges.

Doing its part for the needy in the community, and keeping up the plan of a dance-a-month, students brought old clothes and canned food as admission to a Welfare Frolic on February 23, 1932.

There was a guest speaker who discussed Middle East issues, while faculty speakers created new interest in different ways as they reported on curricular trends such as fields of concentration, survey courses, and senior examinations.

The Women's Athletic Association held its annual Diasia, a great costume festival with prizes in this case for two women who dressed as George and Martha Washington. Held every February, the Diasia was named for an ancient Greek festival.

Professor Don Allen of English was named head of the Illinois Wesleyan Night School, a non-credit program that began in March, 1932. The October 6, 1932, edition of the *Argus* reported: " . . . members of the liberal arts and music school faculties taught courses of a cultural as well as a vocational nature. It is estimated that about fifty students were enrolled in this school. The expenses were defrayed by a small tuition charge for each course . . . [The night school has acted] as an agent for good will between the people of the community and those of the University."

More than 300 women showed up for Woman's Day on April 8, 1932. The spring Water Carnival and another dance were part of this visitors' weekend. On the admissions and marketing fronts, too, were the 700 students who converged on the campus from 86 high schools on April 22-23. They came for the Illinois Wesleyan Music and Literary contest, at the end of which the University gave out 32 scholarships in music and liberal arts. For those who missed that round, the *Daily Pantagraph* announced an essay contest on "Why [Illinois] Wesleyan Attracts Me." Essay-contest awards were 20 scholarships to Illinois Wesleyan, valued at $2,170.

The Founders' Gates circa 1920.

THE DEPRESSION YEARS

On April 22, 1932, the Masquers, the theatre group that began in 1915, produced a classic French play, *Love and Chance,* a comedy by Marivaux first staged in 1730. The production, the 1933 *Wesleyana* reported, was the fourth American production of the play. Among cast members were football standout Tony Blazine, class of 1935, and future retailing executive Virgil Martin, class of 1932.

The Greek houses showed great spring activity on April 27 with a Stunt Show. The winners were the Sigma Kappa sorority and the Phi Gamma Delta fraternity. Then May 12 was declared another Piker's Day and seniors went off to Lake Bloomington for a fun-filled day. Once they returned to campus, they made Dean William Wallis an honorary member of their class.

May was filled with the Junior and Senior Prom and fraternity and sorority dances, all leading up to commencement. There was little complaining about the dreary times with the authors of the 1933 *Wesleyana* declaring the year "one of the greatest" in the University's history.

There are some paradoxes in the Great Depression years. The first fraternity had a house in 1899. By 1925 only the law fraternity did not have a house. There were eight sororities, none of them with a house, but by 1929 all six fraternities had houses and so, too, did all eight sororities. If the late 1920s brought houses for the women, they also brought varsity sports. The first were volleyball and tennis, a few years later volleyball, basketball, hockey, and "baseball." Title IX, federal legislation requiring equality for female athletics, was long in the future, for men had eight varsity sports, with football, basketball, baseball, track, tennis, golf, swimming, and now sometimes wrestling.

Carl Sandburg and Clarence Darrow

Tight times did not preclude bringing interesting visitors to campus.

In the late spring of 1930 famed poet and Abraham Lincoln biographer Carl Sandburg

appeared. The *Argus* reported: "For one and one half hours the tall slim figure, dressed in plain clothes stood with scarcely a movement, explaining the tendencies in arts and poetry, reading his own verse, telling jokes, and singing folk songs of the prairie." Sandburg offered 38 definitions of poetry, including: "Poetry is a pack sack of invisible keepsakes." He concluded: "'Your faces have been good to see and it has been good to be here'—He left the stage, carrying his guitar stiffly by its neck."

April, 1933, brought Clarence Darrow—the Chicago attorney who had defended Nathan Leopold and Richard Loeb in a celebrated murder case and John T. Scopes in the infamous "monkey trial" over the teaching of evolution. The *Argus* summarized: "Mr. Darrow with his cutting sarcasm laid bare the crime of the rich people upheld by religious faith which I [the article's author] did not include in my article because your new editorial writer is planning on graduating in June."

Musicians were no less impressed in October, 1937, when Marcel Dupre played in Presser Hall. Organist of St. Sulpice in Paris, Dupre was known for his amazing improvisations and during the course of the evening improvised an entire symphony in four movements.

McPherson's Accomplishments

President Harry McPherson's accomplishments went considerably beyond the University's balance sheet. During the 1933-34 school year, for example, health programs were established for students. Times were improving by January, 1935. Mary Hardtner Blackstock gave $10,000 toward a women's residence hall and the following January community supporters sought to raise $30,000 and eventually tallied about $45,000. In June, 1937, when the University bought the Benson residence on North East Street it became Blackstock Hall.

Mary Hardtner Blackstock

Campus improvements were made during the McPherson era. Historic Amie Chapel was remodeled and converted into a smaller auditorium with a seating capacity of about 300. The balance of the space was transformed into classrooms. A house on Park Street became the President's Home and the University acquired a radio station, when WJBC moved from LaSalle, Illinois, to Bloomington and was located in Old North, broadcasting as "WJBC at [Illinois] Wesleyan."

Wilder Field continued much as it had in the 1890s. The federal Works Progress Administration (WPA), a New Deal agency, offered a major upgrade, as the University joined the community and the Bloomington Association of Commerce in turning the park into a community stadium. The proposal went to the WPA in March, 1937, and the *Argus* on September 14 reported ground had been broken for the stadium "where, in the future, 3,500 spectators would see contests in football, baseball, and track." Four years later the $200,000 stadium was completed.

Curriculum changes in the College of Liberal Arts followed the faculty's commitment to give students a broader world view. A divisional organization plan was introduced and majors and minors were replaced by fields of concentration, adding flexibility to the curriculum. Seminars and individual conference courses at the junior level also were added.

"The Ole Bus"

In the midst of the Great Depression the University bought a bus. The *Argus* described the impact of "The Ole Bus" in an April 12, 1935, appreciation.

The [Illinois] Wesleyan Bus, purchased in 1933, accommodated 36 passengers—including the driver. It toted various student groups around the country, including the football and men's basketball teams, the a cappella choir, the glee clubs, picnickers, prospective students, and others.

In its first two years of operation, the bus logged more than 18,000 miles, including its longest journey to Alabama. "The bus," according to the *Argus*, "has made an average of three trips a week, has a governor which is set to permit a maximum speed of 50 miles per hour, uses a gallon of gasoline every five miles, and holds 28 quarts of oil at a time."

Travelers aboard the bus put it to creative use. "People have been known to sleep in the baggage racks, above the heads of others, even bringing pillows and robes for that purpose," the *Argus* observed.

Wiley G. Brooks

President Wiley G. Brooks

Ohioan Wiley G. Brooks was a distinct departure as McPherson's successor. He was the first

The early studio for WJBC was in North Hall.

president who was not a Methodist minister, although he was the son of a Methodist preacher. He arrived on campus in 1937.

Brooks had studied at Baker University before he graduated from Nebraska's York College in 1910. He took a second bachelor's degree in education from Nebraska State Teachers College the following year, then was superintendent of schools in several districts in Idaho, Nebraska, and Iowa. He was also head of Burlington (IA) Junior College. Along the way he worked in a master's degree from Columbia University and a doctorate from the University of Iowa.

Students dedicated their 1938 yearbook to him, saying that the new president had found a "place at the heart of [Illinois] Wesleyan." Yet a year later he left for the Institute for Educational Research at Columbia University. In 1941 he returned to Nebraska as president of Nebraska State Teachers College at Chadron.

Powell Museum

The Powell Museum of Natural Sciences, a longtime campus landmark, continued during the Great Depression years, still located on the third floor of Hedding Hall, with its collection of pottery, geological and botanical specimens, plus other items. New gifts were still arriving. R. E. Smith gave a collection of Civil War relics, plus a collection of seeds, and there was the George R. Harrison collection of 5,000 geological and archeological items, plus a collection of 1,200 pieces of stone craftsmanship.

Some of the Powell pottery remains today because it was moved to another building, but the rest of the museum, together with the Aldrich collection of paintings, perished in the 1943 fire that consumed Hedding Hall.

Depression-Era Students

Among the students in the Great Depression years of the 1930s was Edelbert Rodgers, class of 1933, an African-American who was born in a shack in rural Mississippi in 1909, according to an August 14, 1993, article in the *Flint Journal*.

Rodgers, the eldest of 10 siblings, worked, earning $18 a week. He saved $17 of that sum for college. In 1929 Rodgers entered Illinois Wesleyan, majoring in sociology and economics. He was one of only four Black students enrolled in the University at the time.

Rodgers, a member of the debate team, fondly remembered Samuel Ratcliffe, a sociology pro-

fessor, in a 1993 interview. "I'd eat at his house," Rodgers said, adding, " . . . [Ratcliffe] was kind of like a father to me."

After Illinois Wesleyan, Rodgers continued his education, earning a master's degree in psychology from the University of Minnesota in 1942 and ultimately a doctorate from New York University.

Another Depression-era student was Melba Kirkpatrick, class of 1932, who earned a bachelor of arts degree in drama and English literature. She headed the drama department from 1936-42 and later served as theatre director at the University of Kansas City for a half-dozen years. She also founded a touring summer stock theatre group.

After graduating, Kirkpatrick continued her studies in New York and earned a master's degree from Northwestern University. She won acclaim for her monologue performances, as well as for roles such as Madame Arcati in Noel Coward's *Blythe Spirit,* and as Elwood P. Dowd's ditsy mother in the popular comedy *Harvey.* Kirkpatrick, who was named Distinguished Alumna in 1968, established the E. Melba Johnson Kirkpatrick Theatre Artists Series in

Play Ball

Scott Anderson received his diploma in 1935—an event that put him on a course that brightened nighttime baseball and other scientific accomplishments. Anderson, who earned master's and doctoral degrees from the University of Illinois, early in his career worked at the University of Chicago's metallurgical laboratories on the development of stainless uranium.

Near the end of World War II, he opened Anderson Physics Laboratories, Inc., of

Champaign, Illinois. There he developed the process to purify salts and amalgams used in the manufacture of electric lamps, pioneering work which earned him patents for crystals used to manufacture lights for baseball fields.

Anderson received an Illinois Wesleyan honorary doctorate in 1960 and the Distinguished Alumnus Award in 1980. In 1982 he established the Anderson Physics Scholarship.

1971. The series brought to some of the nation's most distinguished performers including actress Helen Hayes ("the first lady of the American theatre") and seven-time Academy Award-winning producer-director-actor John Houseman. Illinois Wesleyan's laboratory theatre was named for her in 1993 in recognition for her patronship of the arts.

Campus Organizations

Students were involved in many campus organizations during the 1930s. One of these groups was the Student Union, which the 1935 *Wesleyana* described as "composed of elected members from every fraternal organization on campus . . . [it] exists for the purpose of establishing better relationships and understanding between faculty and students, forwarding student activities."

The Baconian Club was composed of students who had completed at least 30 hours of college work, including a year of natural science and who intended to elect science as a field of concentration. College friendship among students and faculty was a goal of this group.

The English Coffee Club, founded in 1920, provided informal meetings for lectures, music, and other activities. The tradition of serving coffee still exists, remarked the 1934 *Wesleyana*, which observed that the club was open to any student interested in literature.

A Home Economics Club was available to female students who were majoring or minoring in that field. The Upakaraka was another organization for female students. It was organized on campus in 1931 to promote fellowship among non-sorority women and to serve as a conduit for their representation in campus activities. A similar group was organized for men, the Illinois Wesleyan Independents. It was an organization of non-fraternity men chartered, according to the 1934 *Wesleyana*, "to make the social life of each one of its members a worthwhile one."

Other activities in the late 1920s and early 1930s reached out to prospective students. Women's Day, for example, was set aside for female high-school students to visit Illinois Wesleyan. The day included music, art, a luncheon, tea, and a short play.

Sports in the 1930s

The 1930s saw many achievements in sports. In 1930 the baseball team began a decade of unparalleled achievement, compiling a record of 102-11. The baseball team in 1930 took its first spring road trip to the South, marking the start of a decades'-long annual event. Physical-education minors were first allowed for women in 1930-31. A clear sign that women's athletics was taking on greater dimensions was seen in 1931, when the *Argus* added a women's sports editor to cover the increasing number of women's intramural events.

Football coach J. Norman Elliott, class of 1916, twice captain of the basketball team, began a four-year streak in 1931, where the team's record was 19-11-4, for a .618 winning percentage. Part of the football team's success was credited to players like defensive tackle-offensive lineman Tony Blazine, class of 1935, who earned first-team honors on the *Associated Press* minor-college team in 1935. Blazine holds the record for most minutes played in the College All-Star game: 57 minutes. Blazine, the all-star squad's starting left tackle, had several notable teammates: Gerald Ford, the future U.S. president; Don Hutson, who became a famous end with the Green Bay Packers; and Phil Bengtson, who later coached the Packers. Blazine played professionally for the Chicago Cardinals and New York Giants.

Athletics, the Great Depression, and School Spirit

Athletics played important social and educational roles in campus life, especially in the bleak years of the 1930s. During these tough times, athletics added to school spirit and provided uplifting moments.

The 1934 *Wesleyana*, for example, called the past year's football team "the greatest Titan football machine in the history of the school!

Tony Blazine '44 ➤ future NFL player.
HOF/NFL Photos

J. Norman Elliot

Marching through the toughest opposition in the conference to an inevitable championship, the Green and White finished the season undefeated and unscored upon by conference foes."

That same yearbook also offered kudos to the baseball team, noting it took second place in the 1932 Little Nineteen Conference, winning all but three conference games out of a stiff 23-game schedule.

The Illinois "Wesleyan Splashers," the swim team, placed first in every event, according to the 1934 *Wesleyana*, "to win the Little Nineteen Swimming Championship," while setting four new records for the 100-yard breast stroke, 220-yard free style, 100-yard back stroke, and the 150-yard medley relay.

Tennis also saw its share of triumphs. The 1934 yearbook credited the doubles team with winning its way to the semi-finals of the Little Nineteen State Tennis Meet.

"The 1932 Varsity Golf Team," the 1934 *Wesleyana* reported, "concluded the most successful season in the history of the school by tying for first place with Knox College for the Little Nineteen State Golf Team Championship."

Homecoming 1934 was a classic. Illinois Wesleyan defeated Bradley University in football, there was a Homecoming parade, and fraternities lit bonfires "feared by police as Bloomington's greatest fire hazard." The Saturday of festivities was completed with a

"wind-up dance," which ended "in a blaze of mirth and merriment."

"Athletics for All"

During the early 1930s an intramural program emerged under the leadership of J. Arthur Hill, professor of physical education. The program's motto was simply, "Athletics for All." Earlier structures had emphasized group competitions, which essentially made the games fraternity events. Hill's program was based on "individuality" rather than teams.

During the 1933-34 academic year, Hill added a real cash motivation for students to participate in athletics. For each game played, participants received two points. Being on a championship team meant five extra points for the total. At the end of the athletic season "the man" with the most points received a new Elgin watch, a gift from the athletic department. Intramural sports spanned baseball, track, basketball, volleyball, swimming, and ping pong.

In the 1930s field hockey was the lone varsity women's sport, as it was at many New England colleges. Women in the 1930s participated in intramural volleyball, basketball, and water polo. The 1937 yearbook has "varsity" women's basketball and tennis teams, which seem to be an all-star selection from the intramurals.

A Perfect Season

The men's basketball team had an undefeated season in 1935-36, a record that still stands in the 21st century. The team, led by captain Jack Horenberger, class of 1936, compiled a 20-0 record, winning the Little Nineteen Conference title. Horenberger, a guard, was the first athlete to receive the Senior Award, as voted by the faculty.

The Order of the Titans was established in 1937, recognizing the best varsity lettermen.

The decade also brought another athletic "first" in 1939, when the team played on Doubleday Field, where baseball supposedly was

Tennis courts
circa 1950.

Field hockey in front
of Memorial Gym
circa 1950.

The undefeated 1935-36 basketball team featuring Jack Horenberger (fourth from left in the front row).

first played in 1839. The historic games took place at the opening of the Baseball Hall of Fame in Cooperstown, New York. Illinois Wesleyan defeated the University of Virginia, 9-8, in 11 innings, but lost to Cornell University, 3-2, in 10 innings.

Brooks Resigns

In June, 1939, the University faced another presidential change with the announcement that President Wiley Brooks had resigned, effective September 1. An administrative committee, headed by Dean Wilbert Ferguson, assisted by Dean Malcolm Love and Frank Jordan, Arthur Westbrook's successor as dean of the music school, would have charge of the University until a new president was chosen.

At this time of transition, the financial outlook had improved. Love reported that expenditures for 1938-39 had exceeded income by $7,000. But this deficit was the result of paying off $25,000 in debts—not because of excessive operating expenses.

"This means," Love said, "that there has been an actual surplus this year so far as [the] working budget is concerned." He also announced that for the 1939-40 school year it was estimated that expenses would be $211,430 from an expected income of $222,500.

William E. Shaw Elected

On the eve of the Nazi invasion of Poland and the start of World War II, the trustees met on August 31, 1939, to elect William E. Shaw the

12th president of Illinois Wesleyan University. Shaw, corresponding secretary of the Methodist Board of Foreign Missions in New York, served as president until his death in 1947.

He was born in Minnesota in 1869, the son of a Methodist minister. After graduating from Moores Hill College in Indiana in 1889, Shaw taught school in Kentucky for four years. He entered the Garrett Biblical Institute, where he graduated in 1896. Shaw held pastorates in several Illinois towns until 1910, when he went to the First Methodist church in Peoria, where he remained for 22 years. He had served as superintendent of the Peoria District from 1932 to 1936 and had been secretary of the Board of Foreign Missions for four years when he was elected to the Illinois Wesleyan presidency.

Shaw was no stranger. He had served as a member of the Board of Trustees for nearly three decades. Merrill Holmes, who served as vice president under Shaw and succeeded him as campus chief executive, described Shaw this way: "He was an idealist, and he felt that if there is to be a college at all, it must be a very good college. More specifically, he was a practical idealist."

William Shaw

Shaw's Challenges

Shaw faced two great challenges during his administration. First, he became president when the campus was 90 years old—just one short decade away from the University's centennial.

Consequently, a 10-year centennial campaign was announced to increase the University's endowment from $1 million to $2 million and to secure another $2 million to complete the unfinished stadium, beautify the campus, modernize campus buildings, and erect new ones such as a men's residence hall, a student center, and a chapel building.

Among Shaw's academic objectives, according to historian Elmo Scott Watson, were "securing recognition of all accrediting agencies, a more selective group of students, a stronger teaching staff and an improved curriculum."

Those goals were achieved, in part, through a working partnership with Merrill D. Holmes, who was appointed University vice president (replacing the legendary Wilbert Ferguson, who marked his 84th birthday in 1941) and director of the centennial development program. He arrived on campus in January, 1941, and began raising funds for the endowment and the proposed construction program. Later in 1941 Shaw announced that the University was again accredited by the Association of American Universities and shortly, thereafter, was again placed on the approved list of the American Association of University Women. In 1943 the music school became one of 32 in the United States approved for graduate work by the National Association of Schools of Music.

Malcolm Love, dean of administration and business manager, assessed the University's progress under Shaw's leadership as "phenomenal," citing several facts, including a three year balanced budget and the paying off of all outstanding debt, while the budget for educational programs had experienced a 20-percent increase. "We are now in a position," Love said, "where we can spend more money for the educational program of our students. We are now operating on a sound financial basis."

Over the first three years of Shaw's administration 24 new faculty members and administrative officers were added. Over the last five years, a divisional system of departmental organization was put in place in the College of Liberal Arts.

The permanent chairmen of the University's three divisions were: William E. Schultz, Humanities Division; William T. Beadles, Social Studies Division, and F. S. Mortimer, Science Division.

"Under this organization," Love explained, "a student chooses a divisional field of concentration rather than the older major and minor and his field of concentration consists of work in two closely related departments. This makes for a more unified program of study for each individual student."

The University's improved financial picture and the effectiveness of the new divisional organization permitted faculty members to take leaves-of-absence, enabling them to keep up with the latest trends, thoughts, and practices in their fields.

One result of these positive changes was increased enrollment. During the 1940-41 academic year, enrollment passed the 800-student mark, compared to 764 students in 1939. A slight increase also was posted the next autumn despite activation of a Selective Service System in January, 1941, as a prelude to U.S. involvement in World War II.

At Homecoming, 1941, the state director of the Works Progress Administration, the New Deal agency that helped fund the new stadium

Ned E. Dolan

on Wilder Field, handed the keys to that facility to Ned E. Dolan, president of the Board of Trustees and the Bloomington Association of Commerce. The keynote address was given by Scott W. Lucas, class of 1914, now a U.S. Senator from Illinois. Lucas, an athletic standout when he was a student, dedicated the community stadium "in the name of freedom and liberty to free men and women."

Six weeks later America's freedom and liberty were in question after Japan's attack on Pearl Harbor in Hawaii.

Top: Homecoming 1941 showing (left to right) Robert Miato '43, Homecoming Chair; Senator Scott Lucas '14; and President Shaw. **Bottom:** Illinois Wesleyan Celebrating its 90th Year at Homecoming 1940.

VIII. World War II

Roommates Gordon Dale Ruben King (Rubenking), class of 1943, and Henry Filip (Petrzilka), class of 1944, were playing chess on a quiet Sunday afternoon. As they carefully maneuvered knights, bishops, and pawns around the chessboard, their radio was tuned to a football game.

"Henry and I loved to play chess," King recalled in a 1995 interview with *Illinois Wesleyan University Magazine*.

However, that chess game was interrupted when a radio announcer broadcast a terse news bulletin reporting the Japanese attack on Pearl Harbor.

"We turned up the volume on the radio," King remembered, "and sat there in shock, listening to scraps of news. It was an overwhelming thing."

It was December 7, 1941—and the United States was at war.

King, a sociology major with a double minor in English and history, remembered that in March, 1943, he and 40 other students were called up for active duty. Eventually, King was stationed in Assam Province in India, working as an Army cryptographer, handling coded messages.

Filip, a physics and math major, was hired by the University of Chicago in 1944. In May, 1945, he went to a top-secret laboratory in Los Alamos, New Mexico, to work on "Project Y"— the atomic bomb.

The wartime experiences of King and Filip illustrate the diverse ways students served their country in World War II. Illinois Wesleyan sent 1,250 off to battle—51 never returned. The Memorial Student Center was dedicated in October, 1947, to the men and women who served in World War II. A plaque listing the University's World War II dead, recalling their supreme sacrifice, is located in the Center's chapel. Their uncommon heroism was common.

Wartime on Campus

At the outset of the war, the campus was optimistic. Dean William Wallis in an interview published in the January 14, 1942, edition of the *Argus* said he agreed with British Prime Minister Winston Churchill, who said: "If the United States goes at it heart and soul . . . things might break in 18 months. Wallis characterized student reaction to the war as 'fairly enthusiastic, [they] do not crab about going, and are good sports.'"

Political-science instructor Ross C. Beiler had a more realistic view of the war's outcome. "The fact that we were not properly prepared adds one more year to the war," he said. "I think it will last at least three years . . ."

U.S. Navy on Campus

Kemp Hall was occupied by U.S. Navy V-5 troops, a group of about 40 aviation cadets. Another 38 cadets were transferred to the University in 1943-44 from another program. In total, the 1944 yearbook reported that more than 500 cadets had gone through V-5 training just in the past year. Training consisted of ground-school work in navigation, engine operation, maintenance, communications, and meteorology. While the male campus population was much diminished, the changing sequence of cadets fit right into many familiar scenes as they paraded through Bloomington's streets or relaxed on Kemp Hall's porch. Their singing of *Anchor's Away* in chapel was far more vigorous than other students expected. Some of the V-5 atmosphere on campus was captured in the 1944 yearbook in photos showing cadets and women undergradu-

◄ The campus watches helplessly as Hedding Hall burns on Saturday, January 9, 1943.

ates dancing in the canteen. The Navy unit left campus on July 27, 1944.

Though Illinois Wesleyan students had lived in odd spots around town for years, the Navy took no such chances with housing the V-5 cadets. By war's end the campus was dotted with a half-dozen barrack buildings, which had been constructed quickly to government specification, adding utility but not architectural distinction.

Female Students and the War Effort

Female students were urged to contribute to the war effort. A 1943 pamphlet, published by the Office of the Dean of Women, suggested that "all women capable of leadership or specialized skills [should be guided] into war-related work which fully uses their abilities—areas such as health services, homemaking, business and industry, and community service."

As manpower flowed to the military, the University expedited the awarding of degrees in 1943 with a mid-year commencement in January. This move was prompted by the realization that seniors might be called into military service before the traditional spring graduation. Former President Harry McPherson was the keynote speaker and 14 seniors received their bachelor's degrees.

On the Fighting Fronts

Illinois Wesleyan sent many alumni and students into the military and combat. William Starke, class of 1945—a freshman, class president, and an economics major—joined the U.S. Army Air Corps, eventually fighting in the Pacific from the cockpit of a Lockheed P-38 Lightning. He shot down a Japanese bomber over Formosa in April, 1945.

M. Russell Bramwell, class of 1947, a biology-chemistry-pre-med major, fought in the Philippines, Borneo, and elsewhere in the Pacific. Infantryman Bruce Reeter, class of 1951, a radioman-turned-rifleman, also was a veteran of the Philippines' campaign. He was part of the initial U.S. force that occupied Japan. "We sailed by the U.S.S. Missouri the day they signed

the peace," Reeter said. "It was quite a sight. Twenty ships, maybe, went single file into Yokohama Bay."

Louis Clemons, class of 1940, was a crew member on a B-26 Marauder, when it crash landed into the jungles of Sierra Leone in Africa, breaking his back. Africans found the crew and crafted stretchers for the trek back to their village. "We made it back through the jungle," Clemons said, 'beating the alligators and crossing streams at night. It was a little frightening, but I felt so bad I didn't care." A U.S. flying boat airlifted survivors to a hospital and he recuperated at several locations, including Walter Reed Army Hospital in Washington, D.C.

In Europe, alumni like Paul G. Anderson Jr., class of 1940, were flying the fabled Boeing B-17 Flying Fortress on bombing runs over Germany. Bomber pilot Anderson and a 10-man crew flew the Belle of the Ball. He flew 46 missions and became a squadron and group leader. Anderson was a squadron leader on the first U.S. raid on Berlin. The "King of Hollywood," Clark Gable, was assigned to Anderson's unit, flying five missions as a waist gunner.

Gerald E. Smith, class of 1950, landed on Omaha Beach on June 7, 1944—the second day of the massive D-Day invasion to liberate Europe from the Nazis. He was a Navy Seabee in a construction battalion. When he landed, Smith and perhaps 500 others trudged through shoulder-deep water carrying ammunition, guns, and gas masks above their heads to the beach. During those moments, Smith said: "I was thinking about stepping on mines, and the snipers who were still around. I thought about the rest of the battalion and what happened to them. I was hoping to stay alive."

John E. Cribbet, class of 1940, a history and economics graduate, was a captain in G-3, plans and operations, with the 8th Corps, which was assigned to General George S. Patton's 3rd Army. He was tapped as an aide-de-camp to 8th-Corps Commander, General Troy Middleton. "I went with Middleton all the time," Cribbet said. "I went with him to meetings with Patton," who he described as "the most colorful individual I ever met." Cribbet met General Dwight D. Eisenhower, supreme allied commander, at a luncheon in Normandy, as well as General George Marshall, Army chief of staff, when the "organizer of the victory" was in Europe after the Battle of the Bulge.

Robert L. Behrends, class of 1944, of the Army Medical Corps, was taken prisoner by the Germans in December, 1944, in Belgium. On the march to a prison camp, a seven-day odyssey, the prisoners were fed meager rations twice and slept in ditches, a lumberyard, and in a cow barn with wet manure. At one point, Behrends' weight dropped to barely 100 pounds from a normal 160 pounds. As Soviet troops advanced, he was evacuated by the Germans, and was fired on by U.S. warplanes while the train he was aboard stopped in the Dresden freight yards.

Campus was a sad place during the war, said Colleen Costigan Welch, class of 1946, a political-science major. "We marched to the train station to see people off," for military duty," she said. "We gave everyone a hug, stood on the platform, and waved good-bye. It seemed like an adventure, and everyone was brave. But we were well aware that it was a serious time."

Welch, like many women, wanted to contribute to the war effort. She joined the WAVES—Women Accepted for Volunteer Emergency Services, going on active duty in July, 1944. Welch became an antiaircraft gunnery instructor.

Supreme Sacrifice

February 3, 1943. The *Dorchester,* a troop ship on a voyage to Europe, went down in the icy waters off Greenland, torpedoed by a German submarine. More than 900 souls were aboard, including Methodist Army Chaplain George Fox, class of 1932. Fox was in the company of three other clergymen: a Catholic priest, a minister, and a rabbi.

After the troop ship was fatally struck, the four chaplains handed out life jackets, calming the desperate young men. They instructed the soldiers to get into the water and away from the ship. But there weren't enough jackets or lifeboats. Life expectancy in the frigid waters was only a few minutes—and the *Dorchester* was sinking fast.

When the life jackets were gone, one of the chaplains took off his own, handing it to a soldier. The other three chaplains did likewise. As

Navy Flyer to Retailing Executive

One of Illinois Wesleyan's wartime graduates was economics major Edward R. Telling, class of 1942, who spent the next four years as a Navy pilot. Three decades later, he was the head of the world's largest merchandiser.

In 1978 Telling became chairman and chief executive officer of Sears, Roebuck and Company. He reached that post after

rising through the company's ranks, beginning as a stock clerk-management trainee in his hometown of Danville, Illinois.

He addressed the 300 graduates at the 1978 commencement in an address entitled "Private versus Public Power." He also is remembered through the establishment of the Edward R. Telling Distinguished Professorship in Business Administration.

into the memories of the ship's survivors and others. In 1948 the U.S. government issued a postage stamp bearing the faces of Fox and the other chaplains above the sinking ship. The four chaplains were given posthumous honors and on February 3, 1951, President Harry Truman dedicated the Chapel of the Four Chaplains at Temple University in Philadelphia.

In April, 1945, Illinois Wesleyan paused to offer respects to Franklin Roosevelt, who also gave the supreme sacrifice in pursuing victory. A memorial service was held for the fallen chief executive on April 13, 1945. The memorial program described the dead president as "a gallant spirit," "friend of mankind," and a "world leader." Prayers were offered by President William E. Shaw and others, while history professor William Wallis delivered "A Tribute To Our President." The program closed with Taps.

the ship tipped and plunged into the sea, the four chaplains clasped arms and prayed—in Latin, Hebrew, and English—as soldiers gathered around them.

The chaplains' faith and calm as the *Dorchester* sank was an image that burned itself

A Marine Corps General

Gerald C. Thomas (1895-1984), class of 1919, joined the U.S. Marine Corps in 1917 during World War I, surviving the ugly trench warfare in France. A highly decorated soldier in World War I, World War II, and the Korean War, Thomas retired from active duty as a four-star general in 1956. He served as assistant commandant of the Marine Corps, 1952-54, and was a member of the National Security Council. In a 1993 review of a Thomas biography, *In Many A Strife: General Gerald C. Thomas and the U.S. Marine Corps 1917-1956,* Thomas was referred to as a "gray eminence" of the Corps.

During World War II, as operations officer for the 1st Marine Division in 1942, "... he prepared operational plans for the assault and capture of Guadalcanal and Tulagi,"

Courtesy of Historical Branch of the Marine Corps

according to a Marine Corps' biography of Thomas.

Following action in the Pacific theatre, he served as director of the Division of Plans and Policies at Marine Corps headquarters in Washington, D.C., from 1944 to 1946. A

Marine Corps' historian wrote: "Thomas' efforts helped build the divisions and corps that stormed Peleliu, Iwo Jima, Okinawa, and a host of other Pacific islands."

After serving in several high-ranking posts, Thomas took command of the 1st Marine Division in Korea in 1951-52—a unit whose front stretched 27 miles at one point. Commenting on Thomas' actions in the Korean War, Colonel Angus M. Fraser wrote in the June, 1984, *Marine Corps Gazette:* "Thomas was constantly on the move, sometimes by jeep, other times by helicopter. He went about his long work day with no apparent concern for the North Korean and Chinese reactions to his presence ... "

The University awarded Thomas an honorary doctor of law degree on February 10, 1954.

Building the Bomb

While alumni, students, and faculty were fighting on many fronts, others were toiling for victory in secret laboratories and other installations around the country.

The United States attacked the Japanese cities of Hiroshima and Nagasaki with atomic bombs in August, 1945, ending the war in the Pacific. Among scientists who crafted the war's top-secret weapon were three alumni, who worked on the Manhattan Project: Vernon Struebing, class of 1943, Roger Rasmussen, class of 1944, and Henry Petrzilka (Filip), class of 1944. Another alumnus, Wesley D. Meyers, class of 1937, discovered after the war he had worked on an element of the atomic bomb—the armor plating—at the Naval Proving Ground in Virginia.

Long working hours and tight security marked the months between the time the men arrived at Los Alamos, New Mexico, the focal point of atomic research, and the first atomic-bomb detonation on July 16, 1945. All three—Struebing, Rasmussen, and Filip—did work leading directly to that first test and the wartime atomic bombings of Japan.

Struebing, a chemistry major, worked on the plutonium "source;" Rasmussen, a chemistry and physics major, worked on electronic equipment being installed in a tank that would be used at "ground zero" for the first New Mexico test to get ground samples by remote control after the explosion; and Filip worked on the 64 detonators needed for one model of the bomb.

"I remember the delight of all of us in the laboratory" at the Japanese surrender Rasmussen said. "We were just overjoyed" to have played a part in it. "I still felt a little guilty that I wasn't storming Normandy or Iwo Jima. I felt guilty for those that paid the ultimate price, and I don't know how to apologize to them."

When Filip visited campus for Homecoming in 1994 for his 50th year class reunion, he brought several logbooks and papers from his Los Alamos research—documents that were placed in the University's archives.

Two other alumni from the class of 1943 worked on the Manhattan Project at the suburban Chicago Metallurgical Laboratory that later became Argonne National Laboratory: George Thomas and Elmer Rylander.

Thomas recalled in a 1994 Illinois Wesleyan University Magazine article that Franklin Spencer Mortimer, a chemistry professor, received a letter from the University of Chicago saying they had an ultra-secret project and needed young scientists. This opened the way for job interviews and the hiring of graduates like Thomas and Rylander for the project.

"When they hired us to go up there," Thomas said, "we still had no idea what it was." But they were told several weeks later. Scientists at the Metallurgical Laboratory had obtained the first nuclear chain reaction about six months before Thomas and Rylander arrived. The duo were involved in determining the parameters of a nuclear reaction that would make it effective as a bomb, including the amount of uranium needed, and the material surrounding the bomb that would keep it from exploding until the desired moment.

509th Composite Group

While a handful of alumni were laboring in America's laboratories putting science to work building the atomic bomb, another alumnus was preparing to deliver the terrible weapon to the enemy's homeland.

The B-29 Superfortresses *Enola Gay* and the *Great Artiste* were in the air 45 minutes when Captain George Marquardt, class of 1942, maneuvered another B-29, *Necessary Evil*, into formation off the *Enola Gay's* left wing. The trio of bombers had taken off from Tinian, a Pacific island, and were lumbering toward Japan in the early hours of August 6, 1945. Tucked into the *Enola Gay's* bomb bay was a 10,000-pound atomic bomb. Marquardt's plane carried photographic equipment and a scientist to record the atomic explosion's effects on Hiroshima.

Marquardt, who majored in banking and mathematics before joining the U.S. Army Air

A tribute to the
Illinois Wesleyan
students lost
during World War II
still on display
in the Memorial
Student Center.

Corps, was one of 15 bomber commanders attached to the 509th Composite Group, a super-secret unit whose job it was to deliver atomic bombs to enemy targets.

Marquardt, an eyewitness to the world's first atomic-bomb attack, wrote a memoir, *Field Order #13*, marking the 50th anniversary of the historic mission. When the bomb was dropped from 31,000 feet, exploding over Hiroshima at 8:16 a.m., Marquardt recalled: "There was a brilliant flash, which was partially obscured by the special goggles, which had been issued for the mission. It seemed as if the sun had come out of the earth and exploded. Smoke boiled around the flash as it rose . . . The shock wave from the blast reached my plane and it felt and sounded as if a monster had slapped the side of the plane. This occurred about 15 miles from ground zero as I was flying toward the mushroom cloud, which had already reached our altitude and continued to climb above us. I flew around the perimeter of the mushroom cloud three times. We had been instructed not to fly into the cloud as it might make us 'sterile.' I made my last turn and began my journey back to Tinian."

Marquardt was back in the air August 9. He was flying a weather plane, checking atmospheric conditions in connection with the second atomic-bomb attack on Nagasaki. Marquardt, according to his wife, Bernece, would have commanded a third atomic-bomb mission, but Japan surrendered on August 11. Marquardt spearheaded a fund-raising drive to build a monument to the 509th at the unit's Wendover, Utah, training site, which was unveiled in 1990.

The G.I. Bill

When George H. Bauer, a 1918 graduate of the law school and World War I veteran, met with seven other veterans at an American Legion post in Salem, Illinois, on November 4, 1943, he didn't know he was starting a revolution that would touch millions of lives and cost U.S. taxpayers $14.5 billion.

Bauer and his colleagues drafted a sweeping proposal that in congressional jargon became the "Servicemen's Readjustment Act of 1944." But to 15.4-million World War II veterans, it was simply, "The G.I. Bill of Rights."

President Franklin D. Roosevelt signed the G.I. Bill into law on June 22, 1944—just 16 days after D-Day. The legislation gave veterans education, home-loan guaranty, and jobless benefits.

Explaining his father's support for the G.I. Bill, George J. Bauer, class of 1960, said: "He didn't want a repeat of what happened after the World War I troops came home. They had nothing to look forward to."

The Hedding Hall Fire

On Saturday, January 9, 1943, perhaps the most spectacular event in the University's history happened with the fire that destroyed Hedding Hall in a matter of hours. The fire, reportedly due to faulty electric wiring, burned the 73-year-old campus landmark before the eyes of bewildered students and others. Among items lost were nearly the entire Powell Museum, the Aldrich collection of paintings, Amie Chapel, much equipment, classrooms, and laboratories.

The January 10, 1943, edition of the *Argus* contained many firsthand accounts of the disaster by students and faculty. A page-one story described the heroic actions of football team captain Henry Filip (Petrzilka), class of 1944, who later worked on the Manhattan atomic-bomb project. The January 15 *Argus* published additional descriptions of the fire, including this one: "Inside everyone was running around wildly, but we finally managed to get organized and carry out the office equipment—files, typewriters, dictaphones, and adding machines. The smoke and gas nearly choked us, but we were so excited we scarcely noticed."

The January 15 *Argus* also observed: "On a snowy Saturday night, 73 years of [Illinois] Wesleyan history lighted the starry sky like a flaming torch . . . The building of Hedding Hall itself has disappeared—leaving only ashes and charred ruins in its place. With the crumbling of the pillars of Amie Chapel went a lifetime of memories, traditions, and customs built by men who were

pioneers in a great venture . . . Each creaking step of Hedding could have told a story . . . "

Following the fire came the question of what to do. On Sunday, January 10, administrators, trustees, and faculty met, and Monday morning classes operated as normally as might be expected given the complete dislocation.

The event so affected students that on May 28, 1943, they presented a play, *Sing the Fiery Heart: A Fantasy,* an original production based on the Hedding Hall fire. The back of the play's program explained: "This is the first time Illinois Wesleyan has ever produced an entirely student-written, student-directed theatrical . . . We have tried to show the symbolic link between the burning of Hedding Hall, our most beloved building, and the more ferocious world-fire. Out of this, phoenix-like, is the anticipation of something new and better."

Duration Hall was created by roofing over the remaining basement walls of Hedding after the fire. This was done because the University lacked the funds to construct a new building. Duration Hall, which was demolished decades later, was "made to meet immediate need because of wartime building restrictions," according to the *Argus,* housing classrooms and administrative offices.

Athletics in the 1940s

The decade of the 1940s began with a conference football championship for the Titans. "Bustem" Bob Morrow, class of 1941, led the team and was named to the *Chicago Tribune's* all-star team. Morrow was a bruising fullback, who gained almost four yards per carry. He played on the 1940 College All-Star team, which was walloped by the Chicago Bears. Morrow played with the National Football League's Chicago Cardinals for three seasons in the early 1940s and after World War II with the New York Yankees of the All-America Football Conference, which later merged with the NFL. He returned to campus from 1947-50 to coach the Titans, leading the football team to a 19-16-1 record.

Illinois Wesleyan was among 60 schools continuing to play football, basketball, and baseball during World War II. By 1943 only 112 of 436 students were male, but an influx of Navy aviation cadets training on campus helped the school compete on the varsity level.

"The quality of the athletic teams suffered," *Illinois Wesleyan University Magazine* reported in a 1995 article, "IWU Athletics Mirrored National Trend in War Years." "From 1942-1944, Titan football teams won 9, lost 12, and tied 1 game, playing teams such as Illinois State, Indiana State, and Western Illinois. Basketball teams during the period (1941-42 to 1944-45) won 20 and lost 55, frequently playing teams from Camp Grant, Chanute Air Force Base, and Camp Ellis."

Baseball team captain Robert Fleming, class of 1945, recalled coaching turnover was a problem. "I had four baseball coaches in my four years," he said.

In 1946 Illinois Wesleyan became a charter member of the nine-school College Conference of Illinois (CCI). Two years later, the football team won the Corn Bowl and the baseball team won the CCI baseball championship, the first of 17 such titles. And, the following year, the basketball team won the CCI championship, the first of 23. Lights for night games were installed

The Hedding Hall arch is supported after the fire. The arch will later be used as the entry to Duration Hall.

at Bloomington County Stadium, later Illinois Wesleyan Stadium, in 1949.

Women's athletics in the 1940s largely involved exercise and intramurals. These activities oftentimes were organized by sororities or living units. The Terrapin Club, a swimming group, was a prominent athletic activity for women. Much in the spirit of famed swimmer Esther Williams, participants produced artistic water pageants.

Overleaf:
Duration Hall
circa 1946.

The 1944 Football team.

"Love Rides the Rail"
April 1950.

The Marching Band circa 1950.

The Football bench 1941.

Terrapin Club 1957-58.

IX. Post-War Expansion

With the end of World War II in sight, Illinois Wesleyan began planning for an enrollment spurt as veterans flocked to campuses nationally spurred by the G.I. Bill of Rights, federal legislation offering former soldiers education and other benefits.

Enrollment in the fall of 1945 stood at 523 students, but by the end of the 1945-46 school year, the student body numbered 876. Enrollment in 1946 reached 950 students and the staff increased to 66 full-time faculty members, the largest in Illinois Wesleyan history up to that time.

The decade spanning 1943-53 saw enrollment zoom from a low of 436 students to a high of 1,355 students—and back to 778 students. "You can imagine what financial acrobatics were required," former President Lloyd Bertholf told the class of 1975 in his commencement address, "to deal with a rise and fall of those proportions within a ten-year period."

As veterans flowed to the University after World War II, a housing shortage resulted. At the time, there were no men's dormitories and all housing for women was filled. As a short-term relief, former Army barracks were moved from Weingarten, Missouri, to campus. Four of these buildings were homes to veterans and their families until other residences were constructed. But living quarters remained scarce even with the influx of temporary housing. Subsequently, two residences on North Main Street were remodeled as women's dormitories: Munsell Hall and DeMotte Lodge.

On the drawing boards were a student center, additional dormitories, and a new classroom building. Generous gifts from the late Annie Merner Pfeiffer and the Magill family, as well as other funding, paved the way for construction of these projects. By the mid-1950s, Memorial

Student Center was built, as well as a women's residence hall, Pfeiffer Hall, and two men's residences, Magill and Dolan halls. A classroom building, Shaw Hall, named for the only president to die in office, William E. Shaw, also was constructed, anchoring the east side of campus.

The Death of President William E. Shaw

On February 21, 1947, President Shaw met with Chicago alumni. He told the group about how the University was coping with post-war challenges and wound up his presentation by quoting from the inscription on the campus' west gates: "We stand in a position of incalculable responsibility."

The next day, en route to a Chicago railroad station, Shaw had a fatal heart attack. A statement by students in the aftermath of Shaw's death said: "It is with great sorrow and a feeling of infinite loss that we view the passing of President Shaw, another grand old man of [Illinois] Wesleyan. He worked untiringly for the improvement of the school, in personnel, its buildings, and academic standards.

"Always ready to crown dance queens or to don old clothes and participate in Campus Clean-up day," the statement added, "Dr. Shaw was a very versatile man. All members of athletic teams knew him—he was always a sports booster and a familiar spectator at all kinds of games."

Vice President Merrill D. Holmes, who already had been named to succeed Shaw, assumed the presidency on March 1, 1947.

When Holmes was inaugurated in November, 1947, as the 13th president, representatives from more than 100 educational institutions nationally, attended the ceremony.

Merrill D. Holmes

A New Chief Executive

Merrill D. Holmes (1886-1962) was born in Indianola, Iowa. He took a bachelor of arts degree in mathematics and philosophy from Simpson College. He received a master of arts degree from Northwestern University in 1912 and followed it with a divinity degree from Garrett Seminary. Subsequently, he received a master's degree in theology from Harvard and

was chaplain to the 165th Infantry during World War I. He arrived in Bloomington as University vice president in 1941 after teaching at Dakota Wesleyan University and serving in other posts.

A Construction Boom

The years after World War II saw a construction boom on the campus:

- DeMotte Lodge, a residence on North Main Street, was acquired in 1947 and used as a women's residence hall.
- Munsell Hall, another North Main Street residence, also was acquired in 1947 for use as a women's residence.
- Memorial Student Center was dedicated in October, 1947, as a tribute to the Illinois Wesleyan men and women who served in World War II.
- Pfeiffer Hall, constructed in 1948 as a women's residence, was named in honor of Annie Merner Pfeiffer, an Illinois Wesleyan benefactress.
- Magill Hall, also constructed in 1948 as a men's residence, was named in honor of Hugh S. Magill, class of 1894, and his brother, S. Lincoln Magill.
- Shaw Hall, a classroom and office building constructed in 1954, replaced part of the facilities lost when Hedding Hall burned a

Composer Aaron Copeland and President Holmes, Founders' Day 1958.

(left to right) Senator Scott Lucas, President Holmes, and Aldai E. Stevenson III.

Commencement
Processional
June 7, 1957.

Commencement in
front of Duration Hall,
June 5, 1960.

A Centennial Approaches

In the late 1940s, Illinois Wesleyan was nearing its centennial and a special committee was appointed to direct the program. A Founders' Day Convocation launched the celebration on February 8, 1950. A month later the new Westminster chimes, a carillon, sounded for the first time from Presser Hall. Three weeks later news of the centennial was heard nationwide on a radio broadcast, "America's Town Meeting of the Air," which originated from the Bloomington Consistory. The broadcast was carried by 267 radio stations of the American Broadcasting Company. U.S. Senate Majority Leader Scott Lucas, class of 1914, and others

discussed federal aid to education on the program.

Other centennial celebrations followed: a golden jubilee reunion of the class of 1900; the graduation class of 1950, the largest in IWU history; a reunion of members of the 1910 championship football team during

Homecoming, and a series of alumni meetings across the country.

In 1940 the trustees had announced the University's centennial program, noting: "We recognize that it is impossible for any group to anticipate all the needs of an institution like the Illinois Wesleyan ten years in advance. But this minimum ten-year program is presented with the thought that if it is accomplished, the Illinois Wesleyan will be enabled to begin its second century fitted to make large contributions to the many youth that will continue to seek the opportunities it has to offer."

Top: Memorial Student Center **Left:** Anne Merner Pfeiffer Hall **Right:** Hugh S. Magill Hall.

Left: View of Old North, Holmes Hall and Shaw Hall. **Right:** Ground Breaking for Memorial Student Center 1946. **Bottom:** The Grill 1961.

decade earlier. It is named in recognition of William E. Shaw, president from 1939-47.

• Dolan Hall, a men's residence constructed in 1955, is named in honor of Ned E. Dolan, a long-time trustee.

• Gulick Hall, which was called Southwest Hall when it was completed in 1957, was a women's residence with the Department of Home Economics located in a wing of the building.

School of Art

One of the solid glories of the post-war era was creation of the present School of Art in 1946. K. B. Loomis organized the new art program, a project that had been on the drawing board since he crafted a 1942 memo, "The Development of the Art Department of Illinois Wesleyan University." Over the years, the School of Art had many homes and after the 1943 Hedding Hall fire, the program had moved to the structure that currently houses the English Department. The Gallery Building and the basement of Blackstock Hall also were added as space for the growing program. By 1947-48 the art program had five professors, 25-plus courses,

and 18 studios or workshops, with the University offering a bachelor of fine arts degree.

Rupert Kilgore, an assistant professor, arrived in 1948. He had received an undergraduate degree from DePauw University and a master's degree from the State University of Iowa. Kilgore had taken additional work in art at Ball State Teacher's College. His work had been exhibited nationally at Chicago's Art Institute, Philadelphia Print Club, and other venues. Kilgore taught art history, art methods, crafts, introduction to art, and design. He succeeded Loomis as director of the art program in 1948-49 and for the next quarter century was associated with the school.

George Vinyard, a 1971 graduate and trustee, wrote in *Illinois Wesleyan University: Growth, Turning Points and New Directions Since the Second World War*: "It was Kilgore who established the [Illinois] Wesleyan tradition of quality art education provided by artist-teachers. These traditional qualities led a famous critic and art educator who visited the campus to remark that Illinois Wesleyan possessed something more than a school of art; he called it a 'community of artists.'"

Apollo Quartet 1955-56 (left to right) Lee York, Ed Spry, Robert Cummins, John Cobb, and Mark Snyder, piano.

School of Dramatics

The fine arts made another major advancement when the School of Dramatics was founded in 1947. The following year, however, the School of Dramatics, the School of Art, and the School of Music were combined to form the College of Fine Arts.

Vinyard, in his University history, pointed out that development of the School of Drama paralleled that of the art school. "Dramatics formed a prominent portion of the curriculum in the Department of Speech before the professional program was initiated, and dramatic activities had long been an important traditional aspect of campus life."

Lawrence Tucker headed the School of Drama from its founding until 1968. Just like the School of Art, the School of Drama for many years was in search of adequate facilities. After the 1943 Hedding Hall fire, stage productions shifted to Westbrook Auditorium in Presser Hall.

"Conflicting programs of the School of Music," Vinyard wrote, "led to problems with scheduling and other aspects of this arrangement. Completion of the Memorial Student Center freed the 'Hut', a carriage house adjacent to Kemp Hall formerly used as a snack bar and bookstore, for use as a theatre in 1949."

Summer productions were staged there in what was dubbed, "Spotlight Alley." Drama classes were conducted in Old North. McPherson Theatre was completed in 1963, creating for the first time a modern production and instructional facility for the drama program.

School of Music

The School of Music, a key component of the fine-arts program, also flourished in the post-World War II years. This era for the School of Music, according to Vinyard's history, was characterized by stability and quality. The School of Music, he observed, was less affected by enrollment fluctuations than other portions of the University.

"Throughout the entire period since World War II," Vinyard wrote, "the presence of the School [of Music] has added a unique dimension to the intellectual and cultural life of the University."

The national stature of the School of Music was enhanced over the years by faculty participation in organizations such as the National

Spotlight Alley Theatre

Association of Schools of Music and Phi Mu Alpha, the professional music fraternity. Carl M. Neumeyer, director of the school from 1952 until his death in 1972, headed both of these groups at various times. Neumeyer broadened Illinois Wesleyan's extensive music program, which featured student and faculty recitals, with establishment of the annual Symposium of Contemporary Music in 1952, which brings prominent composers to campus.

Lloyd Bertholf

Carl Neumeyer

Illinois Wesleyan was a performance venue for two jazz greats in the 1950s: Count Basie and Dizzie Gillespie. Count Basie's internationally famous orchestra played Memorial Gymnasium on February 15, 1958. A year later, on April 13, 1959, Gillespie and his quintet also performed in Memorial Gymnasium. Gillespie's concert was sponsored by the Inter-fraternity and Panhellenic Councils as part of Greek Week festivities. Tickets ranged in price from $1.50 to $2.50.

The Presidency of Lloyd Bertholf

Lloyd Bertholf succeeded Merrill D. Holmes as Illinois Wesleyan's 14th president in 1958. Holmes, near age 70, retired after serving as University chief executive from 1947-58.

Bertholf, a native of rural Kansas, attended Friends University, Wichita, Kansas, but graduated from Southwestern College in Winfield,

Kansas. He served in the coast artillery in World War I, stationed at Fort Monroe, Virginia. Bertholf went off for graduate work at Johns Hopkins University in Baltimore in 1921. He began his career teaching biology at the North Carolina College for Women in Greensboro, a post that paid this newlywed just $2,400 a year. For about 15 years he supplemented college teaching with summer work performing research for the U.S. Agriculture Department's Bureau of Entomology and Plant Quarantine in Washington, D.C.

Bertholf taught at Western Maryland College in Westminster for a quarter-century, where he also served as dean of freshmen and dean of faculty. In 1930 he received a postdoctoral fellowship to study in Munich, Germany, on a Rockefeller Foundation Fellowship. Bertholf made a career change in 1948, moving to the West Coast to join the College of the Pacific, where he was a professor of biology and academic vice president.

Bertholf, who served as president from 1958-68, reflected on his years as a campus chief executive in a Spring 2000 *Illinois Wesleyan University Magazine* article, marking his 100th birthday on December 15, 1999. "We increased the endowment considerably," he pointed out, "of course-nothing like it is now, but for those days it was considerable. And, we started January Term-the short term [that eventually became the current May Term] . . . We started a lot of construction.

Nurses in training 1957.

Mary D. Shanks

I was there 10 years and we had a new piece of construction, or were finishing up one, every year I was there."

Among new buildings added to the campus during Bertholf's tenure were: Holmes Hall (1960), Fred Young Fieldhouse (1962), McPherson Theatre (1963), Earl Edward Sherff Hall of Science (1963), Book Store (1963), Ferguson Hall (1963), and Munsell Hall (1966). Moreover, the Memorial Student Center and power plant were expanded and Stevenson Hall and Westbrook Auditorium in Presser Hall were refurbished.

During Bertholf's administration, the enrollment grew from 1,148 students to 1,500 students; the faculty increased from 75 to 109; and the value of the campus climbed from $6.5 million to $14.3 million.

Bertholf also had great faith in students. Among his first acts as president, he gave the Student Senate full authority over student activity fee funds.

When the clock struck midnight on January 1, 2000, the President-Emeritus Lloyd Bertholf crossed a rare threshold becoming one of a handful of people whose life had spanned three centuries and two millennia.

School of Nursing

Among Lloyd Bertholf's lasting achievements as Illinois Wesleyan's president is the School of Nursing, which was founded during his administration.

Bertholf wrote about the school's genesis in his 1984 memoir: "The first major change in the academic program I faced was whether or not to proceed with plans for a Collegiate School of Nursing . . . The University already was in a cooperative agreement with Brokaw Hospital, and had been for some 30 years. The program was essentially a three-year diploma program conducted by the hospital, with collegiate work [at Illinois Wesleyan] added on."

Although the Brokaw program had graduated many outstanding nurses, the initiative to launch a full-fledged baccalaureate program reflected a general movement in nursing in the late 1950s. The nursing school was launched in 1959, with Brokaw continuing to serve as a main laboratory for clinical experience.

Despite skepticism among some University leaders that the school could meet all of the many requirements for accreditation, Bertholf held fast in his support and just three years later "the program achieved National League for Nursing accreditation," wrote Bertholf, "a virtually unheard-of accomplishment for so new a program."

Mary D. Shanks led the nursing school for years. She had a Brokaw diploma and an Illinois Wesleyan degree, as well as a master's degree from Catholic University and a Columbia

Anne Meierhofer

Lee Short '44

William Schultz

University doctorate. She became director of the University's nursing school in 1960. George Vinyard in his booklet, *Illinois Wesleyan University: Growth, Turning Points and New Directions Since the Second World War,* noted that Shanks' "leadership has been a prime factor in [the nursing school's] success. The new School of Nursing completed the course of instruction for the final class of students in the Brokaw diploma program and admitted its first class of 71 degree students in 1959."

The School of Nursing eventually was housed in the old science building (rededicated as the Edgar M. Stevenson Hall), a facility that became available when the departments of biology, chemistry, mathematics, and physics moved in 1964 to Sherff Hall, the new science building.

The Bertholf Team

After Bertholf assumed the presidency, he wrote: " . . . I soon came to be very proud indeed of the staff I had inherited from Dr. Holmes."

William T. Beadles, class of 1923, was dean of the University, vice president, professor of business administration and insurance, and a respected and influential force on campus for 40 years. John Sylvester Smith, who had been dean at Dillard University in New Orleans, succeeded Beadles in 1959, serving for two years. And, Everette Walker filled the post in 1961.

George T. Oborn, an ordained Methodist minister, joined the history faculty in 1946. However, in 1953, he assumed responsibility for fund-raising activities and was valued for his knowledge of charitable giving and estate planning. Business Manager Philip W. Kasch had joined the University in 1948, bringing expertise in budgeting, accounting, investment, purchasing, contracting, and other fields.

Anne Meierhofer was dean of students, having come to Illinois Wesleyan in 1946 as dean of women. "Anne had the happy faculty," Bertholf wrote, "of being able to enter into the lives of students, their concerns and problems, as if these were her very own affairs."

Bertholf characterized Director of Admission Lee Short, class of 1944, as "a great idea-man. He was always thinking up new ways to advertise the University, new reasons for bringing prospective students to the campus, new devices for telling our story to the local business and professional men, new ideas for Homecoming or Alumni Days, new ways of making our catalog and other literature more attractive." Short's success as an admission and public-relations officer, according to Bertholf, was that "he believed wholeheartedly in the thing he was 'selling.'"

Joseph D. Kelley, Jr., a member of the class of 1939, was appointed registrar in 1956. An Air Force veteran and former public-school

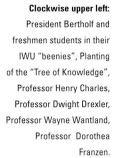

Clockwise upper left:
President Bertholf and
freshmen students in their
IWU "beenies", Planting
of the "Tree of Knowledge",
Professor Henry Charles,
Professor Dwight Drexler,
Professor Wayne Wantland,
Professor Dorothea
Franzen.

teacher and coach, Kelley had a reputation for knowing every student by name. Tragically, he died from injuries sustained in a traffic accident in 1964, while on his way to officiate a high-school football game.

Nurse Velma Arnold, a member of the class of 1930, joined the staff in 1942. Bertholf recalled that "Nurse Arnold" set up "a highly successful nursing service here, one of the few such programs which provided for nursing visits to student rooms under certain conditions."

Russell Troxel, class of 1923, was named executive secretary of the Alumni Association in 1957 after serving as a public-school administrator. "Russ vigorously carried on the process of organizing the alumni in various centers all over Illinois and all across the nation," Bertholf said, "with the result that when I came on the job there were literally dozens of groups ready for me to visit."

The Faculty

"I was much impressed by the quality of the faculty . . .," Bertholf observed in his memoirs.

Among faculty he cited as "genuine assets to the University" were William Eben Schultz in humanities (who died at his desk on April 16, 1964), Wayne Wantland in natural sciences, Bunyan Andrew in social sciences, Rupert Kilgore in art, Lawrence Tucker in drama, and Carl Neumeyer in music. "They were a team that would do credit to any college," Bertholf said, "in their respective fields, both as teachers and administrators."

Among other faculty of note, according to Bertholf's reminiscence, were Elizabeth Oggel, Lucile Klauser, and Joseph and Doris Meyers in English; Patricia Deitz and Constance Ferguson in French; Pedro Labarthe in Spanish; Paul Hessert, James Whitehurst, and Charles Thrall in religion; Richard Leonard in history, and Ralph Browns in philosophy. In the natural sciences there were Dorothea Franzen in biology and Owen York in chemistry. In the social sciences there were Oliver Luerssen in business, Emil Kauder in economics, and Paul Ross and Dewey Fristoe in education. In physical education there were Jack Horenberger, Don Larson, Bob Keck, Marian Niehaus, and June Schultz. In political science there were Glenn Mower, Jr. and Donald Brown; in psychology there was Frank Holmes; in speech Marie Robinson and Ed Carpenter; and in sociology Samuel Ratcliffe and Clark Bouwman.

In the College of Fine Arts, Bertholf recalled, Fred Brian and Nona Craycraft in art; in drama, John Ficca; and in music, Dwight Drexler (piano), Henry Charles (voice), Lillian McCord (organ), Mario Mancinelli (violin), Varner Chance (music education), Ruth Erickson (voice), John McGrosso (band), Zela Newcomb (piano for children), Wilbur Ogden (composition), John Silber (theory), Maurice Willis (wind instruments), Ruth Krieger (violoncello), Lewis Whikehart (choral music), and Virginia Husted (music history and cello).

Dennie Bridges '61
against Illinois State
Normal University.

Baseball Team
on their Spring
trip 1958.

X. The 1960s

hange was the signature trademark of the 1960s. The decade was marked by tumult great and small in politics, economics, and society. Illinois Wesleyan was not immune to this great spirit of change in the wider world and in the University.

For example, changes in the academic program accompanied transformation of the University's campus in the 1960s.

Psychology, a subject long taught, had been housed in a wide variety of academic homes, ranging from philosophy to education to humanities. However, by the 1960s experimental psychology was giving the field more of a "scientific" character, a trend that contributed to the program's placement in the natural sciences in 1961. A social-work major joined the academic program in 1963-64. Anthropology was added to the title of the sociology department in 1967-68 and an anthropology major was added the next year.

Speech and drama programs also saw organizational changes in the 1960s. The speech department was shifted from humanities to social sciences under the leadership of Marie Robinson. Speech courses were removed from the School of Dramatics and Speech and the School of Drama was born.

"The 1958-68 decade," President Lloyd Bertholf recalled, "also witnessed the beginning of a great new interest on the part of students in business courses. Computers were coming into use, government regulations were increasing, taxation was greatly increasing in complexity, and business was becoming more worldwide in its operations."

These trends prompted the University in 1967 to combine business administration, economics, and insurance into a subdivision of the Division of Social Sciences. In 1968 a fourth division of the College of Liberal Arts

◀ Commencement 1957 as viewed through the Hedding Arch.

—business and economics—was established under the directorship of William T. Beadles.

Insurance courses, a trademark of the business program, were first listed in the University's catalogue in 1929-30. A single course, "Insurance," evolved into "Mathematics of Life Insurance" and by the mid-1930s other courses were added: "Fundamentals of Life Insurance" and "Life Insurance Salesmanship." As the program evolved, other courses appeared, including "Fundamentals of Property Insurance." By the late 1950s insurance was a department, offering a major in the field.

"Professor Beadles had been associated with the work ever since it began in 1929," Lloyd

Freshmen being fitted for their beenies in 1965.

Bertholf wrote, "and the State Farm Insurance Company had become so pleased with our program that it began, about this time, to give us an annual gift to help with the expenses."

During Bertholf's presidency an internship program was added to the insurance curriculum. "This gave students," he wrote, "the opportunity, after completing three years toward the major, of working for a commercial company for a 10-week period during the summer, thus gaining valuable practical experience."

January Term

A landmark academic reform during Bertholf's administration was the introduction of the January Term. "J" Term eliminated the "lame duck" portion of the fall semester—the three weeks or so between the Christmas-New Year vacation and final exams at the end of January.

"I saw a great need," Bertholf said, "to make more opportunity for creative instruction, for increased student motivation, and for stimulating students to assume more responsibility for their own learning."

Bertholf floated the idea of a 14-week fall semester, five-week "short term," and a 14-week spring semester in January, 1963. A committee was appointed to study the proposal. Since 16-week semesters would be shaved to 14-weeks, Bertholf suggested lengthening class periods by 10 minutes to an hour. Opinion was divided and studies continued, however, the issue was referred back to Bertholf for a final decision. The plan was put into effect in the fall of 1965. As experience with the "short term" grew, it was modified to a 14-4-14 calendar with an earlier start to the fall semester.

Other Innovations

The 1960s also saw the birth of an innovative program—College Credit in Escrow—the brainchild of Lee Short, director of admission. The plan offered certain high-school students the chance to take a three-hour college course during the summer before their senior year and apply the credit later toward a college degree. The program was started in the summer of 1963 with 10 students enrolling in a general sociology course.

President Bertholf and Senator Everett Dirksen at Commencement 1968.

Demolition of Old North.

A summer independent study program was reactivated in summer of 1963. In the fall of 1967, the Academic Challenge Elective (ACE) program was initiated under the leadership of Everette Walker, academic dean. Upper-class students in good standing could take a single ACE course per semester, receiving a "credit" or "no-credit" grade.

"When the grade of 'credit' was given," President Lloyd Bertholf explained, "the hours thus earned would apply toward graduation, but there would be 0 grade-points given, and the student's record would be neither hurt nor helped by having to take such a course."

Graduate courses were offered at Illinois Wesleyan as early as the 1870s. For three decades such courses were available to students

in absentia by correspondence leading to about 250 dissertations. However, this program ended in 1906 and no graduate work was offered again by the University until 1932, when the School of Music offered a master of music degree. In 1951 a master of music education degree was introduced. Later in the 1950s a master of science teaching degree was offered, a 30-hour course taken in three eight-week summer sessions, plus a final essay. National Science Foundation grants supported the program, which ran from 1958-68.

The Demise of Old North

Illinois Wesleyan lost a strong link with its past in 1966, when Old North—the University's first building and only building for 15 years—was razed to clear the way for what became Sheean Library.

President Lloyd Bertholf wrote in his memoirs that the building, constructed in the 1850s, "was enveloped in an aura of sentiment" by many alumni. Consequently, the building was reluctantly demolished only after several other alternative plans had been examined.

"But a careful architectural appraisal of its condition," Bertholf wrote of Old North, "showed that during its 110 years it had deteriorated to a point where its restoration to modern usefulness would have been more expensive than to tear it down and rebuild it."

The wrecking crew began its work on July 9, 1966, and, according to Bertholf, "within hours it was reduced to rubble."

"Thus," Bertholf concluded, "a symbol of the University's first building is preserved for posterity, and is displayed at each University function where there is a faculty procession."

Bertholf was referring to the fact that a few years after Old North was razed, Professor Anthony Vestuto of the School of Art crafted a wax sculpture of Old North's bell tower, which was cast in bronze and mounted on the head of the University mace, a symbol at the head of all faculty processions.

Old North had served a myriad of purposes over the decades. At various times it housed classrooms, offices, the academy or preparatory school, dining hall, library, print shop, physics laboratory, a radio station, and chapter offices for two fraternities. Old North's rich and varied history prompted the *Argus* to observe in 1960: "Thus Old North, with the great variety of activities which have gone on there, typifies the spirit of a liberal arts college."

Students protest the demolition of Duration Hall 1965.

Duration Hall
demolition with Magill
Hall through the
windows.

Sherff Hall of Science under construction.

The End of Duration Hall

Illinois Wesleyan had lost another enduring bond with its history and heritage the year before Old North was razed. What remained of Old Main—later known as Hedding Hall—was bulldozed in 1965. The building had been destroyed by fire in January, 1943. All that remained was a basement area, which was roofed over, and the original arch over the main door. For the next 20-plus years, the structure was known as Duration Hall and was used largely to house administrative offices "for the duration" until a new structure could be constructed. It served other uses after the new administration building, Holmes Hall, was completed in 1960.

"I must confess," Lloyd Bertholf wrote in his presidential memoir, "that it was a rather sad day for me when on that October morning in 1965 a huge bulldozer moved in and began at the north-west corner of the building to push down the remaining walls of old Hedding Hall.

"So much history," Bertholf added, "resided in these 95-year-old walls—so much of struggle and uncertainty, of faith and perseverance—that it pulled at the heartstrings to see the great stones treated with such disrespect and violence by a mechanical monster."

New Buildings Constructed

But while the University lost some of its historic buildings in the 1960s, new ones sprouted, a sign of the campus' vibrancy and growth.

Administrative offices in Duration Hall were scuttled about New Year's Day 1960, when quarters were taken up in the new administration building—Holmes Hall—which was constructed at a cost of $443,000 and dedicated at the 1960 commencement ceremony.

The need for improved theatre facilities was apparent since "Spotlight Alley," an old carriage house, was transformed into a theatre. The widow of the 10th president, Harry McPherson (1932-37), deeded a family farm to the University, consequently, the new facility would be called McPherson Theatre. The $498,582 building was completed in early 1963.

A new science building—in the age of *Sputnik* and space flight—was another top priority. At that same time, the Illinois Agricultural Association (IAA) was eyeing office space in

Fred Young Fieldhouse

Bloomington-Normal for its headquarters after a move from Chicago. The idea was that IAA would construct a temporary facility, while its permanent headquarters was under construction, and when the organization vacated the temporary building it would be given to the University.

"IAA agreed to build one concrete-and-block three-story building of 33,600 square feet to become our science building," Lloyd Bertholf recalled in his memoir, "and a 26,000 square foot Quonset-type building entirely free of supporting columns inside, one suitable for a field house."

The $454,750 Quonset-type building became Fred Young Fieldhouse, which was dedicated on March 2, 1962. The three-story structure, completed in 1964, became the $1-million Earl Edward Sherff Hall of Science. Sherff (1886-1966) had written Illinois Wesleyan as early as 1931 about a "relative" who was thinking about naming an educational institution as a beneficiary in a will. He had taught at Chicago Teachers College and was a research associate at Chicago's Field Museum.

A second grant from Philadelphia's Presser Foundation—the first had been used to construct

Fred Young

the School of Music building in 1929—came in the 1960s to refurbish the building's auditorium, which was rededicated and named for Arthur Westbrook, dean of the school from 1922-39. Two years earlier, a $30,000 gift from V.C. Swigart supported purchase of a new Schantz organ—named the Swigart Memorial Organ in honor of his late wife, who was a musician—which was located in the auditorium.

The new School of Nursing was located in the old science building, which became available when Sherff Hall was opened. The building, dating to 1910, was remodeled with support from a fund-raising effort spearheaded by the nursing school's director Mary Shanks and a group of prominent women, as well as a $158,000 grant from the National Institutes of Health under the Medical Facilities Act. A conditional matching gift from Hazel Buck Ewing in honor of her friend Dr. E. M. Stevenson resulted in naming the building Stevenson Hall. The $278,000 remodeling project was dedicated on October 9, 1965.

Center from 1947-1960. The facility was dedicated on October 19, 1963.

A second high-rise residence hall was started in October, 1965, at the same time that a second addition to the Memorial Student Center was undertaken. The two projects had a $2.8-million price tag and were dedicated at Homecoming, 1966. The residence hall was named for Charles W. C. Munsell, the University's financial agent from 1857-73, and his brother, Oliver S. Munsell, University president from 1856-73.

Astronaut Frank Borman setting the Evans Observatory cornerstone.

Borman with Representative Leslie Arends.

As a result of burgeoning enrollment in the late 1950s, plans were drafted to expand the Memorial Student Center. In 1960 the University received a low-interest matching loan from the federal government to support the project, which added a recreation area, the DugOut snack-bar area, and other facilities. The $212,451 addition was dedicated on October 28, 1961.

Increased student enrollment also put pressure on residence halls. Financing this initiative was eased as a result of the federal government's policy of providing low-interest loans for income-producing college facilities. The University obtained a $625,000 loan in 1962 for what would become Ferguson Hall, named for Wilbert Ferguson, a distinguished professor and administrator from 1894 to 1944, and his daughter, Constance Ferguson, a professor of French from 1926-1952 and director of the Memorial Student

"None of the building projects during my administration received as much planning attention as did the new library," President Lloyd Bertholf recalled.

Initially, the thought was to build an annex onto Buck Memorial Library. However, a library consultant from Emory University concluded that Buck could not be adapted to contemporary library use and advised a new building be constructed. Eventually, that approach was endorsed and a Library Fund Campaign Committee was established. Librarian Rodney Ferguson visited other campuses with new libraries to help shape the plans. The new library, which was completed in the summer of 1968, cost about $1.2 million for construction and $114,470 for furnishings and equipment. A three-part package financed the project: a federal loan, Illinois Wesleyan funds, and a federal grant under the Higher Education

Facilities Acts of 1963. In 1978 the library was named for Jack Sheean after his widow made a generous contribution to the University.

By the mid-1960s there was renewed interest in astronomy probably in part the result of the emerging space age. However, the Behr Observatory, which dated to the 1890s, was badly deteriorated. Orme Evans, a member of an architectural firm that designed many University buildings, proposed that the Evans family contribute a sum that would cover about one-third of the cost of a new observatory as a memorial to his father, Mark Evans, a World War I-era trustee, who played a leading role in the fundraising campaign that resulted in Memorial Gymnasium and other projects. Project financing also came from University funds, a federal grant, and Kresge Foundation support. The cornerstone for the facility—located on the site of the former Behr Observatory—was laid on March 18, 1969. Astronaut Frank Borman, commander of the Christmastime, 1968, *Apollo VIII* mission, the first manned space flight to orbit the moon, headlined the ceremony.

The Career of "Coach"

The mid-1960s saw the retirement of legendary Jack Horenberger, class of 1936, as men's basketball coach. He was succeeded by Dennie Bridges, class of 1961, a four-year letterman in basketball as a guard, baseball team shortstop, and a three-year letterman in football as a quarterback.

Horenberger began his 37-year coaching career at his alma mater in 1942. Over the years, the captain and guard of the only undefeated men's basketball team, also coached baseball and served as athletic director and dean of men.

An appreciation, published in 1993 in *Illinois Wesleyan University Magazine,* described Horenberger this way: "'Coach' is, of course, Jack Horenberger '36 as permanent a fixture at Illinois Wesleyan for the past 50 years as Buck Memorial Library. Countless students, colleagues, and friends consider him "Mr. [Illinois] Wesleyan' for his contributions in the classroom,

Jack Horenberger

on the athletic fields, and as the school's most beloved goodwill ambassador."

The Horenberger record includes coaching the men's basketball team to a 264-212 record and seven College Conference of Illinois and Wisconsin (CCIW) championships from 1942-65, and coaching the baseball team to a 509-401 record and 16 CCIW championships from 1943-81. He received the University's Distinguished Alumnus Award in 1962.

"Jack Horenberger '36 epitomized what was good and different about [Illinois] Wesleyan athletics for 39 years," wrote Robert S. Eckley in his memoir. "More than any other individual, he set the tone for [Illinois] Wesleyan's student athletes.

"When athletic scholarships were eliminated in a shift to need-based awards in the 1960s," Eckley explained, "Jack went along but thought it would not work. When it did, he was among the first to acknowledge that fact and to become a vocal supporter for aid based on need. His record in coaching basketball and his sport of choice, baseball, speak for themselves—it was the way he did it that attracted attention and respect, along with his ever-present congeniality."

Sports Landmarks over Two Decades

The 1950s began with a landmark event in Illinois Wesleyan football history with the Titans going undefeated and untied in the 1951 season, compiling an 8-0 record and winning the CCI

(left to right)
Coaches Larson,
Keck and Bridges

championship. The 1951 team's accomplishment recalled the gridiron accomplishments of the 1888 squad and anticipated undefeated seasons in 1965 and 1992.

Football also marked an important milestone in 1955, when Don "Swede" Larson, class of 1950, began a 31-year career as football coach. Over the years, he amassed a record of 142-121-6. The 1950s also saw Illinois Wesleyan win five straight CCI baseball championships from 1956-60.

The decade of the 1960s marked many milestones for Titan basketball. In 1961 the University for the first time won the National Association of Intercollegiate Athletics (NAIA) state basketball championship and headed to Kansas City for the national tournament. The team made similar trips to Kansas City in 1966, 1970, 1971, 1975, 1976, 1977, and 1980.

Fred Young Fieldhouse opened in 1962. The first men's basketball game played there was an 85-59 conference championship clinching win over Lake Forest College.

And, in 1967, the College Conference of Illinois (CCI), Illinois Wesleyan's athletic affiliation, was broadened into the College Conference of Illinois and Wisconsin (CCIW).

A great rivalry ended in 1969, when cross-town foe, Illinois State University, played their last football game—a 27-6 defeat for Illinois Wesleyan. In 1970 the basketball rivalry between the two universities ended with a last-second Titan victory, 69-68.

Martin Luther King, Jr.

The decade of the 1960s was a period of great hope and tragedy. This era, filled with contradictions, was symbolized by the civil-rights revolution and manned space flight, as well as hippies, the Vietnam War, and a trio of tragic assassinations.

The 1960s was an era when the nation's campuses exploded in protest—protests fueled by the Vietnam War, the emerging counterculture, and a passion for a racially just society. Illinois Wesleyan wasn't immune to these forces.

One of the social forces students probed beyond the campus was the civil-rights crusade at a time when Freedom Riders and others were challenging America's segregated society. Consequently, Illinois Wesleyan became a stop on the long march to a fairer and more equal society, when civil-rights champion Dr. Martin Luther King, Jr., visited the campus in 1961 and 1966.

King's 1961 message of non-violent social change, years before he was awarded the Nobel Peace Prize, was summed up in the *Argus*, when the newspaper described the clergyman-social activist as "a man who never forgot to 'love his enemy;' he made suffering a virtue."

King addressed an audience at a banquet convened in the Main Lounge of the Memorial Student Center, advocating peaceful movement toward racial equality. He condemned the notion of separate but equal rights for America's black citizens.

"Non-violence is the most effective weapon for oppressed people," King told his audience. "Violence in our struggle would be impractical and immoral . . . to deal with a moral problem we should use a moral means."

A Return Visit

King returned to campus in 1966 after winning the Nobel Peace Prize and *Time Magazine's* 1963 "Man of the Year" award. This visit was sponsored by the Student Senate. More than 3,000 people crowded into Fred Young Fieldhouse to hear his remarks. Additionally, the renowned civil-rights leader made classroom appearances and addressed local clergy.

Receiving standing ovations, when he entered and left the fieldhouse, King said: "We must build a greater America. It cannot be built on bombs. It cannot be built on riots. We must work to change the climate that makes for bitterness that causes individuals to turn to these types of self-destruction."

Two years later, King was dead after an assassin's bullet cut him down in April, 1968. Illinois Wesleyan remembered him with a candlelight vigil. About 25 African-American students also held a memorial gathering.

Sara Ellen Long, class of 1964, wrote in the *Argus* that King "challenged us to accept the responsibility of taking the best of our culture and redirecting it and remaking it so that equality . . . might reign, and so segregation . . . would be eliminated."

Illinois Wesleyan and the Civil-Rights Movement

King was not the only civil-rights leader to use the campus as a platform to advocate social justice. The Reverend Jesse Jackson, a close associate of King, spoke at the Religious Activities Commission's symposium in 1967.

Illinois Wesleyan's interest in civil rights went beyond attracting prestigious speakers to campus to discuss the pivotal issue.

Congress passed sweeping civil-rights legislation in 1964 and the federal government required applicants for U.S. grants and loans to sign a statement stating strict compliance with the new law.

"I willingly signed this statement and sent it in to Washington in January of 1965," wrote President Lloyd Bertholf in his memoir, "and told both students and faculty what I had done. We were therefore on record that as an institution we did not practice racial discrimination in any form."

Concern over the slow pace of integration on college campuses nationally in 1965 triggered a statement by the Human Relations Committee of the Student Senate, which proclaimed an intent to pursue "actively the practice of integrating [Illinois] Wesleyan affiliated groups and organizations." This sparked a campuswide debate over the "risks" and "consequences" of imposing integration on university groups, especially the impact on fraternities and sororities.

Sociology Professor Emily Dunn Dale offered a statement to clarify the Human Relations panel's declaration, saying: "It means that we believe in an integrated community. . . It means

that we intend to practice what we affirm rather than paying mere lip service to an ideal. And it means that we pledge our encouragement to those organizations as yet unintegrated which affirm their support of the ultimate goal, rather than disowning or disavowing them."

Through the Eyes of the Argus observed: "After the Human Relations Committee ensured that the rights statement would not shut down any University organization, Senate approved it on December 12, 1965. (In 1968, five black students chartered [Illinois] Wesleyan's first predominantly black fraternity. The organization disbanded in 1971)."

The Bertholf years did more than invite minority speakers. For the first time an African-American joined the faculty with the appointment of John Martin in sociology in 1961. He came from New Orleans' Dillard University, where he had been an associate professor since 1957. Martin had received an undergraduate degree from Knoxville College and master's and doctoral degrees from Atlanta University and Indiana University, respectively.

Assassinated Leaders Remembered

Tragically, the 1960s was a decade filled with assassinations. Gunmen killed President John F. Kennedy in 1963 and civil-rights leader Dr. Martin Luther King, Jr., and U.S. Senator Robert F. Kennedy (D-N.Y.), the slain president's brother, in 1968.

Students, faculty, and others attended a service in Memorial Gymnasium for the murdered president on November 25, 1963. A newspaper account observed: "Many faces were still petrified with the horror of the assassination which greeted them on Friday."

When King was gunned down five years later, the civil-rights leader who had twice visited the University was memorialized at a commemoration. Paul Bushnell of the history faculty said: "Dr. King gave a vision to our generation, which was short on dreams and long on know-how . . . While he taught us that hatred corrupts

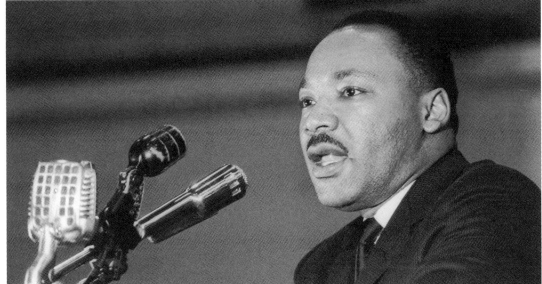

The visit of
Dr. Martin Luther King, Jr.
October 1966.

Buck Memorial Library

The Vietnam War

The first U.S. combat troops landed in South Vietnam in 1965. U.S. troop strength in the beleaguered Southeast Asian nation stood at 190,000—with 1,350 deaths already recorded. President Lyndon Johnson halted bombing of North Vietnam, but a peace overture was stymied. Nineteen hundred and sixty-five also saw about 100,000 people—mostly students—on 100 campuses attend a teach-in on Vietnam. Twenty-five thousand demonstrators marched in Washington, D.C., to protest the growing war.

The next year, U.S. troop strength in Vietnam topped 400,000 and a three-day inter-

and destroys, he also taught us that anger and passion are constructive dimensions of life. . . Non-violence is power and justice demands the right use of power."

national protest against the war took place in seven U.S. and seven foreign cities. The 19th annual congress of the U.S. National Student Association voted to halt all offensive military operations in Southeast Asia.

Despite these trends, the *Argus* reported student and faculty support for the Vietnam War. While not citing polling evidence to support its conclusion, the newspaper in November, 1967, offered a range of student opinion. One student, reflecting Cold War-tensions of the time, said the war was "halting a Communist threat to strengthen democratic policy." Another student took the opposite view, declaring: "I don't feel we are fighting for democracy, freedom, liberty and all the other high sounding words we pound into the 19 year-old GI's heads, but are fighting to save a certain somebody's face in Washington."

Books found during the renovation of Buck Memorial Library.

Vietnam Week, a three-day forum, was convened in 1967. Mutual Broadcasting System newsman Craig Spence, recently back from the conflict, and anti-war activist Staughton Lynd—among others—squared off on war policy.

Anti-war protests swept U.S. campuses in 1968 after the North Vietnamese launched the massive Tet Offensive in the South. The sentiment on campus was captured in *Through the Eyes of the Argus:* "The May 3, 1968 *Argus* reported that more than 600 students attended the first protest event, which featured speeches and readings from 10 faculty members and students."

Through the Eyes of the Argus added: "During the 1969-70 school year, the campus literally came to a halt when faculty and students voted in favor of a moratorium on October 15, 1969,

to discuss pro- and anti-war viewpoints. Over 1,000 students attended the debate, which ultimately revealed a campuswide anti-war bias."

Student Senate expressed an anti-war position by voting to remove U.S. troops from Vietnam, while the faculty voted to adopt a resolution condemning North Vietnamese treatment of U.S. prisoners of war. Furthermore, the School of Drama staged two anti-war plays in 1970 and 1971.

Thomas H. Keeslar, class of 1969, was a Marine stationed in DaNang, site of many North Vietnamese attacks. He wrote the *Argus:* "There are some people that snuff these men and their loyalty to their country, ideals and morals . . . Is loving your country so wrong? Is trying to protect home, family and loved ones wrong?"

XI. The 1970s and 1980s

The 1970s dawned with bloodshed on American campuses. Four students were killed at Ohio's Kent State University when National Guardsmen opened fire on anti-Vietnam protesters. Two students also were killed in a demonstration at Mississippi's Jackson State University. The American academic spring gave way to sweeping campus unrest on May 4, 1970, within hours of the Kent State tragedy.

The 1971 *Wesleyana* captured reactions, where the news "set off a planned program of protest and community education unlike anything previously seen at [Illinois] Wesleyan."

"The outraged reaction of a small group," the yearbook continued, "followed by their request that the University's flag be lowered, soon began to awaken more students to the tragedy at Kent State. Typically [Illinois] Wesleyan, students worked through channels, consulting the administration, who consulted the Senate, who said 'Yes.' . . . Other students, incensed by the action, stood around in menacing groups, some attempting to argue with the 'peace creep Commies' around the flagpole. A campus divided."

The flag was lowered with a flower-filled coffin at the foot of the flagpole on May 5, while the Wednesday chapel was transformed into a memorial service and students and faculty organized a forum on Kent State and the war in Southeast Asia.

President Robert S. Eckley stood firm in a May 7 statement, declaring: "I feel our students have acted sensibly in setting up a series of programs aimed at showing their concern with events of the last few days on both domestic and international fronts. I am as certain that they will continue to act in a responsible manner." Summer at least allowed a respite for planning. Administrative, faculty, and trustee colleagues reached consensus. As Eckley remembered the direction in his memoir: "If the unrest takes no more serious form than blocking of facilities, if

the operation of the University is not immediately threatened . . . our response should be mild and not resort immediately to physical methods of removal . . . Whether or not we would have the patience to wait out the occupation of facilities as was done at Brandeis for eleven days or at the University of Chicago for sixteen days is an open question."

Robert Eckley

Arson in Presser Hall

May was far from over. Presser Hall went up in flames, clearly the work of arsonists setting two separate fires. Eckley would remember later, "If there was a darkest day in my [Illinois] Wesleyan years, this is the most likely candidate."

More than two years passed before three Bloomington-Normal juveniles confessed to the crime. Another two years passed before they were brought to trial. The group's leader retract-

◄ Snowball fight in front of Dodds Hall 1978.

The stage of Westbrook Auditorium after the 1970 fire.

ed his confession and was acquitted by a jury. The building suffered extensive damage in two fires set by the youngsters. The case remains officially unsolved.

Incidentally, fires have played disastrous and historic roles in Illinois Wesleyan's history. The Tau Kappa Epsilon house had burned in 1930 and 13 years later a blaze destroyed Hedding Hall, while the Kappa Delta house caught fire in 1957. Five other fires took place on the campus between 1968 and 1986.

Robert S. Eckley becomes President

Thus ended the second year of Robert Eckley's presidency in an era when college presidents survived on campuses a shorter time than the average undergraduate course. Paradoxically, Eckley was just beginning the longest tenure in the University's history.

After 14 years at the heavy-equipment manufacturer, Caterpillar, Eckley was manager of the business-economics department, when he was named president of Illinois Wesleyan in 1968. A native of Kankakee, Illinois, he had graduated in economics from Bradley University in 1942 and finished an M.B.A. at the University of Minnesota before three years in the Coast Guard on the U.S.S. Davenport. After the war he was at Harvard for an M.A. and Ph.D. in economics. Two years as assistant professor at Kansas led to an appointment as an industrial economist at the Federal Reserve Bank in Kansas City. From there he went to Caterpillar, where he continued to publish in economics.

Eckley's connections to Illinois Wesleyan stretched to his paternal grandfather, a Methodist minister, who was a graduate of Hedding College, and his uncle Wayne Eckley, who was a 1927 mathematics and physics alumnus, taught nuclear engineering at the U.S. Naval Academy for years.

The University interested Eckley for other reasons, too, as he recalled.

President Eckley and
his cabinet (left to right)
Wendell Hess, Lee Short,
Glenn Swichtenberg,
President Eckley,
Phil Kash, Randy Farmer,
Larry Hitner, and
Jim Ruoti.

Left: President and
Mrs. Eckley **Right:**
President Eckley
arriving on campus.

"I had long been interested in higher education and liberal arts colleges, in particular because of their exemplary record in preparing people for leadership positions."

"Their performance," he explained, "is enhanced by a close relationship between faculty and students in a teaching environment. [Illinois] Wesleyan's commitment to the fine arts and the existence of pre-professional programs in business, nursing, and teaching as well as the liberal arts were compatible with my educational interests and philosophy."

As Eckley embarked on his presidency, he sensed a dual mission at the University. "Two of the key requirements would be to increase its academic and financial strength, something I thought I knew how to do."

Faculty and Student Achievements

The Eckley years were filled with many headlines and highlights on the academic and scholarly fronts.

As the curtain was dropping on the 1970s, two faculty members revealed important insights into the 1700s in an interesting work of scholarship.

It took four years of research, writing, and editing but in 1978 the story of a young man's life and experiences during and after the Revolutionary War came to light with publication of *The Diary of a Common Soldier in the American Revolution, 1775-1783: An Annotated Edition of the Military Journal of Jeremiah Greenman*, prepared by Robert Bray, Colwell Professor of English, and Paul Bushnell, professor of history.

The book was the 200-year-old journal kept by Greenman, a Rhode Island resident. The journal was owned by Greenman's great, great, great granddaughter, a Bloomington resident. The book related Greenman's war experiences, as well as his business ventures and career as a sea captain after the revolution.

A glimpse into some other noteworthy academic achievements included:

• By the time economics major Peter B. Berg, class of 1983, won a Fulbright grant for study in Germany in 1983-84, it was the ninth time in 10 years that at least one student had received a Fulbright, created by federal legislation.

• The Nautilus, a scientific journal, reported the discovery of a new species of mollusk by Dorothea Franzen, professor of biology-emeritus, in a 1983 article she authored. Franzen, who joined the faculty in 1952 and retired in 1977, discovered the snail-like species on the shore of Long Lake in Michigan in 1967, but conducted research during the ensuing years to determine the discovery's validity.

• English Professor James D. McGowan drew high praise in 1985 for his translation of 66 poems from Charles Baudelaire's "The Flowers of Evil." One critic called the work "a new high standard of imaginative excellence and inventive fidelity."

Teaching Excellence

When sociology professor Emily Dunn Dale became the 29th Century Club honoree in 1988, she also became the first recipient of the Sears-Roebuck Foundation Award for Teaching Excellence and Campus Leadership. Over the years, Illinois Wesleyan has had countless faculty—far too many to name—dedicated to quality teaching in the classroom, laboratory, on stage, and in the studio. This commitment to first-class teaching has defined the University over the decades. But what makes for a top-notch teacher-scholar?

When Jared Brown, professor and former director of the School of Theatre Arts, received the DuPont Award for Teaching Excellence in 1997, he said: "A good teacher has a love for his or her discipline, students, and the academic life. A good teacher is curious, always attempting to learn more. And, of course, the teacher wants to share his views, his knowledge, and his passions with students. But, in the best of times, that's a reciprocal process, for the students share as well, in some mysterious way, we come to enlighten and inspire one another."

Two years later, Michael Seeborg, the Robert S. Eckley Distinguished Professor of Economics,

tifying with the modern aspirations and goals of the black man in this country."

President Eckley said the University would make "extra efforts" to employ African-American faculty, yet he had to add that since

James Farmer, President Eckley and Jeff King '72.

Frank Starkey

was the teaching-excellence award recipient. "I really enjoy working with student-research projects," he said, commenting on his teaching philosophy. "To see students' critical-thinking skills improve—mature—brings a lot of satisfaction."

An "Urgent Concern"

Consensus sometimes was elusive in the America of the 1970s. However, there was agreement on one key point at Illinois Wesleyan. Faculty and staff were determined to increase the number of African-American students and enhance the quality of their experience.

The Black Student Association (BSA) was formed in 1968. John Martin, the first African-American faculty member had joined the sociology department in 1961, but he had left and once more the University had no African-American professors. The new BSA advocated a goal of 10 percent black faculty by the fall of 1969. These faculty were needed, according to an *Argus* article, "to complete the black students' educational experiences and to aid them in iden-

blacks held only 2 percent of doctorates in the liberal arts at that time, "there is little likelihood that a major portion of the specialized positions can be filled by black candidates, even with the extraordinary efforts we are prepared to make."

In the meantime, alternate tactics could provide an improved environment. "We had no black faculty or administrative staff initially," Eckley wrote, "so we sought to present African-American role models through invited guest speakers and performers."

Over the years, the University and the Black Student Union collectively invited nationally prominent African-American personalities like Andrew Young, a colleague of Dr. Martin Luther King, Jr; Georgia legislator Julian Bond; civil-rights leader James Farmer; soprano Kathleen Battle; Ralph David Abernathy of the Southern Christian Leadership Conference; and Yolanda King, daughter of Dr. Martin Luther King, Jr.

"Because our black students came from segregated backgrounds and few joined fraternities or sororities," Eckley wrote in his memoir, "I granted their request for a house for their activities and meetings, and the Afro-American Cultural Center became a part of the campus scene in the spring of 1970." Operated by the Black Student Union, the center featured original works by several art majors, discussion rooms, a record collection, and a library named in honor of Alfred O. Coffin, a Ph.D. and one of the University's first African-American students.

Hiring efforts paid off. From 1970 onward, the University had at least one black faculty member. Among these faculty were Frank Starkey, who taught chemistry from 1971-80, and Pamela Muirhead, a member of the class of 1968, of the English department. In 1983 the University elected its first black trustee, David Wilkins, class of 1974. And the Student Senate provided funding for a Black Fine Arts Festival, beginning in 1970-71, and a gospel choir, style show, and other activities.

Eckley remembered, too, that "four social or service fraternities and sororities with chiefly black membership appeared for a number of years, and two were still functioning when I retired."

The civil-rights revolution quite logically appeared in the curriculum. Professor Paul Bushnell introduced African-American history in 1968 and by 1974 the catalogue had much to report: "Several courses in the University curriculum include material on various aspects of the Afro-American heritage. In addition, there are specific courses in Afro-American History, Minorities, and Contemporary Black Literature as well as other experimental courses and independent study opportunities."

Commitment Beyond Tumult

As the academic community packed for the summer of 1970, it feared a fall worse than May. Yet summer calmed emotions of the spring, without leaving commitments any less intense. Politics and human rights remained a focus of many campus events, and the panoply of visitors showed the vibrancy of campus life.

Former Irish Prime Minister Terrance O'Neill talked about unrest in his country, while Julian Bond, the black Georgia state legislator and civil-rights leader, discussed social unrest and political movements in the United States. Former Vice President Hubert Humphrey urged abolition of anti-ballistic missiles as he gave the fifth annual Adlai E. Stevenson Lecture on International Affairs; experimental poet Allen Ginsberg, who coined the phrase the "beat generation," read his poetry during a campus visit; and Bill Russell, the perennial Boston Celtics all-star and the first black to coach a professional basketball team, discussed the relationships among sports, athletes, and contemporary events. Other visitors included Apollo VIII astronaut Frank Borman, plus Illinois Poet Laureate Gwendolyn Brooks, Nancy Hanks, chairman of the National Endowment for the Arts, and Sears, Roebuck board chairman Edward R. Telling, class of 1942.

And, once the fire damage from arson was repaired, Presser Hall continued to offer the classics, while other concerts brought *The Lettermen* and the hard rock group, *Blood, Sweat, and Tears*.

Curricular Developments

Overall curricular developments were not lost among vibrant political currents. In his inaugural address, Eckley observed that the University was a distinctive combination of undergraduate professional programs in the fine arts and nursing, as well as a balanced liberal-arts college. "The direction of curricular reform necessary at [Illinois] Wesleyan in 1968," Eckley noted, "was the improvement of programs and departments within the Liberal Arts College."

He explained: "With the resources available, we were close to being over-extended. We had a tenuous master's program in music and at least two other elements of the University aspired to offer master's degree work. At the same time, there were weaknesses within the undergraduate programs—our core undertaking—which required attention."

Liberal-Education Model

Campus leaders focused on the combination of professional schools and liberal arts which the University's history had created. A distinctive mix seemed possible in a professional model of liberal education. Along those lines the University had grants in 1976 from the Lilly Endowment and the Kellogg Foundation. The Lilly grant was tapped to craft a liberal arts-professional model for undergraduate education and the Kellogg project focused on bolstering career opportunities for liberal-arts college students and led to a Career Education Center in 1977.

"While we fell short of establishing a distinctive model for American higher education," Eckley remembered later, "the work was highly beneficial to the University in providing incentives for curricular and support services innovation."

However, on the career-education front, the Kellogg grant spurred improvements in career advising, including establishment of the pre-medical advisory committee in 1972, the pre-law committee in 1974, the graduate business committee in 1979, and the pre-engineering and graduate fellowship committees in 1982.

To promote programs with a competitive edge and to upgrade other areas, the University launched a five-year planning process, and over several years the faculty established a course-unit system which had faculty teaching seven courses a year as the students took nine. A General Education Task Force in 1974 brought greater options as the number of required courses was reduced from 16 to 14 out of 34.

The University's Outlook

In the fall of 1972 the University had a record fall enrollment of 1,685 full-time students, which continued a 10-year trend. The College of Liberal Arts accounted for 67 percent of the total enrollment. Staff and faculty could be especially proud that efforts to help students stay through graduation had increased junior and senior enrollments by 17 percent.

Financial aid was growing as a student need and budgetary necessity, with 62 percent of students receiving some kind of aid by 1973.

In October, 1975, board approval culminated a planning process which aimed at a stable enrollment of 1,650 students. At the time it was a brave move, for American colleges were full of committees planning for decreased enrollments which inevitably would come with the declining cadre of 18-year-olds. The experience of the next decade proved that visible quality and strength filled a university despite national numbers. In fact, enrollment was not only stable, it reached new heights with the 1,693 full-time students in 1986-87.

The 1980s brought a new phenomenon— the annual appearance of new college guides. The University's increasing profile was put in sharp focus in 1981, when Illinois Wesleyan was included among 246 U.S. colleges and universities in The Competitive Colleges: Who Are They? Where Are They? What Are They Like?, published by Peterson's Guides of Princeton, New Jersey. Director of Admissions James Ruoti, class of 1963, could report three applications for each student accepted for a freshman class of 510. The 1,608 applications for that class set a record.

January Term

During the 1970s, the innovative January Term evolved, proving itself especially appropriate for foreign and domestic travel courses, internships, and student immersion in a single course for concentrated study on campus. By the mid-1970s, themes appeared for "J" Term such as: the Bicentennial (1976), World Hunger (1977), Living with Technology (1978), and Human Rights (1979). The January Term also provided a venue for guest speakers to visit campus and for the staging of plays.

By January Term 1973 faculty could report that 266 students—about 16 percent of enrollment—participated in travel courses in the United States or overseas to locales including

Glenn Dodds

England, France, Germany, Austria, Russia, Switzerland, and the Netherlands. One student traveled to Singapore to conduct a home-economics research project on foods as they relate to culture. Other students studied poetry, healthcare, opera and music, international business, insurance, and the making of foreign policy in various nations.

The Age of Computers

No one at the time would realize the profound implication of one purchase order, as the University bought an Apple II computer in 1978. When the box was opened, Illinois Wesleyan moved into the computer age. Forty-four such machines were in use by 1984, with that total soon climbing to 100 computers of various types. By the early 1980s more than 80 percent of students had some exposure to computers, especially after a National Science Foundation grant helped develop new programs.

"Laboratories were established in the science and liberal arts classroom buildings and in the library," Eckley explained, describing the computer revolution on campus. "Many faculty were dispatched to summer short courses to enable them to teach the introductory course in computing."

A new five-course sequence in computer science led to a joint major in mathematics and computer science starting in 1981.

Looking back on the growth of computers in higher education over his 18-year presidency, Eckley observed there was a "continuous evolution and expansion of computer education, enabling faculty and students with significant interest in computers to develop that interest, and equipping practically all students with an opportunity to become familiar with microcomputers by gaining first-hand experience."

Campus Buildings

The late 1960s and 1970s saw several facilities added to the campus. In 1968-69 a new president's house was constructed. Dodds Hall—named in 1975 for Glenn Dodds, class of 1926 and his late wife—was completed in 1970 and is a residence hall known for its suite-living arrangements.

Evans Observatory replaced the former Behr Observatory in 1970, giving the University new capabilities in astronomy, physics, and optics. The ground floor of Stevenson Hall was renovated for the psychology department in 1972. Renovations also were made to Buck Memorial Library and the football stadium, adding a press box in 1974.

Lloyd and Martha Bertholf

Bertholf Commons

The Commons, the student dining area in the Memorial Student Center, was named in honor of Lloyd Bertholf, the University's 14th president from 1958-68, and his wife, Martha, in 1983.

Installation of the copper cupola of Evelyn Chapel.

This action was especially appropriate since Bertholf's presidency is remembered for his many "pro-student" policies, including giving the Student Senate full authority in handling the student activity fee. He also launched a policy of including students as members of University committees.

Evelyn Chapel

Until the 1980s, Illinois Wesleyan didn't have a separate chapel building. Evelyn Chapel was completed in 1984 and became the center of campus religious activity. The chapel's brick exterior, laid in the Flemish bond pattern, repeats an element of the Georgian style, consis-

tent with colonial architecture at the time of American Methodism's founding in 1784.

"Evelyn Chapel was designed to provide acoustical brilliance for its custom-designed Casavant organ and other musical programs," according to a pamphlet marking the chapel's 1984 dedication program series. David Gehrenbeck, associate professor of organ and sacred music, inaugurated the organ with a September 16, 1984 concert.

The American Institute of Architects bestowed an award on the chapel in 1985, calling it a "very skillful project . . . classic quality . . . decorative, ornamented . . . [with its] undulating balcony proficiently handled [with] strong interior architecture." The chapel also was the subject of a cover story in the January, 1985, edition of Architecture, the official magazine of the American Institute of Architects. The $1.8-million chapel is named in honor of Mrs. Jack (Evelyn Howell) Sheean in recognition of her efforts as a member of the Volunteers for [an Illinois] Wesleyan Chapel and in appreciation of her philanthropic gifts.

Other Facilities

Beadles Hall, constructed in 1907 and the home of the Sigma Pi fraternity, was named in 1980 to honor William T. Beadles (1902-1991), class of 1923, a professor of business administration and insurance. Beadles joined the faculty in 1924 as an economics instructor and assistant registrar. Over the years, he held various administrative posts, including chairman of the division of social studies, dean of the college of liberal arts, dean of the University, and vice president before returning to the classroom to teach in 1960. Beadles was the first recipient of Illinois Wesleyan's Century Club award for excellence in teaching in 1960. He retired in 1968.

Wilder Hall, acquired in 1980, was named in honor of William Wilder, president from 1888-98.

The Velma J. Arnold Health Service was established in 1941 and named in 1987 in honor of its founder and first University nurse. It is located in the lower level of Magill Hall, a student residence hall. The health service provides primary healthcare and professional referral services for students, faculty, and staff.

Kemp Hall's development as the International House dates from the 1980s. It is a living and learning center for students interested in international issues and concerns.

The Fine Arts

The Alice Millar Center for the Fine Arts was dedicated in 1973, marking the 25th anniversary of the founding of the College of Fine Arts. The new art building (28,000 square feet) replaced several old houses, Presser Hall was renovated, a new music building (25,000 square feet on three levels) was added, and a facility for experimental theatre was constructed. The art building featured a large ground-level gallery, a large lecture

Millar Fine Arts Center Dedication 1973.

Landscaping the
Quadrangle.

Nelva Weber-Sammataro

hall, and separate areas for painting, printmaking, silk screening, lithography, ceramics, sculpture, welding, design, commercial art, and drawing, plus studios for faculty and students.

A Fine Arts Festival was launched, a new music-theatre degree was inaugurated in 1977 and an arts-management program was established in 1978. An accreditation team from the North Central Association wrote in 1982: "Programs are sound, facilities are superior, and equipment and library resources are substantial

. . . great efforts have lately been made to integrate the fine [arts] and liberal arts."

The strength of the Fine Arts Festival early in its history is seen in the 1978 program, "The Arts: Real to Reel," which attracted famed filmmaker Frank Capra (*Mr. Deeds Goes to Town* and *It's A Wonderful Life*), as well as author-screenwriter Larry McMurtry (*The Last Picture Show*), and others.

The keyboard program also excelled with faculty such as Dwight Drexler, class of 1934, Larry Campbell, David Gehrenbeck, and Bedford Watkins. The band programs were led by Thomas Streeter and Steven Eggleston. Key faculty members of the voice program were Henry Charles, David Nott, Robert Donalson, and Sammy Scifres, while Todd Tucker led the music-theory program.

The Illinois Wesleyan Civic Orchestra, under the baton of Steven Eggleston, director of bands, held its inaugural concert in 1985 in Presser Hall. The 51-member orchestra—including five faculty, 23 students, and 23 community musicians—was formed in November, 1984.

1970's aerial view of the campus.

The School of Art responded gamely to enrollment challenges in the early 1970s. Printmaker and painter Fred Brian, class of 1950 and a professor of art, provided leadership for the school after the death of long-time director Rupert Kilgore, while Miles Bair became director in 1979.

Some artistic endeavors reflected the era's social consciousness and concerns. *Black Resurrection: Pure Suffering*—a depiction of the black experience from the earliest days in Africa to the present—was produced in April, 1978, and involved nearly all of the University's 80 African-American students. The multi-media production, presented by the Black Student Union, featured a slide presentation, choral numbers, dances, dramatic skits, and oral presentations.

Landscaping the Campus
Before construction began on the first campus building in the 1850s, the campus site was a small portion of Franklin K. Phoenix's Bloomington nursery. Those 10 acres—purchased for $2,000 in 1854—supported a honey locust tree grove. The last of those trees, it is believed, died in 1948.

About a decade later, Dutch Elm disease attacked the campus trees, killing more than 100 elms. Sixteen years later, however, a wave of new life swept over the campus. Illinois Wesleyan embarked on a mission to transform the prairie-like quad into a flourishing vision of foliage under the guidance of Nell Eckley, wife of President Robert S. Eckley, and landscape architect Nelva Weber-Sammataro, class of 1931. Basic to the new conception was vacating University Street between East and Park, and then upon completion of a new walkway system, planting began.

Weber-Sammataro recommended the planting of oak, sugar maple, ash, sweet gum, tulip, and various other trees. The $100,000 landscaping project brought 600 new trees to Illinois Wesleyan. The project also involved constructing 2,650 feet of new sidewalks, installing 26 new light fixtures, and the addition of several benches.

Manager of Grounds Services Eric Nelson explained: "Our goal is to create an atmosphere for reflection and serious thought. A quiet and serene place, with pockets of color, where people can mingle or be by themselves without having to go into a building."

The Naked Truth

Campus capers—from panty raids to bogus issues of student newspapers on April Fool's day—are part of the legend and lore of American higher education. While these high jinks change with the generations, they often are memorable.

In 1974 "streaking" was the memorable fad that hit the campus. The March 8, 1974, edition of the *Argus* earmarked a large portion of page one, along with photos, to record the latest such romp, when a group of Sigma Chi fraternity members scampered naked across the quad.

Through the Eyes of the Argus: 100 Years of Journalism at Illinois Wesleyan University reported: "However, the Sigs were not the campus' only group to take it all off. During one of the fraternity's nude chorus line acts that faced Munsell

Hall, women danced naked in blackened dorm windows while five nude independents ran past the dorm and eventually disappeared behind the Sheean Library. One spectator told the *Argus*, 'It's better than goldfish.'"

Robert Montgomery

Alumni Affairs: A Death in the Family

Robert M. Montgomery, class of 1967 and director of alumni affairs and annual giving from 1969-73, was killed in 1976 in a head-on car-truck collision in Oklahoma. Montgomery was director of development and executive assistant to the president of Phillips University in Enid, Oklahoma, a post he had taken in 1973 after leaving Illinois Wesleyan.

Montgomery's death at age 31 led to the establishment of the Robert M. Montgomery Outstanding Young Alumnus Award, announced annually at Homecoming.

Presidential Scholars

The Presidential Scholars' program was unveiled at the 1978 President's convocation. The original idea was that just three or four students from the entering freshman class would be selected each year for their high scholastic potential and be known as Presidential Scholars.

The first Presidential Scholars were from the class of 1982: Kathryn Ann Kasley, Janet Carol Pauls, Pamela Diane Little, and Tim Joseph Vega.

University Finances

During Robert S. Eckley's 18-year presidency, 1968-86, the University's operating budget almost quadrupled. "To accomplish this general rate of increase with a balanced budget," Eckley wrote, "even faster increases in current gifts and endowment income were necessary because of rapid growth in several important categories of spending."

Among those categories was student-financial aid spending, which climbed almost seven times during Eckley's presidency. "Fortunately," Eckley explained in his memoir, "we were able to increase endowment income even more rapidly to accommodate the need. By 1985-86 gift and endowment income was still exceeding the almost $1.9 million in University aid . . . "

The 30 largest gifts during the Eckley administration totaled about $15 million. Among these was a $2-million gift commitment by Foster G. McGaw of the American Hospital Supply Corporation for the Fine Arts Center, named for his mother, Alice Millar. Veteran trustee R. Forrest Colwell and his aunt made a gift in 1971 establishing an endowed chair in American Literature. Additional endowed chairs were added during the Eckley years, including the Adlai H. Rust Chair in Insurance and the Robert S. Eckley Professorship in Economics. After a 1971 visit, artist and painter Arrah Lee Gaul of Philadelphia bequeathed most of her estate and more than 200 paintings to the University in honor of her father, who was a member of the class of 1899. Bloomington office furniture supplier Jack Sheean left a major gift when he died in 1977. His widow, Evelyn Sheean, increased the bequest and the library was named in Mr. Sheean's honor.

The value of the endowment rose sevenfold between 1968-86. The University owned 16 farms in 1968 totaling 5,357 acres, but by 1986 these holdings had grown to 22 farms and 6,000 acres.

"Investments in securities—almost exclusively marketable stocks and bonds—were the chief emphasis of endowment holdings," Eckley explained in his memoir. "They rose from $2.3 million at market value in 1968 to $35.2 million in 1986."

Eckley summed up the investment strategy this way: "The results speak for themselves. For the first time in its 130-year existence, the University could face the future with an assurance of financial undergirding. After 1980, Illinois Wesleyan had an endowment valued among the top 10 percent for colleges with less than 3,500 students."

By 1977 the University ended a $10-million fund-raising program. "A little over one-fourth of the $10 million has been raised in Bloomington-Normal and the surrounding area," Larry Hitner, former director of development, reported. "That means nearly $7.5 million was raised elsewhere, the proceeds of which will be used for education in this community." A total of 209 gifts were made by 197 donors, with 57 percent of the total coming from friends of the University and 22 percent coming from alumni, while 15 percent came from trustees and 6 percent from foundations and corporations.

These positive financial trends continued into the 1980s and beyond. For example, C. Virgil Martin, class of 1932 and retired chairman of Carson Pirie Scott & Company told the Board of Visitors in April, 1983, that the Alumni Campaign for Endowment (ACE) was on schedule to raise $15 million by mid-decade. Martin, campaign chairman, reported receipts of $10.1 million in cash and pledges. The campaign, said Martin, a former Illinois Wesleyan business manager, was needed to retain the University's "qualitative edge." Two years later, the Board of Visitors learned that ACE, launched in 1979, had surpassed its goal, reaching $15.2 million from 610 donors by mid-decade.

Record gifts of $1,065,171 were contributed to the 1988-89 Illinois Wesleyan Fund. Marvin Bower, class of 1945 and chairman of the trustees' Development Committee, announced the record Illinois Wesleyan Fund tally in

August, 1989, observing that more than 84 percent of the students received some portion of their financial assistance from scholarships funded through the annual Illinois Wesleyan Fund. Since 1981, the average amount of Illinois Wesleyan-funded scholarships had nearly tripled, going from $821 per student in 1981 to $2,244 per student in 1989.

On the Air

WESN, Illinois Wesleyan's radio station, began operations in January, 1972, adding another dimension to the University's student-run media. The 10-watt stereo station was located in the basement of Kemp Hall, while its transmitter was atop Ferguson Hall, a high-rise residence.

"Besides providing the campus and the community with enjoyable and educational FM stereo listening," the University's 1972-73 catalogue pointed out, "the station offers opportunities for students and faculty to gain technical knowledge and experience in station operation.

The opportunities for involvement in program production also give an added dimension to the academic and cultural aspects of the campus."

Special Events

By the 1980s several special events were enshrined on the annual calendar. One day was set aside in the fall and spring for Dads' Day and Mothers' Day, respectively. Special Student Senate committees planned these events with the assistance of parents. Homecoming remained an annual fall highlight, featuring a varsity football game, alumni reunions, the Titan Games (intramural contests), a parade, selection of a Homecoming queen, and a dance or concert.

The College of Fine Arts, in cooperation with the Student Senate, sponsored a spring Fine Arts Festival. Typically, the two-week event featured a theatre production, guest artists, and composers who joined with School of Music faculty and students in the Contemporary Music Symposium. Film presentations and appearances

Athletes in Professional Sports

Jack Sikma wasn't the only athlete to find success in professional sports. Shortstop Bobby "Ace" Winkles, class of 1952—who hit .400 and led the baseball team in home runs, triples, hits, runs batted in, and total

Bobby Winkles, center

bases—signed with the Chicago White Sox as a shortstop after his junior year. Eventually, he became head baseball coach at Arizona State University, winning NCAA national championships in 1965, 1967, and 1969. He went on to manage the California Angels and Oakland Athletics in the major leagues.

Doug Rader, class of 1966, lead the Titans to a College Conference of Illinois title in 1963 and a second-place finish in 1964. Through the Eyes of the *Argus* reported: "Rader, a gold glove third baseman and a .251 lifetime hitter in 11 major league seasons, played for the Houston Astros, San Diego Padres and Toronto Blue Jays, and later managed the Texas Rangers, Chicago

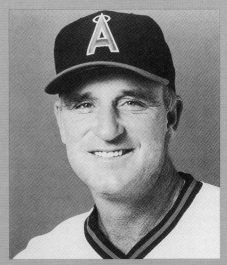

Doug Rader

White Sox and California Marlins," and was a hitting coach with the Florida Marlins.

Calvin (Cal) Neeman, class of 1951, played baseball for the Chicago Cubs, Pittsburgh Pirates, and the Philadelphia Phillies.

Jack Sikma

by authors and literary critics rounded out the festival.

Each spring, residence units planned social and philanthropic activities. Three all-University convocations—President's, Founders' Day, and Honors—provided forums for guest speakers.

Fort Natatorium

The early 1980s brought a consensus that the University needed a new swimming facility. Memorial Gymnasium had been built more than 60 years ago for a student body about one-third of the University's current size.

A new swimming pool would be located on the northeast corner of Emerson Street and Franklin Avenue. It was to be modeled on what was ideal for Illinois Wesleyan, rather than what was merely practical and simple. Thus, plans called for eight lanes, a separate diving area, locker rooms, spectator seating, classrooms, and an office-management area.

In 1965 Judge Arthur C. Fort, class of 1897, bequeathed three farms and other assets as a

trust which passed into University hands in 1986. With these assets, the new building was named Fort Natatorium in memory of G.L. Fort, class of 1877, and his children, Judge Fort and Clara E. Fort, class of 1903.

The Jack Sikma Era

In the early 1970s the University gained title to Bloomington Community Stadium, changing its name to Illinois Wesleyan Stadium.

Athletic achievement continued at record level, particularly for men's basketball. Jack Sikma, class of 1977, was a business-administration major and a GTE Academic All-American. During his last three seasons at Illinois Wesleyan, the Titans won conference titles and 44 of 46 conference games. Between 1975-78 the men's basketball team tallied a 31-game winning streak at Fred Young Fieldhouse. Sikma also established several individual men's basketball records, including most career points, 2,272.

"After establishing all-time records" at Illinois Wesleyan, President Robert S. Eckley

"The Super Seven Plus One" from 1976-77 basketball team.

wrote of Sikma in his memoir, "the small-college star unexpectedly was the eighth choice in the first round NBA draft in 1977. The choice was a good one for the scholar-athlete—in his second year with the Seattle Supersonics, he came home wearing an NBA championship ring. In fourteen seasons, including six with the Milwaukee Bucks, he was involved in eleven playoffs." A seven-time NBA All-Star, Sikma finished his NBA career in 1991.

As the decade drew to a close, the University joined NCAA Division III in 1977. Three years later, in 1982, women's sports joined Division III.

Athletics in the 1980s

Jack Horenberger retired in 1981 as athletic director and baseball coach. He was succeeded as athletic director by Dennie Bridges, class of 1961, who also had succeeded Horenberger as men's basketball coach.

The Women's CCIW was formed in 1984. The women's basketball team began six seasons of play at Fred Young Fieldhouse in 1988, compiling a 19-4 record the last two years at the fieldhouse.

In his memoir Robert S. Eckley rightfully praised coaches for combining academic excellence with winning. "Much credit goes to the coaches and athletic directors: Jack Horenberger, Dennie Bridges, Don Larson, Bob Keck, and Barb Cothren. They not only fielded excellent teams, they helped keep the focus where it belonged, on student academic priorities."

Eckley added: "The excellence of our athletes is confirmed by the number elected as first-team Academic All-Americans by the College Sports Information Directors of America."

Task Force on 1990

In 1984 Dean Wendell Hess was appointed to lead a nine-member faculty, staff, trustee, and student group in planning priorities for the last half of the 1980s.

"Hopefully, they will dream about what this institution may become," President Robert S.

Eckley said, "as they weigh alternative directions and suggest the most rewarding course for us to follow. We anticipate their report in June, 1985."

The report concluded the University must "build from strength." The Task Force agreed that success will require the University to "constantly engage in efforts to stretch its vision." It focused on a six-part strategy: developing new academic programs; enhancing pre-professional opportunities; integrating educational experiences; fostering the faculty's professional growth; financing excellence; and evaluating and communicating quality.

Specifically, the task force report called for establishing an International Studies program and a communications concentration; requiring a flexible, but university-wide senior capstone experience; exploring aggressive program development in pre-engineering; and initiating a comprehensive curriculum review.

A Nation at Risk

An 18-member federal commission released a landmark report in 1983, charging that the "educational foundations of our society are presently being eroded by a rising tide of mediocrity that threatens our very future as a nation and a people." President Robert S. Eckley conceded the accuracy of the conclusions contained in A Nation at Risk: The Imperative for Educational Reform in a presentation to the Board of Trustees.

However, he pointed out that the University was successfully swimming against the tide. "I believe," Eckley said, "that I am accurate in saying that the quality of work done by [Illinois] Wesleyan students . . . has not deteriorated, but we are the exception, and we are being affected in many ways by conditions in the schools and in higher education generally."

Eckley pointed out that the University had not scuttled general-education requirements, like many campuses. Illinois Wesleyan's posture, he added, "is that academic work should not be compromised in quality and this is likely to position it well to lead in the reversal of trends described in the National Commission study."

125th Anniversary

As the University approached its 125th anniversary it was reported in October, 1974, that 80 percent of students were enrolled in business and economics, nursing, music, teacher education, pre-medicine and related sciences, pre-law, art, and drama, with the greatest enrollment increases in recent years in pre-medicine and pre-law. Two-thirds of the College of Liberal Arts faculty had doctorates, compared to 40 percent in 1958.

Illinois Wesleyan marked its 125th anniversary in 1975. In 1974 it was announced that the University would hold many "birthday parties" the following year—Founders' Day, the Fine Arts Festival, Alumni Day, the President's Club Dinner, the opening all-school convocation in the fall, commencement, and Homecoming— with anniversary-related themes.

At the Founders' Day convocation, it was announced that the congressional papers of

Leslie C. Arends, a member of the U.S. House of Representatives from 1935-75 and a trustee from 1937-68, would become part of the library's special collection. Arends' papers, photos, memorabilia, and 250 books filled 200 boxes and crates.

The Alumni Weekend, convened May 16-18, gave graduates the opportunity to celebrate the University's past, present, and future. Reunion classes met from 1915, 1920, 1925, 1930, 1935, 1940, 1945, 1950, and 1955. About 40 members of the class of 1925 attended for their golden anniversary. A slide show chronicled the University's history and there was a tour of Bloomington's historic houses, including the David Davis Mansion, once the home of a U.S. Supreme Court justice, U.S. Senator, and University benefactor.

At the Alumni Day dinner the University received the original manuscript of the University's "Cheer Song," written in 1910 by Ralph S. Freese, class of 1911, and Chalmers H. Marquis, class of 1910. Freese wrote the music and Marquis scripted the lyrics. The document

Opera Stars Around the World

One gauge of the music program's success is the roster of opera singers it produced between the 1960s and the 1980s, including: Roger Roloff, class of 1969; Z. Edmund Toliver, class of 1970; Susan Quittmeyer-Morris, class of 1975; Karen Huffstodt, class of 1977; Brenda Hemann Harris, class of 1979; Andrea Huber-Burda, class of 1981; Dawn Upshaw, class of 1982, and others.

The accomplishments of 10 international opera stars from this era were recounted in the Spring, 1997, edition of *Illinois Wesleyan University Magazine*, in an article headlined: "The World is Their Stage: IWU Alumni Sing Opera from Sydney to Vienna."

Speaking of the world of opera in Europe, Andrea Huber-Burda said: "There are so

many opportunities here, it's wonderful. There are something like 60 opera houses in the German-speaking countries, all with complete seasons of 46 weeks a year, and all with acting companies, ballet companies, and opera

companies attached. That's not to mention all the orchestra and concert work available."

A 1999 *Illinois Wesleyan University Magazine* profile of three-time Grammy Award-winner Dawn Upshaw pointed out: "Part of what makes Upshaw so different is that her choices have taken her down an astonishing variety of musical roads. A favorite at the Metropolitan [Opera in New York City] and other world-class opera houses for her roles in classic 18th-century works by Handel and Mozart, she is equally at home in the 20th century," including the lead role of Daisy Buchanan in the world premiere of "The Great Gatsby"—an adaptation of the F. Scott Fitzgerald novel—at the Metropolitan Opera."

was presented to the University by Donald Freese, class of 1943 and son of the song's co-author. The sheet music was accompanied by a photo of the entire student body of 1910 standing in front of Old Main.

The Ferguson Cane

When Louise Behr Empson died in April, 1980—five days after her 103rd birthday—Illinois Wesleyan lost its last link to the University's fabled Behr Observatory of the 1890s.

Sylvester Melvin at age 102 with the Ferguson cane.

Empson was a member of the class of 1898 although she had to quit college during her sophomore year to care for her ill mother. She grew up on Chestnut Street, just a few blocks from the campus, and frequently visited the Behr Observatory, which her uncle C.A. "Anton"

Behr, presented to the University in 1894.

One of her last visits to campus was on May 13, 1978, Alumni Day, when she received the Ferguson Cane, which traditionally was held by the oldest living University alumnus. In a 1979 *Argus* interview Empson noted that Wilbert Ferguson, for whom the cane is named, was her favorite professor. Ferguson served as a faculty member and administrator from 1894 until his death in 1944.

After Empson's death, Julia Baker Gray, who was approaching her 93rd birthday, became the keeper of the cane. Gray—who received a teacher's certificate from the College of Music when it was located on the second floor of the Hoblit Building at Main and Mulberry Streets—was one of only a half dozen remaining members of the class of 1906.

The tradition of the Ferguson Cane began in 1941, when Ferguson—a professor of Greek and German—gave it to the University. He had purchased it in 1892 in Leipzig, Germany, as a gift for his father.

The first recipient was attorney Eli P. Adams, class of 1875. He kept it until his death in 1947 at age 98. His successor was classmate Samuel Van Pelt, who died in 1953 at age 98. Sylvester Melvin, class of 1878 and a founder of the Mutual Insurance Company possessed the fabled cane until 1962, when he died at age 110. John Robert Van Pelt, class of 1882 and brother of Samuel, was presented the cane in 1962, but he died later that same year.

Community Service

Over the years, countless faculty have made landmark contributions to their disciplines, research, and community service. Samuel C. Ratcliffe, who taught sociology from 1927-60, was a symbol of that spirit of community service—especially when he delivered the inaugural Emeritus Professor lecture in 1982 at a youthful 95 years of age.

Ratcliffe, a Canadian by birth who became a U.S. citizen in 1935, left a lasting mark on the

Samuel C. Ratcliffe

Bloomington-Normal community. He assisted in organizing the McLean County Senior Citizen's Advisory Board. He was a participant and organizer of the local Office of Economic Opportunity, as well as serving as a member of the McLean County Social Service Council. He was a Head Start director, worked with the State Commission on Prevention of Sex Delinquency, and served on the War Labor Board. Ratcliffe was cofounder of the Bloomington-Normal Child Guidance Clinic and the Social Service Exchange, and was on the board of directors of the Western Avenue Community Center, Red Cross Home Service Board, and the Bloomington-Normal Church Council.

The nonagenarian Ratcliffe, one of 11 siblings, was admitted to college based on his performance on proficiency exams since he had no high-school training. He received degrees from Canada's University of Mt. Allison and the University of Alberta, as well as a doctorate from the University of Chicago. He taught at the University of Illinois for seven years before coming to Illinois Wesleyan in 1927—the year Lindbergh flew the Atlantic—as head of the sociology department. He introduced one of the first internship programs for undergraduates to study welfare in the United States. He died at age 103 in 1990.

XII. Toward a Sesquicentennial

That Bloomington would have a college seems a given, based on the eastern background of the early European settlers. Its form and specifics, though, depended very much on politics and details.

In September, 1985, President Robert S. Eckley turned age 65. Lloyd Bertholf, his predecessor, had retired at age 68, while Merrill Holmes had served in the presidency until 72 years of age, and William Shaw had died in office at age 78. That fall Eckley announced he would retire at year's end, making him the longest serving president in the University's history.

"I have been privileged to serve Illinois Wesleyan students, faculty, staff, alumni, and trustees for 18 years and now I am looking forward to a sabbatical," Eckley said.

The search process named Wayne Anderson the University's 16th president and he arrived in August, 1986. A graduate of the University of Minnesota, he did master's work in public and international affairs at Princeton's Woodrow Wilson School before receiving a Ph.D. from Georgetown University. He had been on the staff of the Association of American Colleges and his nine years as assistant to the president at Johns Hopkins prepared him to be president and professor of political science at Maryville College at age 39. He knew well the tasks of his new office as he took over a planning process already in place.

Anderson brought new sense of vision as he urged his new colleagues to be leaders in many spheres. Provost Wendell Hess chaired the Task Force for 1990, and as the group continued its work, Anderson pushed an agenda focused on overseas programs, community interaction, programs for women and minorities, development of the University's visibility and academic profile,

and plans for new construction and its funding. Anderson saw great vigor in the accumulated results of the previous decades and urged his colleagues to help consolidate them for national visibility. His tenure was brief as he announced his resignation after barely 18 months in office, yet his departure left many new currents afoot. Far sooner than expected the University was in a presidential search mode again. The faithful veteran Provost Wendell Hess became acting president. Hess joined the faculty in 1963 as a chemistry professor and already had been dean of the University for 11 years when Anderson appointed him provost in 1987. There was hardly an aspect of the institution he did not know well. An admired professor, who won the University's top teaching award in his sixth year, Hess had been a department chair, division director, and leader of the planning process.

A New President Named

Minor Myers, jr., became the 17th president of Illinois Wesleyan University in 1989. An alumnus of Carleton and Princeton, Myers taught for 16 years at Connecticut College, where he wrote five books and headed the board of a local museum. Previous to arriving in Bloomington, he had spent five years as provost, dean of faculty, and professor of political science at Hobart and William Smith Colleges.

University Finances

In Vice President for Business and Finance, Kenneth Browning, the University has contin-

The atrium of the Center for Natural Science.

The Sesquicentennial Gateway

ued its tradition of balanced budgets. Head of the Massachusetts Institute of Technology's student paper as an undergraduate and then a housing officer there, Browning has a natural sensitivity to students as well as balance sheets. The tradition of the balanced budget reached its 42nd year in 2000, a spring in which the endowment touched the $225-million mark.

Special credit for the endowment's success goes to Rex James Bates, a former trustee and former head of the investment division at State Farm insurance. He volunteered vision, advice, and management skills during decades in which he helped to grow the endowment from a cushion into a resource. Today, five fund managers do what he did alone for years.

Assets are only as good as the planning for them and recent years have allowed the University to balance other needs with the continual enhancement of a student-aid budget that has exceeded $10 million annually. More than 80 percent of students receive some sort of financial assistance because of careful planning, alumni enthusiasm, and the endowment.

Development work has excelled. Under the leadership of Vice President for University Advancement Richard Whitlock and Director of Development Ben Rhodes, class of 1969, alumni and friends have operated a campaign that has exceeded $125 million in commitments. Whitlock knows colleges well as an alumnus of Gustavus Adolphus College, while Rhodes, an IWU alumnus, has family roots in Bloomington going back to the 1820s. Their leadership has allowed faculty and students to move forward.

The 1990s inherited a strong financial outlook. Even periodic economic slowdowns, which devastated the northeast in the decade's early years, were something only read about in Bloomington. The founders would have been amazed. Elements of financial solidity and academic success are interrelated. Consequently,

Board President E. Hugh Henning explained at an October, 1988, trustees' meeting that balanced budgets were the product of careful financial management, increased student retention, and record support from alumni, friends, and foundations. Board Treasurer Craig C. Hart also reported that the market value of the endowment stood at $54.7 million. Acting President Hess noted that the University had a record enrollment of 1,732 full-time students. President Wayne Anderson's efforts to recruit international students brought together representatives of 27 countries, while two dozen students were studying off campus in London, Paris, Vienna, Washington, D.C., New York City, and elsewhere.

A Campaign

Trustee Edward B. Rust, Jr., class of 1972, is chief executive officer of State Farm insurance, which is ranked the 15th largest corporation among the *Fortune 500*. Yet, he readily agreed to chair a fund-raising campaign for his alma mater. He announced in May, 1992, that the University

Ed Rust announcing the Campaign for Illinois Wesleyan.

already had received $30.1 million in gifts and pledges. The initial $58-million goal was passed in 1995.

Ebullient leadership among alumni accumulated $125 million of new support by the summer of 2000 and their enthusiasm very quickly

translated into new buildings, programs, and needed scholarship resources for students drawn from around the globe.

The Fort Natatorium proved far more of a model than anyone imagined, when the Memorial Gymnasium pool looked ripe for replacement. When the Shirk Center was designed to go with the Natatorium, Russell Shirk, class of 1943, in his quiet way set the example, which has pervaded each construction project that followed. University leaders have traveled the entire country, looking at the best undergraduate facilities they could find and asking what was good and what could be improved.

Faculty

The faculty of the 1990s gave vigorous demonstration that scholarship and teaching were not antithetical. Indeed at selective colleges they reinforce each other. Hardly a faculty meeting went by without the provost displaying a new faculty publication. Among some of those pieces were a cover article in *Nature* on Assistant Professor of Biology Elizabeth (Susie) Balser's work on light-emitting octopi to a two-book set authored by four Illinois Wesleyan chemists *Integrated Chemistry: A Two-Year General and Organic Chemistry Sequence*, published by Houghton Mifflin in the late 1990s. The authors are David Bailey, professor of chemistry; Forrest Frank, associate professor of chemistry, who retired in May, 1999; Jeff Frick, associate professor of chemistry and department chair; and Timothy Rettich, associate professor of chemistry.

Academic Leadership

Ellen Hurwitz followed Wendell Hess as provost. With the additional title of dean of faculty Hurwitz stayed until 1992, when she left to become president of Albright College and subsequently president of New England College. Janet McNew followed as provost and dean of faculty in 1993. She and Associate Provost Roger Schnaitter and Associate Dean Mona Gardner

The dedication of the Center for Natural Sciences.

have worked with faculty colleagues to develop new curricular offerings, hire new colleagues, and design buildings—assignments that have enriched the University.

The joint success of development and admissions supported a buoyant expansion of the faculty. More than 50 percent of Illinois Wesleyan's young and vigorous faculty have been appointed since 1994. They pride themselves on teaching and there is great pride and competition for the annual duPont teaching award, yet scarcely a faculty meeting goes by with the provost announcing important new books, papers, or other achievements by productive colleagues. John Wesley Powell would be proud of those who have followed in his tradition.

It is perhaps out of that pride that the faculty has named the John Wesley Powell Research Conference, the annual spring showcase of student-faculty collaboration. In the spring of 2000, 82 students took part. No one found a new species that year, but Karen Lindahl, class of 1999, had done so the previous year, as she and Professor Elizabeth (Susie) Balser found a creature barely a millimeter long, a tardigrade, Milnesium, in a lichen-covered roof-top area outside of Balser's apartment.

Science Education

Science took a great step forward in 1995, when the University opened the Center for Science Learning and Research. Designed by an architectural consortium of Anderson DeBartolo Pan, Inc., of Phoenix, and Shive-Hattery of Bloomington, the building provides nearly 130,000 square feet for biology, chemistry, physics, mathematics, computer science, and psychology, all organized as a community of science. The massive building with its sweeping atrium contains 440,000 bricks, 77 miles of wire, 17 miles of conduit, and 1,400 electrical outlets. It was designed for periodic technological updates. A key to the building's design is the 22 student-faculty research laboratories in which junior and senior students may maintain research projects throughout the year.

◄ Center for Natural Sciences

The science center caught the attention of Project Kaleidoscope, a science-education program sponsored with support from the National Science Foundation. The project featured it as a model building, while *Barron's 300 Best Buys in College Education* wrote: "With the addition of a new science facility and equipment, the undergraduate program [at Illinois Wesleyan] could surpass that at any national university."

Biology continues to attract almost 100 students in each class of 560, yet the total roster of physics majors is often more than 50 students, a fact almost unknown on other liberal-arts campuses of 2,000 students. About a fifth of Illinois Wesleyan students have a science as one of their majors. Consequently, John Wesley Powell's great scientific tradition continues to thrive, as does his spirit of exploration.

January Becomes May

Generations of Illinois Wesleyan students had loved the January Term and when the faculty decided to move it to May, there was considerable doubt among students and alumni about the efficacy of this decision. Now students cannot imagine it any other way, and we sense some alumni may be envious.

For the inaugural May Term in 1996, almost 200 Illinois Wesleyan students had their passports stamped for destinations including the People's Republic of China, Australia, England, Ireland, Greece, and the Czech Republic, while others traveled to Hawaii, Texas, New York City, and points along the old Oregon Trail. University Chaplain and Professor of Humanities Dennis Groh, class of 1961, was a veteran of 15 archaeological expeditions to Israel in 1997, when he took 25 students on an archaeological adventure as part of May Term.

Other Programs Abroad

May is only one option for study abroad and many students spend a year or term elsewhere. Across the curriculum from music to nursing, students explore other continents, enriching the campus on their return.

A program with Pembroke College, Oxford, for example, launched in 1997 with six students is particularly popular. Each year students have the option of studying and living at the college of Samuel Johnson, the dominant figure of 18th-century English letters. Though the oldest buildings date from 1624, the great dining hall was going up just as Illinois Wesleyan was getting started.

By 2000 Illinois Wesleyan had participated in about 10 international exchanges with Technos International College in suburban Tokyo. The primary goal of the two-week program is to provide participants with a first-hand glimpse into Japanese culture through travel, seminars, and other activities.

Humanities and Social Sciences

When the new science center opened, the old science facility, Sherff Hall, was abandoned. Planning led to its complete renovation with architectural plans by Jack DeBartolo, who had worked on the science building and the Shirk Center. In 1997 after a $5.1-million renovation it became the Center for Liberal Arts (CLA), a three-floor brick building housing 60 faculty offices, classrooms, seminar rooms, and various other facilities. History, philosophy, classics, education, religion, political science, sociology and anthropology, economics, and business all moved into the CLA. However, the English Department opted to remain in its elegant house at 1101 N. Main Street.

The CLA features laboratories for social-science research such as the political-science laboratory, which houses computers, phone banks, and other facilities needed for survey research, analysis, and downloading information from electronic data banks.

Foreign Languages

Language study has grown in offerings and interest. The complete renovation of Buck Library into a computer and language center in 1990 carried language study to a new level. Russian

was consolidated as a major, and with the help of the Tanaka Memorial Foundation Japanese was added as a new language, as part of a burgeoning program in Asian studies. Annual trips to Japan, sponsored by the Tanaka Foundation and Technos International College, have created many more friends for things Japanese, just as has the exchange program with Obirin University in Tokyo. Both of these spirited programs serve as a worthy reawakening of the Japanese heritage of our first international students 110 years ago.

Perhaps least imaginable of all developments from the perspective of the 1970s is the reemergence of the classics. Once more the University had specialists in Greece and Rome, centered in classics and in history. But the classics of India, the rest of Asia, of Latin America, and of Africa found a place in the modern curriculum, too, which seeks the best and most interesting of all continents and centuries.

Dean of Students

After 21 years as dean of students, Glenn Swichtenberg retired in 1996, leaving many generations of successful and grateful students. He was followed by Debra Wood, who came from Coe College and left for Scripps College. She was followed by James Matthews, drawn directly from the faculty and the Department of Modern and Classical Languages.

Matthews had first come into student affairs when Dean Wood put him in charge of a Greek Affairs Task Force. When she departed, he seemed a natural to work with students to reach new levels of programming. In the fall of 1999, he and associate deans Malinda Carlson and Darcy Greder could count some 700 separate events available to students during a semester.

A New Student Center

Student enthusiasm reached new levels once Tom Hansen, class of 1982, got involved. In the fall of 1999 he returned to campus to announce a major gift to transform the old Memorial

Past and present Student Senate Presidents and a student Senator review plans for the Hansen Student Center, From left to right: Matt Glavin, president 2000-2001; Harold Gauthier, president 1999-2000; Greg Adamo, president 2001-2002; Jerry Pope, president 1977-1978, and Tom Bowen, senator 1998-2001.

Gymnasium into a vibrant new student center, featuring a two-story bookstore, cafe, grille, information center, offices for student government and other student organizations, conference rooms, newsstand, and an outdoor patio.

A $2-million gift from Hansen, a business-administration graduate, and his family spearheaded the student-center project. "I wanted to make a gift," he said, "which benefits all students at Illinois Wesleyan and the student center project was perfect. The design of the center caters to the diverse needs of all students and is very conveniently located."

The student-center project got off to a unique start in 2000, when students swung sledgehammers at a "wallbreaking" ceremony. "Students have been part of the student-center planning since day one," said Dean of Students James Matthews, "so we wanted them to have a role—a physical role—in the demolition work that's the first step in constructing the new facility. The Hansen Student Center is their building."

Rust House

The deans of student affairs have been involved in considerable other real-estate work as well. After Jack DeBartolo's master plan suggested the need and place for a new residence hall, the trustees turned to BLDD of Decatur, Illinois, to design the building that opened in 1997. Dean Wood and students led the programming, which created a four-floor residence hall offering four-, six-, and eight-person suites. Its 54,000 square feet accommodate 118 students. The building also includes kitchenettes, floor lounges, a recreation room, laundry facilities, and access to the Internet and cable television.

The Board of Trustees needed little reflection to come up with an appropriate name for the structure, for the students of the University for decades had no better friend on the board than Harriett Fuller Rust, who also was a daughter-in-law of a trustee, wife of one, and mother of another. In her cheerful way she championed the cause of students and their scholarship needs, as

she organized annual fund support on their behalf. All were saddened when she died only weeks after her name was emblazoned on the stones over the door.

Earlier construction had created a building at 111 E. Emerson, occupied by Sigma Chi, just as all but one of the other fraternities occupy University buildings. Phi Mu Alpha on Franklin Park owns its own building, while the sororities own all their own structures.

Portfolio Class

The line between student activities and course work is often thin, as the portfolio class shows. In 1992 John Liston, class of 1949, and C. Leroy Benner were having lunch in Savannah, Georgia, as they did every week, but this time it was different. They ended that meal convinced that Illinois Wesleyan should have a student-investment fund. If biologists have frogs to work on, why shouldn't business students have a fund to manage? Not much later former trustee Elmo Franklin had exactly the same idea and within a few months Professor Mona Gardner was working with a trustee client board, as she led that first group of students in investing $200,000, which those first discussions had produced. Benner was so pleased with the progress that he added another $50,000. Not quite a club, the class is an ongoing organization managing a portfolio and quite often outperforming key market indices and the University's own portfolio managers. Now under the guidance of Zhenhu Jin, associate professor of finance, the fund crossed the $1-million mark for the first time on March 24, 2000. In addition, the fund contributes 4.75 percent of its principal each year to student scholarship funds as a functioning part of the endowment.

Concern for Others

A key component of a liberal-arts education is developing a keen sense of public service as seen in the twin coast-to-coast ventures—Make a Difference Day and National Volunteer Week—

◀ Harriett Fuller
Rust House

The atrium of Rust House.

that Illinois Wesleyan participates in annually. When Illinois Wesleyan joined the National Volunteer Weekend in 1994, 32 students participated. By 1998, the roster included more than 250 students. The 1998 National Volunteer Weekend was typical with students painting the local Red Cross office, picking up trash along Bloomington-Normal's Constitution Trail, and helping the elderly at Path Senior Services.

In the 1990s Habitat for Humanity became a popular public-service project for students. In 1995, for example, about 30 students spent spring break working on Habitat for Humanity homes in Conway, South Carolina. Others worked in the Bloomington-Normal area. In 1996 students were involved in a bike race to raise $10,000 toward construction of a home locally. Mary Kern, a 1997 business and psychology graduate, said she was attracted to Habitat for Humanity because "it's an active service organization— you're not just raising money for a national organization to divvy up. You go out and accomplish much yourself and that is satisfying."

Illinois Wesleyan brought to campus in 1996 about 15 youngsters from Cabrini Connections' Tutor/Mentoring Program. Daniel Bassill, class of

1968, started the after-school nurturing program for seventh to 12th graders from Chicago's Cabrini-Green neighborhood. "The main reason Illinois Wesleyan wants to do this is to show students from Cabrini Connections that higher education is attainable," said Monica Taylor, director of Multi-Cultural Affairs and a 1988 graduate.

In 1996 the University began cosponsoring a summer Sports & Scholars program, which helped 24 Bloomington high-school freshmen sharpen their math, science, and writing skills. The innovative program—a creative partnership among the Bloomington public schools, State Farm insurance, and GTE—was described as an excellent example of a public school-university collaboration by Bloomington School Superintendent Richard Sens.

The University promoted these types of community-campus efforts nationally in its 1996 President's Report, *Touching the Future—American Collaborations*. The report was the product of an eight-month canvass of more than 160 national liberal-arts campuses and selected corporations to find out what they were doing in collaboration with civic groups and others to replace hardship with hope in neighborhoods nationwide.

And, in an entrepreneurial venture, a group of students produced a CD, *A Musician's Christmas*, in 1998 with proceeds from the recording—which featured 16 holiday songs and carols—earmarked for the *Peoria Journal-Star's* Christmas Fund, a charity.

Gospel Festival

The annual Dr. Martin Luther King, Jr., Gospel Festival became a fixture on the annual calendar in the 1990s. The event—slated for the national holiday weekend commemorating the slain civil-rights leader's birth—became a model of campus-community cooperation. It celebrated the life and teachings of King, the Nobel Peace Prize winner who visited Illinois Wesleyan twice in the 1960s.

The festival, launched by Corine Sims and the United Community Gospel Singers of Bloomington-Normal, became a venue for bringing to campus noted human-rights leaders committed to keeping alive King's vibrant message of non-violent social change and social justice.

The festival also became a magnet attracting to campus many members of the King family and other civil-rights leaders, including: Martin III (son), Bernice (daughter), Yolanda (daughter), Vernon (nephew), as well as noted civil-rights attorney Morris Dees and former Virginia Governor Douglas Wilder.

In addition to keynote and other speakers, the Gospel Festival program typically includes a community-wide fellowship dinner and an eight-hour musical and educational program.

Alumni Support

At its sesquicentennial, Illinois Wesleyan has 17,481 living alumni distributed all over the globe. Recent years have brought notable success re-establishing the active alumni clubs of an earlier era, and alumni enthusiasm has risen sharply with continuing student achievement and the Ames challenge.

When B. Charles Ames, class of 1950, and his wife Joyce Eichhorn Ames, class of 1949, made the landmark gift, which named the new library, they equally challenged their fellow alumni: if the alumni contributed $1 million each for three years they would match it. As this book went to press, two of those challenges have been met.

A New Magazine

Bob Aaron joined Illinois Wesleyan in 1991 as director of University Communications. Within months he had conceived the new *Illinois Wesleyan University Magazine*, which published its inaugural issue in the fall of 1992. Four times a year it brings campus news to 23,000 alumni and friends, at the same time it celebrates alumni achievements. Aaron came to campus after an 18-year career in Washington, D.C., where he was a public-relations specialist and a journalist, who covered national politics and reported from Moscow and Beijing.

Illinois Wesleyan University Magazine hit its stride during its first eight years of publication under two visionary editors—Elaine Graybill and Tim Obermiller—and Senior Graphic Designer Gary Schwartz. The professional editorial staff, supplemented by a talented group of student workers, some of whom went on to successful careers in journalism and public relations, included Stew Salowitz, class of 1976 and director of news services; Sherry Wallace, assistant director of university communications; Tina Williams, office coordinator; and University photographer Marc Featherly.

Movie Guide

By 1998 the seventh edition of *Illinois Wesleyan at the Movies* had rolled off the press. The *Wall Street Journal* took note of the first edition, while Gannett News Service covered release of the fifth edition.

For the seventh edition the guide reported that 34 alumni from the classes of 1932 to 1997 had appeared in 315 feature and made-for-television films. They have been in Academy Award-winners like *The Silence of the Lambs* and *One Flew Over the Cuckoo's Nest*. Alumni also have had roles in critically acclaimed films like *The Hustler, The Right Stuff, Hannah and Her Sisters,* and *Mississippi Burning*. Among these alumni are William Duell, class of 1949; Kevin Dunn, class of 1977; Frankie Faison, class of 1971; Stephanie Faracy, class of 1974; Richard Jenkins, class of 1969; Alison LaPlaca, class of 1982; Sam Smiley, class of 1952; and James Sutorius, class of 1967.

Athletics and the Shirk Center

Athletic vigor has flourished with academic success. In the late 1980s Russell Shirk, class of 1943, was a devoted alumnus, known worldwide wherever aficionados of his Beer Nuts products gathered. A basketball and tennis standout as an undergraduate, Shirk remained a spirited Titan fan, who nurtured the idea of a new athletic

The performance gym in Shirk Center.

complex. He thought about it for many years and soon he and Dennie Bridges, class of 1961 and athletic director, were making plans for a structure conceived beyond the standard of any other building. Trustee Marvin Bower, class of 1945, Shirk, and Bridges flew around the country studying various athletic centers.

When Russ Shirk and his wife, Betty, made a commitment of $5 million toward the project,

Coach Keck
at his final game.

the future Shirk Center was no longer a theoretical investigation. Designed by the St. Louis firm Hastings and Chivetta and in conjunction with the Fort Natatorium, the new building rose in proportions that awed even those who studied the plans daily. The performance gymnasium for varsity basketball seats 2,500, while an adjacent basketball court allows another team to practice when the arena is in use. The huge activity center has 200-meter, six-lane track with flexible space in the center for tennis, volleyball, basketball, indoor batting practice, or as we have sometimes seen even cricket.

With the opening of the $15-million Shirk Center for Athletics and Recreation in 1994, the men's basketball team ended 33 seasons of play in the Fred Young Fieldhouse, where it had a 311-80 record, winning 79.5 percent of its home games. Women's basketball had come into its own in the fieldhouse, and the women chalked up a win for their last game there, a 74-61 win over North Central College.

Athletics: The Decade of the 1990s

The decade of the 1990s opened with NCAA Division III All-American Malik Jones, class of 1990, winning the national indoor 55-meter high hurdle championship.

Essai! (Touchdown!)

American football was catching on in France in the early 1990s and three pioneering coaches of the French gridiron visited the campus for a week in 1993 to sharpen their coaching techniques and game plans. They tapped Illinois Wesleyan for their tutorial after reading an article co-authored by head football coach Norm Eash, class of 1975, "Exploiting the Defense: Illinois Wesleyan's Short Side Passing Attack," which appeared in the American Football Coaches Association 1993 Summer Manual.

"We want to learn things we can integrate in France," explained Emmanuel Gorce, assistant coach in charge of the offensive and defensive lines for the Saint Etienne Giants. "Illinois Wesleyan's approach is best for us. We can reproduce it in France and I'm sure we will win with this type of program."

Three years later, the Titans traveled to Hamburg, Germany, for Charity Bowl IV, a gridiron contest pitting them against the Hamburg Blue Devils, who lost in the 1995

German Bowl finals. The first three Charity Bowl contests raised about $81,000 for children's-care programs. Illinois Wesleyan football players raised funds to cover trip costs.

"I want the trip to be fun," football coach Eash, said in a pre-game interview, "but at the same time I want the team to be competitive—we're playing for the United States not just Illinois Wesleyan, so there's some added pressure."

Illinois Wesleyan was more than competitive, defeating the Blue Devils, 37-7.

Coach Bob Keck retired in 1991 after serving 34 years as a professor and assistant coach in football, wrestling, men's track, and cross-country. He coached 10 NCAA Division III All-Americans.

The 1992 football season forever will be remembered for "the catch." Chris Bisaillon, class of 1993, a GTE Academic All-American, won national acclaim when he shattered San Francisco 49er and NFL all-pro receiver Jerry Rice's NCAA all-division touchdown-pass reception record of 50 catches in a college career. Bisaillon broke the record during his senior year, finishing with 55 TD catches. Among the people calling with congratulations was Jerry Rice.

The women's softball team won the CCIW championships in 1994, 1995, and 1996.

The football and men's basketball teams saw post-season action in 1996. The basketball team captured third place in the NCAA Division III tournament. The football team advanced to the quarterfinals of the NCAA Division III playoffs, losing to Mt. Union, the eventual national champion.

1996 also inaugurated women's golf competition.

National Distinction

Athletics had a banner year in 1997, with a national championship and several distinctions for individuals.

The men's basketball team won the NCAA Division III national championship, defeating Nebraska Wesleyan, 89-86, while All-American forward Bryan Crabtree, class of 1997, earned NCAA Division III "Player of the Year" honors from the National Association of Basketball Coaches. Crabtree, a GTE Academic All-American, also was spotlighted in "Faces in the Crowd," a *Sports Illustrated* feature on amateur athletes.

Coach Dennie Bridges was named "Coach of the Year" in 1997 by the National Association of Basketball Coaches for the 1996-97 season when the Titans went 29-2.

Chris Bisaillon

"The Catch" -
Chris Bisaillon breaking
Jerry Rice's record.

Korey Coon

That same year Quarterback Lon Erickson, class of 1997, won the Gagliardi Trophy as best NCAA Division III football player. He also was selected as *the* Academic All-American of the Year for college division players.

Female athletes also were honored in 1997. Nicole Frank, class of 1998, of the track team won the NCAA Division III national high-jump championship. Laura Carroll, class of 2000, won All-American honors and two events at the NCAA Division III swim meet.

In the spring of 2000 guard Korey Coon, class of 2000, won the Jostens Trophy, recognizing the outstanding student-athlete in NCAA Division III basketball for the 1999-2000 season. Coon, too, was named the College Division "Academic All-American of the Year," no surprise since he graduated with a 4.0 average. He

also was named to All-America teams selected by the National Association of Basketball Coaches and by the *Basketball Times*.

Another award-winning student-athlete in 2000 was long jumper Martez Clark, class of 2000, who was named to the first team of the Arthur Ashe Jr. Sports Scholars Awards for track and cross-country athletes. An English-writing major and political-science minor, Clark headed off to Stanford's law school after two years on the NCAA All-American list.

Horenberger Field

The 1999 baseball season began with the opening of the $1.65-million Horenberger Field, which a stadium plaque declared, "is dedicated to the students of Illinois Wesleyan University, the youth of McLean County and all those who love baseball." The ballpark, named for the legendary baseball skipper of 38 seasons Jack Horenberger, was a first step in upgrading other fields.

Dr. Elmer Beadles, class of 1934, gave the University three more tennis courts in honor of his wife, the late Marjorie Morse Beadles, class of 1934, while Tom and Marilyn Neis, the classes of 1970 and 1971, respectively, honored several in their family in presenting the Neis Soccer Field, which opened in the fall of 2000. The gift of William C. and Susan Nazha, parents of two students, brought lights to Horenberger field,

Hoop Dreams

Luther Bedford, class of 1959, had taught physical education and coached since the early 1960s at Marshall High School, a 1,700-student inner-city public school on Chicago's West Side. As Marshall's basketball coach in the late 1980s and early 1990s, he mentored Arthur Agee, one of the two high school

players featured in the critically acclaimed 1994 film documentary *Hoop Dreams*.

The film won the 1994 Sundance Film Festival award for "Best Documentary." It tells the story of two high-school basketball players dreams of some day playing professional basketball and the pressures in their lives as they work toward that goal and others.

"A modest Luther Bedford would be the first to admit he is an unlikely movie 'star,'" a 1995 *Illinois Wesleyan University Magazine* article pointed out. "Bedford's role (as himself) in the film reinforces his calm dignity as a coach in a difficult neighborhood. . . "

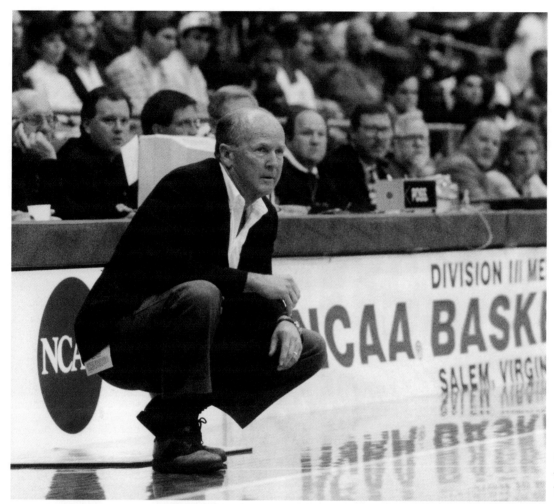

Coach Bridges during
the Championship
Tournament 1997.

Bryan Crabtree
and Buck Cowdell
lift Coach Bridges
in celebration.

Bryan Crabtree
and Korey Coon
congratulate
Coach Bridges.

The first game at Horenberger Field.

Russ Shirk and Coach Horenberger at the dedication of Horenberger Field.

and very quickly to the planning of other fields as well, including the new softball field. A new standard 400-meter oval running track around the football field also took shape in the summer of 2000.

As the 21st century dawned, the University gained its 96th berth on the roster of GTE Academic All-Americans, placing the University fourth nationally.

At the Close of the 20th Century

As the 20th century came to a close one of its distinguishing landmarks in athletics was the emergence of women's varsity sports. This development was spurred by Title IX, federal legislation requiring campuses receiving U.S. funds to offer equivalent sports opportunities, equipment, and funding for female athletics. The spirit of this legislation is seen in Illinois Wesleyan's athletics history as early as 1923 when the Women's Athletic Association was formed.

The importance of athletics to women was described by then-students and alumni in the 1996-97 *President's Report: Achievements: Mind & Body*. Kirstin Rajala Sexson, class of 1990, volleyball team co-captain and a GTE Academic All-American, said: "Volleyball taught me analytical skills. It taught me the ability to put the ball where you want it to go. It's a mind game—that's what sets top players apart from average players, thinking ahead and learning to think quickly." Laurel Hardesty, class of 1995, credited playing basketball with improving her teamwork, communications, and endurance skills. "No matter how bleak things look," she explained, "you can't give up, you have to keep going. Playing sports—especially team sports—gave me the confidence I need today in medical school."

Student Profile and Selectivity

New buildings, student achievement, and alumni support all translated into a very solid admissions profile.

With the dawn of the 1990s, Illinois Wesleyan continued to buck the national trend of a shrinking pool of freshmen applicants. The University reported a 10-percent hike in applications in August, 1991, compared to the previous year. Applications for the class of 1995 reached 2,913 of which 45 percent were accepted and 520 students enrolled.

"We were only able to admit 45 percent of those who applied for admission," explained Dean of Admissions James Ruoti, class of 1963, "which is a very low figure compared to the majority of colleges and universities. Our incoming freshman class is smaller this year as a result of the high retention rate of current students."

Choosing from a large pool of applicants enabled Illinois Wesleyan to be more selective. The average score on the ACT college-entrance exam for incoming freshmen was 26.9, while the average SAT score was 1,172 compared to national averages of 20.6 and 900, respectively, at that time.

The academic profile continued to sharpen throughout the 1990s. When classes began for the 1997-98 school year, Illinois Wesleyan boasted a record enrollment of 1,995 students. The freshman class was composed of 560 domestic students from 16 states and included 37 high-school valedictorians, 22 National Merit Scholars, 10 international students, and 56 minority students (African-Americans, Asian-Americans, and Hispanics).

"This year's freshman class," Ruoti said, "seems to have a larger number of students who are multitalented. They are outstanding students academically, but they have done a lot of other things in terms of extracurricular activities."

And, when the class of 2002 entered in the fall of 1998, the average ACT score of its members had reached 28. "Based on standardized test scores and class rank," Ruoti said, "this is the academically brightest class in the history of the University."

The 1999-2000 school year began with a record enrollment of about 2,075 full-time students, including 545 first-year students. Ruoti credited the academic strength of this multitalented freshman group to several factors, noting, " . . . the word is out due to the national recognition that we receive in a lot of the college guides."

U.S. News & World Report, Ruoti pointed out, ranked Illinois Wesleyan 48th among the 162 national liberal-arts colleges and *Kiplinger's Personal Finance Magazine* ranked the University 12th among the nation's best 100 private colleges in providing a top-quality education at an affordable cost.

Ruoti explained: "To me, the *Kiplinger Guide* is probably one of the strongest recommendations we have received because it combines quality with value."

At the start of the 21st century, Illinois Wesleyan was using technology—particularly the Internet—as a marketing tool. Consequently, in 2000 the website was ranked No. 8 in the United States by the non-profit National Research Center for College and University Admissions. The study, conducted during the summer of 1999, included more than 800 colleges and universities.

A National Liberal Arts University

America's Best Colleges, annually published by *U.S. News & World Report*, shifted Illinois Wesleyan from a top regional ranking to the national liberal-arts university category in 1994. President Minor Myers, jr., noted that the change was expected and welcomed.

The change was expected because of a change in the University's classification—along with many other campuses—by the Carnegie Foundation for the Advancement of Teaching. Now, the University was classified a "Baccalaureate (Liberal Arts) I campus, a category traditionally home to colleges like Williams, Amherst, Carleton, and Swarthmore. The change was prompted, according to Carnegie, because the undergraduate degrees Illinois Wesleyan awards were in liberal-arts fields and "the admissions policies of the college are very selective."

Dean of Admission Ruoti pointed out, "Illinois Wesleyan competes for students primarily with schools in the national liberal arts category rather than in the regional category."

Around this same time, another college guide, *101 of the Best Values in America's Colleges and Universities*, described the University as "undoubtedly one of the finest small colleges in the country," adding, "Illinois Wesleyan has surged to national prominence on the basis of its reputation as a school with a rock-solid academic program."

◄ Brad Sherman, Matt Willson and Elizabeth Cazel on the quad.

Other College-Guide Kudos

When Illinois Wesleyan was ranked No. 1 in the Midwest for the fourth consecutive year in 1992 by *U.S. News & World Report*, the 2.3-million circulation news weekly profiled freshman Tim Culbertson—a National Merit Scholar and an Presidential Scholar—as an example of the type of student attracted to Illinois Wesleyan. "Some of Illinois Wesleyan's more ambitious students, like Tim Culbertson . . ." *U.S. News & World Report* wrote, "try to take advantage of both the University's high-quality programs in the sciences and those in the performing arts. Culbertson, a tuba player who is studying music, is thinking about adding an unlikely second major: physics.

"He was drawn to Illinois Wesleyan," the magazine added, "not just by the breadth of its curriculum but also by its commitment to individual students, something he decided would be lacking at the larger Big 10 schools he considered. The summer before he arrived on campus, Illinois Wesleyan made a gesture that convinced him he had made the right decision. The school lent Culbertson a tuba until he could save enough money to afford to blow his own horn."

Illinois Wesleyan was among only 359 campuses nationally included in *Competitive Colleges 1993-94*, published by Peterson's, the Princeton, New Jersey-based education and career-information publisher. At this same time, the University also was included in *Barron's 300 Best Buys in College Education, Barron's Profiles of American Colleges, Comparative Guide to American Colleges, Fiske Guide to Colleges, The Multicultural Student's Guide to College: What Every African-American, Asian-American, Hispanic, and Native American Applicant Needs to Know about America's Top Schools* and *The Best 100 Colleges for African-American Students*.

Just days after *U.S. News & World Report* ranked the University the top regional campus in the Midwest for the fifth consecutive year in 1993, it picked Illinois Wesleyan as a "best buy" among colleges and universities in its *America's Best College Values*.

B. Charles and Joyce Eichorn Ames

As Illinois Wesleyan moved full throttle into the information age, its efforts were recognized nationally in 2000, when the magazine *Yahoo! Internet Life* ranked the University the eighth "most wired" college in the nation.

The Ames Challenge

A new $12-million fund-raising challenge targeted to Illinois Wesleyan alumni was announced at Homecoming 1998. It was made by B. Charles Ames, a business-administration graduate of 1950, and his wife, Joyce Eichhorn Ames, a class of 1949 art graduate.

"This challenge," said Craig C. Hart, president of the Board of Trustees, "represents the largest financial commitment in the history of Illinois Wesleyan University."

In a statement to alumni, the Ameses said: "We believe Illinois Wesleyan University has a unique opportunity to rank among the top 40 national liberal arts institutions in the United States within the next few years. For this reason, we are willing to make a substantial commitment of funds if our fellow alumni will join us to achieve this goal."

The Ameses proposed to match—on a dollar-for-dollar basis—all gifts to the Alumni Annual Fund, if alumni contribute a minimum of $1 million annually for the next three years for a total of $3 million. Furthermore, the Ameses proposed to match—on a dollar-for-dollar basis, up to $9 million—all gifts earmarked for the proposed new library.

The first and second years of the Ames' Challenge were met by alumni by the time this book went to press.

B. Charles Ames is a senior partner with Clayton, Dubilier & Rice, Inc., a New York City-based investment firm and has been chairman at various times of Uniroyal Goodrich, Lexmark, and Kinko's.

The Ames Library

Design of a new library followed the model of other buildings, as constituents of our community asked what the ideal building should be. The University called on the Boston firm of Shepley Bullfinch Richardson and Abbott (SBRA) as architects. No strangers to libraries, SBRA counted among their clients Princeton, Yale, and Dartmouth.

Ground was broken for the $26-million Ames Library on November 6, 1999. The library's design calls for 103,000-square-foot-building, compared to Sheean Library's 37,000 - square-foot-area. The five-story library—an architectural blend of traditional elements and modern technology—will form a new University entryway in tandem with a new, two-section curved gateway, marking the University's 150th anniversary.

The Ames Library, which is estimated to go into operation in the fall of 2001, will accommodate 400,000 volumes and a minimum of 100 computer-equipped workstations. The new library also will feature group study rooms, study carrels, space for special collections and University archives, an auditorium, and an Information Commons.

Architect's sketch of The Ames Library.

Callback to Washington

When actress Heather Siemsen, class of 1993, stepped onto the Kennedy Center's stage in Washington, D.C., in April, 1993, she performed in a setting that annually honors the dramatic talents of legends like Katharine Hepburn.

Siemsen was one of 16 students nationally who were finalists in the Irene Ryan Acting Scholarship Competition, sponsored by the American College Theatre Festival and the John F. Kennedy Center for the Performing Arts. Participation in the Irene Ryan competition is widely regarded as the highest honor a college actor can earn.

While Siemsen did not win the competition, she had the chance to take classes with Tony Award-winning Broadway actress Uta Hagen, who visited the campus in 1975 as part of the E. Melba Johnson Kirkpatrick Theatre Artists Series.

Siemsen earned her way to the Kennedy Center stage by winning a regional acting competition, involving about 200 college students from five states. Two other students have won Irene Ryan regional competitions: Linda Sterling, class of 1980, in 1979, and Andrea Huber, class of 1981, who won the national competition in 1981.

Centennial of the *Argus*

When editor-in-chief Clarence E. Snyder sent the first issue of the *Argus* to press on September 17, 1894, Grover Cleveland was in the White House and Thomas Edison had just publicly shown a newfangled invention—motion pictures. A century later, the *Argus*, the University's campus newspaper, still was rolling off the press every week, an achievement marked in February, 1994, by three events:

• Publication of a 256-page history of the newspaper, *Through the Eyes of the Argus: 100 Years of Journalism at Illinois Wesleyan University*, written by staffers Chris Fusco and Jennifer Barrell, both of the class of 1994.

• A centennial dinner keynoted by *Chicago Tribune* columnist Bob Greene. Also participating in the festivities was Bob Page, class of 1958—former United Press International (UPI) executive vice president and former president-publisher of the *Chicago Sun-Times* and *Boston Herald*—who was *Argus* editor in 1956-57.

• A Founders' Day Convocation address by UPI's veteran White House bureau chief Helen Thomas.

Commencement
on the Eckley
Quadrangle 2000.

The Center for Liberal Arts.

Interesting People Doing Interesting Things

The 1990s saw a wave of interesting and challenging activity sweep through the campus, engaging students and faculty in a wide range of eclectic and exciting projects. Here's a sample:

• The Helene Fuld Health Trust awarded a grant to the School of Nursing in 1990 for interactive video hardware. This equipment, said Donna Hartweg, director of the nursing school, "is viewed as a high-tech approach to increase clinical decision-making skills."

• The Illinois Wesleyan "Select 100" hit bookshelves in 1991. It was a collection of 100 must-read books, a compilation based on nominations received by the Bookstore Advisory Committee. The compendium included well-known classics—*The Odyssey* by Homer, *Great Expectations* by Charles Dickens, and John Steinbeck's *The Grapes of Wrath*—but it also contained lesser-known works like *Johnny Got His Gun* by Dalton Trumbo.

• *Rolling Stone* magazine in 1991 recognized biology professor Thomas Griffiths as one of the top college teachers in the United States. Griffiths, who came in 1981, is a nationally recognized authority on bats.

• Two physicists worked with the federal space agency in the summer of 1992 on projects involving superconductivity and studies of data beamed to Earth from satellites exploring planets at the edge of the solar system. Narendra Jaggi conducted research on superconductivity and Herman (Lew) Detweiler studied data from the International Ultraviolet Explorer and Voyager II, a satellite launched in 1977, which probed the mysteries of Jupiter, Saturn, Uranus, and Neptune.

• A $110,000 federal education department grant received by the University in 1992 helped launch three new international-studies programs, expand the teaching of Russian, and establish a new Japanese-language program.

• The 46-member Collegiate Choir capped its 10-day, six-state spring concert tour in 1992 with a performance at New York's famed Lincoln Center, home of the Metropolitan Opera and the New York Philharmonic Orchestra. The Camerata, a 23-member chamber music group, took its "Music for Peace" program on a three-concert east coast tour in 1993, including a performance in New York City's Carnegie Hall.

• Donna Hartweg, Rupert Professor and director of the nursing school, joined the deans of about 45 nursing schools nation wide in 1993 for a peek into President Bill Clinton's health-care reform proposals at a White House meeting.

• The scholarship of faculty also was reflect ed in the books they authored. W. Michael Weis, professor of history, wrote *Cold Warriors & Coups D'Etat—Brazilian-American Relations, 1945-1964*, and Carolyn Jarvis, adjunct assistant professor of nursing, wrote *Physical Examinations and Health Assessment*, used by almost 200 nursing schools and 10,000 students nation-wide—both books appeared in 1993.

• The estate of Aaron Copland, one of America's foremost composers and music educators, bequeathed to Illinois Wesleyan more than 150 of his published works in 1993. Copland, who died in 1990, received an honorary doctorate from the University in 1958 and participated in the Symposium on Contemporary Music.

• *Discover* magazine, the 1.1-million circulation monthly, profiled former Illinois Wesleyan geochemist Wendy Wolbach in 1994. It described her pioneering work in connection with the hypothesis that an asteroid's collision with the Earth 65-million years ago triggered the death of the dinosaurs.

• In 1994 Illinois Wesleyan became the first private college and the first campus outside Michigan to join the Wade H. McCree, Jr. Incentive Scholarship Program, which guarantees that talented minority high-school students from Detroit will have the chance to attend college.

• James Plath, professor of English, won a Fulbright Scholarship in 1995, to teach courses on the American novel and short story at the University of the West Indies-Cave Hill campus.

• Economics Professor Margaret Chapman, Political-Science Professor Emeritus John Wenum, and a co-author in 1995 probed the political, social, and economic impact of a U.S.-based Japanese auto factory in *Mitsubishi Motors in Illinois: Global Strategies, Local Impact*. The *Chicago Tribune's* John McCarron wrote: "It seems that a team of economists from [Illinois Wesleyan University] actually took the time to evaluate the impact of one of these public-private ventures . . . The [Illinois] Wesleyan team dissected one of the biggest 'giveaways' in Illinois history—the $183 million bag of goodies that the state and local governments put together in 1985 to convince Chrysler/Mitsubishi to build its $500 million Diamond-Star automobile plant in Bloomington."

• Retired Army General William Westmoreland, who commanded a half-million U.S. troops in Vietnam, was inter viewed at his Charleston, South Carolina, home in 1995 by two classes of 1995 history majors—Christopher La Jeunesse and Matt Nelson—for an oral history tracing his life and career as part of a January Term research project.

• Neal Vermillion, a class of 1996 political science and history major, took time off from the Washington, D.C., Semester Program and a Capitol Hill internship in 1995 to appear on the top-rated TV quiz show, *Jeopardy!* Cheering him on at the Culver City, California, studio was a contingent of alumni, wearing Illinois Wesleyan sweat-shirts, and Ellen Myers, wife of President Minor Myers, jr. "I won $5,000 for an hours' work. You can't beat that," Vermillion said about his appearance on the *Jeopardy! College Championship*, which involved students from 15 campuses nation-wide, including Harvard and Stanford.

• The National Science Foundation award ed a grant to Illinois Wesleyan in 1996 to purchase scientific equipment earmarked for experiments to pinpoint pesticide levels in migratory birds and other environmental studies.

Buck Memorial Library

• By 1996 the annual student-research conference had evolved into the John Wesley Powell Research Conference, named for the post-Civil War faculty member who was the first U.S. professor to use field work to teach science. In the conference's seventh year it attracted as a keynote speaker the famed Harvard evolutionary biologist and best-selling author Stephen J. Gould. Research projects on Alzheimer's Disease, divorce, methods to detect cocaine metabolites in urine, and coronary-artery disease highlighted the two-day conference.

• In 1996 junior Kurt Galbreath, a biology major, was among 264 college sophomores and juniors nationally—out of a field of 1,200 students from 516 campuses—to win scholarships named for former U.S. Senator Barry Goldwater of Arizona, the Republican party's 1964 presidential nominee. Two members of the class of 1998 won Goldwater Scholarships in 1997: Nathan Mueggenburg, a physics-mathematics major, and Jeremy Kotter, a physics major. And, in 1999 Matthew Dearing, a class of 2000 physics major, was a Goldwater Scholarship recipient. Goldwater Scholarships are considered the foremost undergraduate award of their type in mathematics, the natural sciences, and engineering.

• Former Vice President Dan Quayle profiled Darnell Burtin, class of 1996, his sister, DaToya, class of 2000, and their parents in a 1996 book he co-authored, *The American Family—Discovering the Values That Make Us Strong*.

• Shelley—Illinois Wesleyan's version of R2D2, the cinematic robot of Star Wars' fame—had a coming-out party in 1996. She was designed and built by students and faculty and was a key tool in cognitive-science teaching and research. Shelley was designed to play the piano, recite poetry, and solve puzzles.

• Celebrity photographer Annie Liebovitz had a new assistant in the summer of 1997, Lisa Hillmer, an art major from the class of 1998. After sending a slide portfolio and "self-promotion piece" to Leibovitz, Hillmer flew to New York for an interview and won the job.

• Michael Votava, class of 1997, won Honorable Mention honors in *USA Today's* 1997 All-USA College Academic Team Competition, recognizing "the best and the brightest," according to the newspaper. He was recognized for his alcohol and drug-education work with high-school students, as well as his scholastic performance and long list of community-service activities.

• A $2-million gift was made in 1998 to endow the School of Art building. The gift was made in tribute to Joyce Eichhorn Ames, class of 1949, by her husband, B. Charles Ames, class of 1950, through the Ames Family Foundation. "The Ames family desire," said B. Charles Ames, "is to make the School of Art the finest school of art in the nation for a college the size of Illinois Wesleyan University." In addition to the naming of the school of art building, the Joyce Ames Scholarship Fund was established to support students majoring in the fine arts.

• Illinois Wesleyan's scenic quad was named The Eckley Quadrangle in 1998 in honor of former President Robert S. Eckley and his wife, Nell. It was through the Eckleys' efforts that the quad's beautification and current land scape design took shape.

• The first Freshman Fall Festival took place in 1998, introducing the class of 2002 to Illinois Wesleyan in a sweeping new orientation program. The festival, an annual event, helps classes develop an identity, as well as expose first-year students to the people, places, and issues they will come in contact with at the University.

• Three faculty were appointed to endowed professorships in 1998. Donna Hartweg, professor and director of the School of Nursing, was the recipient of the Carolyn F. Rupert

Professorship of Nursing. Lawrence Campbell, professor of music and chair of the piano department, was named the Fern Rosetta Sherff Professor of Music. Thomas A. Griffiths, professor of biology, was appointed to the Earl H. and Marion A. Beling Professor of Natural Sciences.

• The First-Year Experience program was introduced in 1999 to assist "rookies" in making a smooth transition from high school to college through a semester-long calendar of seminars, workshops, and other activities.

• Susan Anderson-Freed, professor of computer science, won a contract in 1999 from publisher Prentice Hall to author a book—*Weaving Arachne's New Web*—about programming worldwide web pages.

• Chicago's Victory Gardens Theatre was the site of the 1999 world premiere of *Friday in America*, a play written by John Ficca, professor of theatre arts, and featuring a 10-member cast of Illinois Wesleyan alumni—all theatre professionals.

• The 24-member Jazz Ensemble traveled to Japan in 1999, bringing the sound of the great Duke Ellington to Bloomington-Normal's sister city, Asahikawa. It also released its first CD recording, *It's Swinging at IWU*, featuring 14 1940s-era swing tunes.

• Eight Russian nurses from Bloomington's sister city, Vladimir, studied U.S. nursing and medical practices at Illinois Wesleyan and elsewhere in 1999 under a federal grant. Charla Renner, an associate professor of

Campus in Spring 2000.

nursing emeritus, was among community-nursing leaders who coordinated the Russians' visit.

• Cancer-causing agents found in the environment that trigger lung and colon cancer were the target of 1999 research conducted by Ram Mohan, assistant professor of chemistry, and four students under a grant from the Petroleum Research Fund. Mohan was awarded a $124,000 National Science Foundation grant in 2000 to develop environmentally friendly compounds using bismuth, a metal whose various compounds are found in pharmaceuticals.

• David Vayo, professor of music, won a Guggenheim Fellowship in 2000 to support writing a composition for a chamber orchestra.

VIPs on Campus in 90s

The 1990s flourished as a time when Illinois Wesleyan showcased its robust tradition of providing a forum for the marketplace of ideas by inviting to campus a wide range of guest speakers. This tradition extends formal education beyond the classroom and draws its strength from America's coveted First Amendment freedoms. This tradition gives students and faculty—as well as the community—the unique opportunity to see and hear first hand men and women who shape our times.

Illinois Wesleyan's guest book for the 1990s and into 2000 included five Nobel Prize winners: Oscar Arias, former president of Costa Rica (Peace, 1987); Mairead Maguire, the Northern Ireland peace activist (Peace, 1977); Derek Walcott, poet-playwright (Literature, 1992); Jean-Marie Lehn, a scientist (Chemistry, 1987), and James D. Watson, the co-discoverer of the structure of DNA (Medicine, 1962). The University also hosted statesmen such as former Jamaican Prime Minister Michael Manley, former British Prime Minister Sir Edward Heath, and Slovenian Prime Minister Janez Drnovsek.

A wide range of political and government figures visited the campus in the 1990s, includ-

ing: U.S. Senators Paul Simon (D-Ill.) and Richard Durbin (D-Ill.), former State Department spokesperson Margaret Tutwiler, U.S. Navy Admiral Leighton Smith (Ret.), the former NATO commander in war-torn Bosnia, environmentalist and consumer advocate Ralph Nader, and former Defense Secretary, White House Chief of Staff and U.S. Representative Donald Rumsfeld (R-Ill).

Donald Rumsfeld, Secretary of Defense

A wide range of personalities, sharing a common commitment to civil and human rights, addressed Illinois Wesleyan audiences: black nationalist leader Kwame Ture (formerly Stokley Carmichael), AIDS activist Jeanne White-Ginder, civil-rights fighter Morris Dees, NAACP chair Myrlie Evers-Williams, Holocaust survivor Benjamin Jacobs, Chinese freedom fighter Harry Wu, women's-rights advocate Gloria Steinem, and Maulana Karenga, the educator and author who created Kwanzaa, the African-American and Pan African cultural holiday.

Pioneering scientists and groundbreaking researchers also shared their insights with students and faculty, including: archaeologist and Dead Sea Scrolls researcher James F. Strange, National Medal of Science recipient Harry B. Gray, and the father of the asteroid-dinosaur demise theory Walter Alvarez.

Men and women of literature and ideas visited the Univesity, including: award-winning

Mexican novelist and diplomat Carlos Fuentes; Cornel West, one of America's leading African-American philosophers; civil-rights Freedom Rider, author, and former Yale University Chaplain William Sloane Coffin; Kurt Vonnegut, author of Slaughterhouse Five and other critically acclaimed works; poet Gwendolyn Brooks; and author Maya Angelou.

Many of America's outstanding journalists shared their eyewitness experiences with various Illinois Wesleyan groups, including: Pulitzer Prize-winner Peter Kann of the Wall Street Journal, New York Times' science reporter Laurie Garrett, United Press International's White House bureau chief Helen Thomas, ABC News Correspondent Chris Wallace, Emmy Award-winning newsman Ken Bode, and James Fallows, then editor of U.S. News & World Report.

Celebrities from the world of entertainment spoke out about the stage, screen, and television professions, including: filmmaker Spike Lee, veteran actor John Randolph, film producer Ismail Merchant, and Reinhold Weege, creator of the wacky world of television's long-running and award-winning sitcom, Night Court, who attended the University in 1970.

Conclusion

The sweep of Illinois Wesleyan's history is striking. The University with its trademark single building and lone sidewalk in the 1850s has matured into an elegant campus with a strong national reputation over a century and a half. But, first and foremost the Illinois Wesleyan saga is the story of people—people with big ideas, people with imagination, people with perseverance.

This can-do spirit is what we celebrate upon the university's Sesquicentennial in 2000-2001—a time when we remember and honor

Redesigned plaza of Sheean Library.

the great personalities and landmark events that shaped Illinois Wesleyan. As we survey it's history, it is remarkable that our founders had the vision and determination to commit themselves to establishing "an Institution of learning of Collegiate Grade"—and that the many generations who followed them did their best to remain faithful to the founders' bold vision.

One of those founders wrote, " . . . but most especially and emphatically I say success to Illinois Wesleyan University . . . may her endowments and facilities, and buildings and apparatuses and libraries . . . be speedily and abundantly enriched . . . "

This book is a tribute to the achievement of that lofty prophecy.

Overleaf: ➤ Entry bridge to the Center for Natural Sciences.

Index